RE-THINKING ABORTION

Psychology, gender, power and the law

Mary Boyle

London and New York

First published 1997
by Routledge
11 New Fetter Lane, London EC4P 4EE

Simultaneously published in the USA and Canada
by Routledge
29 West 35th Street, New York, NY 10001

Typeset in Baskerville by Routledge
Printed and bound in Great Britain by Clays Ltd, St Ives PLC

British Library Cataloguing in Publication Data
A catalogue record for this book is available from the British Library

Library of Congress Cataloguing in Publication Data
Boyle, Mary.
Re-thinking abortion: psychology, gender, power, and the law/
Mary Boyle.
p. cm.–(Women and psychology)
Includes bibliographical references and index.
1. Abortion–Psychological aspects. 2. Abortion–Government policy.
3. Women–Psychology. 4. Women–Legal status, laws, etc.
5. Men–Psychology. 6. Social psychology. 7. Social policy.
I. Title. II. Series.
HQ767.B63 1997
363.46–dc21
97–14933
CIP

ISBN 0–415–16364–1 (hbk)
ISBN 0–415–16365–X (pbk)

CONTENTS

CONTENTS

ACKNOWLEDGEMENTS

Writing a book on a topic as sensitive as abortion can be a rather lonely experience – I certainly became used to conversations faltering or moving sharply in another direction when I answered questions about the book's subject matter. Fortunately, it wasn't always like that. Many people discussed the book enthusiastically with me and some told me of their own experiences of abortion. I am grateful to everyone who strengthened my conviction that psychology urgently needs to re-think its relationship to this controversial topic. Particular thanks are due to Jane Ussher for encouraging me to write the book and for being so supportive of it; to Patricia Lucas for administrative help without which progress would have been much slower; and especially to Clive Gabriel for invaluable discussion and support throughout the project.

1

INTRODUCTION
Psychology and abortion

In 1994, more than 166,000 women had legal abortions in England and Wales; the average figure for the years 1989–94 has been over 176,000[1] and around four million abortions have been carried out in England and Wales since the implementation of more liberal abortion legislation in 1968 (Office for National Statistics 1996a). In spite of the large number of women who have abortions, and men who experience it indirectly, British psychology has had little to say on the topic. For example, a search of the *British Journal of Psychology* and the British Journals of Clinical, Medical and Social Psychology, and all issues of *Psychology and Health* for 1981–1994, produced four papers. Similarly, an unselected sample of ten texts on health psychology published in the last eight years produced a total of less than half a page in one text and two lines in another. The *Journal of Reproductive and Infant Psychology*, however, has produced one issue on the related topic of 'fetal screening'.

The topic has received more attention from psychologists in the United States, where around 1.5 million abortions are performed each year (Hansen 1993). As well as a text on adolescent abortion (Melton 1986), there has been a special feature on adolescent abortion (*American Psychologist* 1987) and a journal issue devoted to psychological aspects of abortion (*Journal of Social Issues* 1992). But although the topic of abortion has been more visible in the US psychological literature, the number of journal articles is very small and abortion tends to be treated as a 'special' topic which is rarely mentioned, far less discussed in detail, in texts on social, clinical, health or life-span psychology. The major US review journal *Psychological Bulletin* has not published a paper on abortion in the last fifteen years.

One possible reason for this relative neglect of abortion, and for the failure to integrate it into the study of people's lives, is the extreme social and political sensitivity which surrounds the topic. Ronald Dworkin, for example, recently suggested that 'the war between anti-abortion groups and their opponents is America's new version of the terrible seventeenth-century European civil wars of

---

1 The exact figures for abortions carried out in England and Wales are 166,876 for 1994 and an average of 176,345 for the years 1989–94.

religion' (1993: 4). A similar sentiment was expressed by a US anti-abortion campaigner who compared himself to a 'soldier in a holy war' (Connell 1994). Although abortion does not appear routinely to inspire such extreme sentiments in the UK and Europe, it remains a highly controversial issue. For example, there have been around twenty parliamentary attempts to restrict the law on abortion in Britain since it was liberalised in 1967, while abortion laws in Northern and Southern Ireland are amongst the most restrictive in the world. In 1992, the Irish Supreme Court barred a 14-year-old girl, who had been raped, from travelling to England for an abortion, although the injunction was later removed. The ban precipitated public protests in Britain and Ireland, with placards such as 'Get your rosaries out of my ovaries' and 'If men got pregnant, abortion would be a sacrifice'. Hadley (1996) has argued that negotiations over abortion legislation created more difficulties than any other issue in the German reunification process.

Small wonder, perhaps, that an issue so obviously laden with moral, political and religious overtones has not been a very popular subject for psychological research and analysis. But is the undoubtedly contentious and sensitive nature of abortion an adequate explanation or justification of this neglect? Can we assume that psychology has little to contribute to an area that uses language and arguments derived from religion, morality and ideology, and which appears to make little use of what psychologists would think of as evidence? In fact, we might argue the opposite: that an issue which arouses such strong feelings and induces extremes of behaviour must have such significance in many people's lives that a discipline devoted to the study of human behaviour cannot afford to neglect it. And leaving aside the political controversy, the official statistics on abortion show that it directly touches the lives of a considerable number of people. A more informal survey in *New Woman* magazine in April 1993 found that almost a quarter of its respondents who were thirty or over had had an abortion. There is also good evidence that when abortion is not legally available, women will often resort to illegal abortion even at considerable risk to their health (Callahan 1970; Brooks 1988; NIALRA 1989). Indeed, Faludi (1992) has claimed that women have been terminating about one in three pregnancies, legally or illegally, for at least the last century. It seems difficult, then, to justify psychology's relative neglect of abortion simply in terms of the socially controversial nature of the topic, although I shall argue that this certainly helps to account for the neglect. But to seek to account for why psychology should pay so little attention to abortion is only part of the story because our attention is not then directed to the ways in which psychology *does* attend to the topic. For example, Smetana and Adler suggested in 1979 that psychological and psychiatric research on abortion tended to emphasise the (negative) character-istics of women seeking abortion and its possible negative effects on women. Adler *et al.*'s 1992 review suggests that the situation has not significantly changed, although there is now less emphasis on the psychological characteristics of women who seek abortion. However, the emphasis on the negative effects of abortion on women remains.

Psychology, then, has approached abortion largely as a health or 'well-being' issue and has tended to focus on individual women. This might seem reasonable: after all, abortion is a health issue insofar as it is performed by doctors on women within a health system. It will also have particular effects, positive or negative, on individual women. It might also seem that, in an area fraught with controversy, psychology can adopt a neutral stance by concentrating on the physical and psychological health of women who have abortions, rather than becoming embroiled in issues which are well beyond its scientific remit. One of the major themes of this book, however, is that psychology is already embroiled in abortion, whether or not it intends or is aware of it, and that its relationship to abortion is not neutral in terms either of its relative neglect of the topic or the kind of research it has generated. The less visible aspects of psychology's relationship to abortion will be discussed in later chapters, but if we look for the moment at its visible relationship through published research, we can identify three main character-istics. The first is the search for an objective and scientific approach to the study of abortion which circumvents its value-laden nature. Adler (1992: 19), for example, has argued that, 'The scientific study of abortion has been burdened by the fact that it is a procedure about which individuals have strong feelings'. In a review of 'psychological factors in abortion', Adler *et al.* also stated that 'it was recognized that differing moral, ethical and religious perspectives impinge on how abortion is perceived. Our mission, however, was not to assess values, but to consider the best available scientific evidence on psychological responses to abortion' (1992: 1194). The second characteristic is the focus on individual women. This often takes the form of the quantitative study of women's responses to abortion, often using standard scales of assumed intrapsychic states such as depression or anxiety. Finally, psychological research on abortion is characterised by a neglect of gender, in spite of the fact that the vast majority of research participants are women. These features, however, are not simply characteristic of research on abortion or a result of the special nature of this topic; they are characteristic of psychology's general approach to its subject matter. We can therefore better understand why the psychological study of abortion should have taken this form, and why it is so problematic and limiting, by looking at the nature of psychology as a discipline and the nature of the subject matter it has set for itself.

PSYCHOLOGY, SCIENCE AND THE INDIVIDUAL

Psychology clearly sees itself as a science. For example, a report on the profession of clinical psychology claimed that 'Scientific method and systematic enquiry determine the way they practice' (MPAG 1990). Reviewers for a major learned journal are told that the primary consideration in considering papers is that they should 'advance scientific knowledge'. Psychology's perception of itself as a science is based on its having publicly adopted both the methods and rhetoric of the natural sciences. In this the discipline has followed the mid-nineteenth century positivist doctrine of Auguste Comte, that the systematic study of society and of humans is possible only by applying the methods of the natural sciences. Comte believed that such methods led to the discovery of secure and irrefutable knowledge. The methods adopted by psychology involved a strong reliance on experimentation, the extensive use of quantification and measurement, the separation of phenomena of interest from their contexts and their study under controlled conditions, and, finally, a commitment to the creation of general laws of behaviour. This latter commitment has led to an emphasis on the form of behaviour, or general features common across groups, rather than on its specific content or social and personal meaning. Psychology's adoption of natural science methods, and of the assumptions underlying them, has been accompanied by what might be called a rhetoric of justification which depicts such methods as neutral, objective, value-free and rational (Venn 1984; Hare-Mustin and Marecek 1988; Harding 1986, 1991). There are a number of problems with the extension of the methods and rhetoric of the natural sciences to the study of humans, but two of the major ones concern the nature of scientific method and its assumed neutrality.

The adoption of natural science methods for the study of behaviour and experience appears to be based on the idea that there exist methods which are intrinsically scientific, which result in secure knowledge, and with which aspiring scientific disciplines can compare themselves. It is an appealing and comforting idea, but it has proved remarkably difficult to substantiate. There has never been an agreed definition of 'science' (Medawar 1984; Chalmers 1990) and philosophers of science have disagreed about what it is that natural scientists actually do (see, for example, Lakatos and Musgrave 1970; Feyerabend 1978). Medawar (1984) has argued that science should not be thought of as the application of an essential method, but as attempts to solve problems using whatever methods appear to produce reliable and useful results. Chalmers (1990) has supported this view, arguing that we underestimate the extent to which methods and standards in the natural sciences have changed – and are still changing – not in pursuit of *the* scientific method, but pragmatically, to suit the circumstances of the time. As Chalmers points out, the fact that the natural sciences have developed methods to suit their subject matter means that the achievements of, say, physics will not tell us how to solve the problems studied by psychologists or sociologists. Scientists do not apply quantification to decontextualised objects in laboratories because to do so is intrinsically scientific, but because they can make useful statements about objects by doing so. These objects have no social life, culture or language; whether studying decontextualised individuals who have all three will enable us to make useful statements about people, is another matter entirely. Similarly, the success of quantification in the natural sciences does not guarantee that it will be equally successful when applied to human behaviour and experience.

The second problem of transferring natural science methods to the study of humans concerns their assumed neutrality or objectivity. The rhetoric of objectivity functions to confer authority, status and trust. It has also, however, absolved psychology of responsibility for examining the value systems which influence choice of research questions, methods and theories, as well as attempts to put theories into practice. Psychology's preoccupation with objectivity has also resulted in a relative neglect of topics which are socially and politically sensitive but which are arguably central to people's lives, such as sexual and racial discrimination, sexual objectification, racial and sexual violence, women's domestic labour and, of course, abortion.

Psychological research on abortion, however, has been characterised not only by its sparseness but also by its emphasis on individual women. The individual has, of course, been psychology's traditional object of study. It is not that this is unreasonable in principle, the problem lies in how we conceptualise the individual and the relationship of individual behaviour and experience to its social context. It is assumed, for example, that individuals carry with them attributes and processes which can be studied independently of the social world – personality, intelligence, aptitude, depression, anxiety, dysfunctional cognitions, attitudes, and so on. Psychology has taken account of social variables such as 'class' and marital status, but these are often conceptualised as separate and discrete entities 'out there' whose impact on internal psychological attributes can be expressed numerically. Even studies of social *inter*action, as Henriques *et al.* (1984) have noted, tend to assume a dualistic relationship between the individual and the social with a pre-given individual subject, on whom the social world impinges, taken for granted.

This approach treats the psychological object of study, the individual, as unproblematic and self-evident. It seriously underestimates the extent to which psychology has not simply studied but *constructed* the individual, as well as the extent to which that construction has been influenced by social and cultural values. Venn (1984) and Rose (1989), for example, have argued strongly that neither psychology's focus on the individual, nor the particular construction of the individual which emerged, was the result of epistemological factors; rather, they were at least partly the result of an intense focus on the utility of the individual which accompanied industrialisation. As Rose points out, for a domain to be governable, we not only need a language in which to speak about it, we also need information about it. It was the mental sciences – psychology and psychiatry – which, in the late nineteenth and early twentieth century, provided both the language and the means for the collection of information about people. And the questions to which scientists directed their attention reflected current social and political concerns. Which children would not benefit from education? Which men would not stand up to the rigours of war? Which workers would be most productive? Which indigents should be excused the workhouse on the grounds of insanity? Mental scientists did not reframe these questions by asking, for example, how we could develop an educational system which would be of some benefit to all children or why so many wars and so much loss of life seemed necessary? Instead, they constructed individuals who possessed important attributes in amounts not easily discernible to the naked eye and developed tests and diagnostic criteria to measure them. Howard (1985) has pointed out that if researchers hold certain models of humans as basic to their understandings of the meaning of their research, then they will accumulate evidence which appears to support these models. They will do this, at least partly, because they will cease to ask questions from outside these models. Thus, notions of the subject matter of psychology and of the nature of the individual come to be taken for granted, to be naturalised, when they are actually historically specific. The fact that the use of techniques for studying individuals, for identifying and measuring their attributes, and for examining the effects of external events on these attributes, have come to seem to be amongst the most important activities of psychology has happened only because we take for granted particular constructions of the individual and of their relationship to the social world.

The intense study of the individual, the construction of individuals as possessing attributes which can be studied without reference to a social context, and the use of a rhetoric of objectivity, function to protect psychology from 'contamination' by the social and ideological, and thus from accusations of bias. Applied to abortion, these ideas help to account both for psychology's neglect of a topic where the social, ideological, political and moral threaten constantly to intrude, and also for its 'neutral' construction of abortion primarily as a health issue, or as one amongst many potentially stressful procedures with objectively measurable effects on individuals who just happen to be women. In this book I shall move away from this traditional framework in order to place the topic of abortion and women's experience of it firmly within a social context. It is important that this is done, not only to provide a fuller account of psychology's relationship to the topic, but also because, whether or not we intend it, psychological research *constructs* the phenomena on which it focuses: it tells people how to think about themselves, about others and about particular experiences. And whether we intend it or not, research informs social policy and is linked in often subtle ways to social regulation. In using a wider framework than that traditionally adopted by psychology, I aim to make these processes highly visible and to provide an account which offers greater choice in constructions of abortion than is currently available in psychology. Two areas traditionally absent from psychological theories – gender and power – will be central to the discussions. Their relevance to abortion and the ways in which they will inform the arguments developed in the book will be briefly discussed in the next section.

ABORTION, GENDER AND POWER

Only women can have abortions, but access to abortion – or at least to legal abortion – is controlled largely by men. In Britain, for example, around 90 per cent of Members of Parliament, who develop abortion legislation, are male;[2]

---

2 Since the 1997 general election, this figure is around 82 per cent.

MASTER *the Art of* READING

over 80 per cent of gynaecologists, who perform abortions, are male, as are around 75 per cent of general practitioners, who may be approached first by women seeking abortions. A participant in a 1984 debate in the Northern Irish Assembly on whether the 1967 British legislation should be extended to Northern Ireland, regretted that debates on abortion 'very often take place when no women are present' (NIALRA 1989: 26). In addition, Lipman-Blumen (1994) and Faludi (1992) have drawn attention to the fact that, at least in the US, the leaders of the anti-abortion movement are predominantly male. The implications of this gender imbalance for the development and implementation of legislation and for women's experience of abortion have been almost entirely neglected by psychological research, as if the gender relations implicit in abortion were simply an artefact of no theoretical or practical interest.

One way of thinking about the relationship of gender to abortion is through abortion's strong and obvious links with female sexuality and motherhood. Control of the procedure can therefore be seen as part of a larger pattern of control of female sexuality and reproduction. French, for example, has argued that 'almost all extant cultures regulate women's procreation, through regulating marriage or women's sexuality or both' (1986: 27). Similar arguments emphasising the persistence and pervasiveness of male practices of control over reproduction have been put forward by many others (e.g. Rich 1976; Ehrenreich and English 1979; Petchesky 1984; Lerner 1986; Vickers 1994). Control over reproduction has often operated by force or in highly visible ways, for example, through the use of chastity belts, confinement of women to the home, chaperoning, making contraception and abortion illegal or sinful, and so on. Although such visible mechanisms are still widely used, they have been accompanied or, particularly in Western cultures, partly replaced by more subtle and less visible mechanisms of control. Michel Foucault (1977, 1979, 1980) has provided a theoretical framework for examining these mechanisms which is particularly relevant for psychology because of the ways in which he linked less visible forms of social regulation to the production of knowledge in the human sciences.

Foucault was strongly critical of traditional essentialist models of power which depicted power as an entity which could be possessed by particular individuals or groups, was located in a centralised source and could be 'seized' or 'passed on'. Within these models, power is mainly repressive, an accumulation of laws, taboos, prohibitions and sanctions often backed by the use of force. Foucault did not deny that such forms of power and domination existed; he argued, however, that essentialist models could not give an account of non-centralised forms of power at the micro-level of society. In the alternative model proposed by Foucault, power is exercised rather than possessed and operates through social relationships and social practices. This emphasis on power as relational and as operating at all social levels highlighted processes of power which had been obscured by essentialist models.

Foucault used the term bio-power to describe those ways in which power is exercised on the bodies and minds of individuals. As Sawicki points out, bio-power emerges as 'an apparently benevolent but peculiarly invasive and effective form of social control' (1991: 67). And it is unlikely to be accidental that these subtle mechanisms of control appear to have developed in parallel with the decline in more direct processes such as absolute monarchies or rule by a social elite (see also French 1986). Foucault described two related forms of bio-power, both relevant to abortion. The first consists of a 'bio-politics of the population', a series of social and economic policies, interventions and laws relating to birth, death, marriage, health and reproduction. The second form of bio-power is disciplinary power which operates through social institutions and social relationships to render individuals more productive and useful, but also more docile and manageable.

The idea of *discourse* is central to this model of power, and particularly to disciplinary power. The term refers to particular ways of talking or writing (and, by implication, thinking) about certain groups or phenomena. Alternatively, as Ransom (1993) puts it, discourse refers to 'structured ways of knowing'. 'Discourse' provides an important link between the production of knowledge about any topic and social regulation. Given that there are potentially many different ways of talking about or construing any group or phenomenon, the important question becomes not whether what is said or known about particular phenomena is true, but, for example: What conditions fostered the emergence of a particular discourse? What status is accorded certain discourses and what status is accorded their alternatives? Who is empowered to produce particular discourses and what devices are used to present them as valid or even factual? Which social practices and power relationships are allowed, maintained or made to seem reasonable by particular discourses and which discouraged? In posing questions such as these, Foucault took it for granted that constructing theories or producing knowledge involved exercising power, whether intentionally or not. Attempts to answer such questions allow us to see the close relationship between the production of discourse, including 'expert' discourse which may be called knowledge, and the practices of social regulation. For example, it would be difficult to justify the social practice of hospitalising some people who behave in deviant or criminal ways without an expert discourse which links deviant behaviour to illness, treatment and medical care, even when no bodily ailment can be found. Yet as Scull (1979) has shown, this way of talking about deviant behaviour gained ascendancy during the nineteenth century for a complex set of social, political, economic and professional reasons that had little to do with the epistemological values which are now used to defend it. Similarly, nineteenth- and twentieth-century medical discourse about women's bodies and minds exists in a complex cause-and-effect relationship to political and social practices of excluding or attempting to exclude women from public life (Jeffreys 1985; Ussher 1989; Kent 1990).

The relationship between discourse, knowledge and social regulation is highlighted further when we consider what Foucault saw as a central feature of bio-power, and particularly of disciplinary power: that it does not so much directly oppress people (although it may do) as *produce* them. It does so by creating desires (for example, the desire to be thin) and personal attributes such as locus of control, self-esteem, attitudes or personality. Bio-power also creates, rather than discovers, particular groups of people – the homosexual, the frigid woman, the agoraphobic, the alcoholic, the borderline personality, the child with attention deficit disorder – and, at the same time, mandates particular ways of 'managing' them. As I emphasised earlier, within psychology these constructed categories have gone hand in hand with an intense focus on the individual so that category names are assumed to refer to attributes or entities possessed by individuals; it is these constructed categories or attributes which so often become the objects of study of psychological and psychiatric research.

Psychological research on abortion has largely been carried out within this discursive framework. Much of the research focuses on whether women 'join' a particular category or develop certain attributes, such as anxiety or depression, after abortion. Not only does this approach take such categories as given rather than constructed, it tends to view abortion as a potentially stressful life-event whose wider social meanings are not central to individual women's experience. It thus creates an artificial separation between the individual and the social context, in which discrete external events impinge on the individual, leaving their mark in the form of a different psychological state but through processes which are not clearly described or analysed. Some studies do take account of the meaning of the pregnancy and abortion for the woman, but this tends to be construed in an individualistic and personal way without reference to the wider social and political context. When the social context is acknowledged, it is often in a limited, descriptive way through the statistical relationship between discrete untheorised variables such as 'class', 'religion' and 'social support' and scores on an intrapsychic measure. It is not simply that this research draws on existing constructions of individuals and of their relationship to the social world, in turn, the research itself becomes a means of reproducing and strengthening these constructions, it becomes part of the mechanisms of disciplinary power.

Some aspects of Foucault's theories, however, have been criticised by feminist scholars (see, for example, MacCannell and MacCannell 1993; Ramazanoglu and Holland 1993). One of the major criticisms has been that in emphasising power at the micro-level of society, in relations among people, Foucault underemphasised the impact of power at the macro or structural level and provided only an outline of the relationship between micro and macro processes of power. Smart (1989) has also criticised Foucault for failing to provide an adequate account of the relationship between juridical (legal) power and disciplinary power, and for underestimating the continued impact of legal power. In writing about bio-power, Foucault implies that female and male bodies and minds stand in the same relation to practices of power; he fails to consider the origins and implications of the fact that both discursive and material power in relation to female and male bodies so often seems to be exercised by men. Nevertheless, the framework provided by Foucault, together with feminist theories which have extended and overlap it, provide a rich source of ideas for

9

re-thinking psychology's relationship to abortion and for uncovering aspects of the relationship which go well beyond those implied by published research. This framework is particularly appropriate because abortion involves one of the most salient and contested sites for the operation of bio-power – women's bodies and women's reproductive processes. Because it is regulated by law, abortion is also an area where we can examine the relationship between juridical (legal) power and bio-power, as well as the complex relationships amongst material entities and processes (bodies and reproduction), discourses surrounding abortion and the operation of professional power. Finally, we can examine the relationship of all of this to women's and men's experience of abortion.

THE STRUCTURE OF THE BOOK

Any discussion of abortion requires a background knowledge of the law relating to it, and this is provided in the next chapter. The chapter is not simply descriptive, but provides a framework for considering the relationship between legal/juridical power and bio-power and for examining psychology's role in this relationship. The third chapter examines the debates surrounding abortion legislation. It provides a detailed study of the discourses about women which participants drew on in these debates and of the relationship of these discourses to legislative proposals. This chapter also highlights the extensive and often hidden role played by psychological and psychiatric research in the abortion debates and offers some explanations for the extraordinary strength of feeling which surrounds abortion. Chapter 4 is concerned with the role of the medical profession in abortion. It continues the discussion of the relationship between different processes of power by looking at the implementation of abortion legislation through the practice of medicine. It examines the ways in which the medical profession is positioned in abortion debates and the decision-making process which doctors are expected to undertake. The process of implementing legislation will be looked at also in relation to women's status and role in the health care system and in relation to the historical and recent role of medicine in defining women's psychology and controlling their sexuality. Chapter 5 focuses on perceptions of the relationship between abortion and contraception and on the fact that a considerable number of women seeking abortion report that neither they nor their partner were using contraception when the woman conceived. Some of the social and psychological issues surrounding the use and non-use of contraception will be examined as well as the possible role of abortion services in reinforcing the view that women are primarily responsible for contraception. In Chapter 6, I shall discuss the experience of abortion, but within a much broader framework than is traditionally used in psychological research. In particular, this chapter examines how the experience of abortion may be related to its social meanings and to the discourses surrounding it. The final chapter will return to the theme with which the book began, that of psychology's relationship to abortion. Drawing on discussions in previous chapters, this chapter examines further psychology's uneasy relationship to social policy and its reluctance to acknowledge the role of social, moral and political factors in the production of knowledge. Finally, I shall suggest some future directions for research and policy which take account of these issues and which acknowledge the close relationship between the production of knowledge and the regulation of behaviour and experience.

2

ABORTION LEGISLATION

The law on abortion, like all legislation, has developed against a background of particular social and moral concerns. The first part of this chapter will describe these legislative developments in Great Britain and Northern Ireland, the Republic of Ireland and the United States (for discussions of abortion law worldwide, see Eggert and Rolston 1994a; Furedi 1995; Hadley 1996). The second part of the chapter will be concerned with the nature of abortion legislation. It will focus particularly on the ways in which the conceptual nature of abortion legislation has changed over the last century or so and on the ways in which these changes illuminate the relationship between the two major mechanisms of power posited by Foucault: juridical (legal) power and bio-power, or power over bodies and minds.

ABORTION LEGISLATION IN GREAT BRITAIN

Access to abortion in Great Britain is controlled by two major laws: the 1967 Abortion Act and the 1990 Human Fertilisation and Embryology Act.[1] The Abortion Act allows termination of pregnancy under two main sets of conditions. Two registered medical practitioners must decide in good faith that continuation of the pregnancy would involve risk to the life of the pregnant woman, or injury to her physical or mental health or to that of any existing children of her family, greater than if the pregnancy were to be terminated. Alternatively, two registered medical practitioners must agree that there is a substantial risk that if the child were born it would suffer such physical or mental abnormalities as to be seriously handicapped. In reaching their decision, doctors are allowed to take into account the woman's 'actual or reasonably foreseeable' environment. Additional clauses specify some of the requirements for abortion services, such as the licensing of premises outside of the National Health Service, and also specify those

---

1 The Human Fertilisation and Embryology Bill was concerned with the regulation of reproductive technology, for example, in-vitro fertilisation, and with embryo research. In the absence of alternative opportunities to change abortion legislation, however, a number of parliamentarians tabled amendments to this bill concerning abortion.

exceptional circumstances, such as immediate danger to the woman's life, where the decision to carry out an abortion may be taken by one doctor.

The 1967 Act did not impose a time limit on abortions. The limit was inferred from a previous law – the 1929 Infant Life Preservation Act – which referred to 'infants capable of being born alive'. Women who had been pregnant for twenty-eight weeks or more were assumed to give birth to infants capable of being born alive. The 1990 Human Fertilisation and Embryology Act set an explicit time limit of twenty-four weeks for most abortions, with exceptions under certain extreme circumstances such as grave threats to the woman's life or health.

The 1967 Abortion Act supplemented what was at the time the most restrictive abortion legislation in Europe – the 1861 Offences Against the Person Act.[2] That Act set a maximum penalty of life imprisonment for attempting to procure an abortion and criminalised anyone, including the woman herself, who attempted to secure an abortion. The Act also criminalised the attempt even if the woman was not pregnant, and attempted to check the supply of 'noxious things' and 'instruments' obtained with intent to procure abortion. The 1861 Act clarified and extended what had been the first criminal statute against abortion – Lord Ellenborough's Act of 1803. Although this Act was ostensibly intended to protect women from the dangers of surgery, Brooks (1988) sees it as partly resulting from the growing interest of medical men in gynaecological problems and their concern with professional status. While abortion might be indicated in some very narrow circumstances, such as to save a woman's life, doctors expressed concern that so many abortions should be carried out by 'irregular', i.e. non-medical practitioners. The 1803 Act, however, had not fully addressed medical concerns. As Brooks points out, its retention of the 'quickening' distinction, in which abortion before the woman first perceived foetal movement was seen as a lesser offence, was a particular irritant to doctors, relying as it did on a woman's subjective judgement about the progress of her pregnancy. The quickening distinction was dropped in an 1838 amendment to the 1803 Act and this change was maintained in 1861. The 1861 Act also referred to the *unlawful* procurement of miscarriage, thus implying that there were circumstances under which abortion might be lawful. While these were assumed to be extremely narrow and were not to be set out in law for over a century, it was widely assumed that only medical practitioners could ever lawfully perform abortions.

The social context of British abortion legislation

One of the most striking features of abortion law prior to 1967 was the extent to which it was disregarded. For obvious reasons, reliable figures on the number of illegal abortions carried out each year are difficult to come by. But even the most conservative estimates suggested tens of thousands per year, while estimates for

---

2 Neither the Infant Life (Preservation) Act nor the Offences Against the Person Act applied in Scotland, where abortion was governed by common law.

the years between 1963 and 1967 reached over 100,000 per year (Callahan 1970; Diggory 1970). There was, too, a great deal of informal evidence that illegal abortion was a common occurrence. A paper published in the 1930s (McIlroy 1936, cited in Brooks 1988), for example, noted with disapproval the existence in one factory of 'a private insurance fund, paid in weekly' which insured both single and married women against the risk of unwanted pregnancy by paying an abortionist's fees. Similarly, Marie Stopes noted that at her birth control clinic she had had:

> In three months...as many as 20,000 requests for criminal abortion from women who did not even *know* that it was criminal...In a given number of days one of our travelling clinics received only thirteen applications for scientific instruction in the control of conception, but *eighty* demands for criminal abortion.
>
> (Cited in Brooks 1988: 6, emphasis in original)

Some women might have been forgiven for believing that abortion was not a crime when advertisements for abortifacients regularly appeared in newspapers and respectable women's magazines. These advertisements did not mention abortion directly, but offered remedies for 'female ailments', 'menstrual irregularity' or 'disruption of the menses', all well-understood codes for unwanted pregnancy.

The number of prosecutions for breaches of abortion legislation was tiny in comparison with the number of abortions carried out. In 1919, for example, sixty people were tried for procuring abortions; forty-two were convicted. In 1934, thirty-three were convicted (Brooks 1988). Prosecution was made difficult not only by the secrecy surrounding abortion but also by popular sympathy with the practice. Brooks, for example, notes one case in which over 10,000 people signed a petition in support of a doctor whose practice had come to legal attention when a woman died. Although many women did die as a result of abortion or were injured in some way, the death rate appears to have been well below 1 per cent in the early decades of this century. As Brooks points out, abortion was therefore an acceptable alternative to poverty, shame, unemployment and homelessness. The very high rates of illegal abortion, coupled with low rates of prosecution, emphasise the existence of strong and reliable networks of advice for women seeking abortion. One Ministry of Health document referred to a sort of 'secret service' among working-class women to help women with unwanted pregnancies (ibid.). Middle-class women, of course, also had such networks, even if they were more likely to lead to the medical profession for a 'small operation' than to a backstreet abortionist.

By the first decades of the twentieth century, there was widespread concern amongst the medical profession, the judiciary and the Government about the extent to which the law on abortion was disregarded. The number of prosecutions under the 1861 Act doubled between 1900 and 1910 and doubled again over the next twenty years. It is difficult to know if this reflected increased recourse to abortion or increased vigilance in the implementation of the law, but it seems likely that the increasing employment of women outside the home, and the social changes brought about by the First World War would have led to an increase in the number of abortions. That women were increasingly choosing abortion is also suggested by figures for maternal mortality and for infant mortality from prematurity. These rose steadily in the early decades of this century and it was widely believed that at least part of this increase could be attributed to increased resort to (often unsuccessful) abortion.

Concern over abortion was reflected in the extent to which it was the subject of public examination. Groups as diverse as the World League of Sexual Reform, the Women's Co-operative Guild, the Eugenics Society and the British Medical Association discussed the issue, voted on it and produced reports. The general attitude was one of support for reform of the law and the Abortion Law Reform Association was formed in 1936 to campaign for reform. In 1937, the Government appointed a Committee of Inquiry, chaired by Norman Birkett, to examine the issue of maternal deaths and, in relation to this, abortion. There is no evidence, however, that the government of the day intended this Committee to act as a catalyst for changes in the law.

Although there was general agreement that the extent of recourse to criminal abortion was undesirable, a number of factors operated to produce what was in effect a stalemate in the law and therefore the maintenance of the status quo. Each argument which seemed to suggest that abortion law should be liberalised could be balanced by another (often from within the same organisation) which suggested that it should not. For example, supporters of eugenics and 'racial betterment' could argue that abortion would help rid society of 'defective stock' and improve the quality of the race. On the other hand, they feared that if abortion became widely available, it would be used as much, if not more, by middle- and upper-class women as by poor women, leading to a serious imbalance in the 'quality' of the population. Nor did concern over maternal welfare lead to a clear conclusion about abortion. While lives might be saved by legalising abortion, the same end could be achieved by proper implementation of the law and by improvements in maternity services. Indeed, as Brooks (1988) has noted, the majority report of the Birkett Inquiry dissociated maternal welfare from criminal abortion by concluding, on the basis of very little evidence, that spontaneous abortion (miscarriage) accounted for the majority of abortions. The solution was thus improvements in maternity services rather than reform of the law.

The medical profession, too, was ambivalent about abortion. There was cautious support for reforms which would allow doctors to carry out abortions to prevent severe deterioration in a woman's health, but doctors had no wish to be associated with the popular image of the criminal backstreet abortionist who destroyed life for profit. The medical profession's stance was further complicated by disagreements between general practitioners, who were often well aware of women's social circumstances, and hospital specialists, distant from the woman's environment but who must agree to carry out the abortion. As Brooks has noted, obstetricians were inclined to view the pregnant woman as 'a case which would be successfully completed by the birth of a healthy child' (1988: 62). Resort to abortion therefore reflected a failure of clinical skill.

The birth control movement was a third area of conflict and ambivalence over abortion law. At first glance, it might seem that those who supported birth control would also support reform of the abortion law. In fact, as Brooks points out, the birth control movement, while supporting women's right to control their fertility, acted to create a distinction between abortion and contraception where previously many women had viewed them as a continuum. This was only partly because many of those involved in the movement believed that there genuinely was a distinction; others believed that the task of the birth control movement would be made easier, and therefore more beneficial to women, if its supporters dissociated themselves from a criminalised practice. The result was that developments in contraceptive services did not go hand in hand with attempts to reform the law on abortion.

One further factor which operated against reform of abortion law was the widespread alarm at women's demands for economic and personal autonomy. Responses to this situation involved both support for and opposition to reform of abortion law. Supporters of reform could argue that a married couple's sexual fulfilment, and a woman's dedication to motherhood, were best served by removing the constant fear of pregnancy. Others argued that resort to abortion was at odds with the self-sacrificing and life-enhancing ideal of motherhood. In the short term at least, this latter ideal proved stronger and was central to the social reconstruction which followed both the First and the Second World Wars. Indeed, Brooks has emphasised the continuity of political goals which underlay the massive social disruption of the two wars. As she points out, the popularity of the post-World War II coalition government's slogan 'Homes fit for heroes' 'went beyond the appeal of a neat council house to the wider emotional resonance of a wife and family. Shaken by the upheaval of war, contemporaries clung to traditional gender roles to provide a sense of stability in a changing world' (1988: 10). These sentiments, combined with post-war unemployment, created an unfavourable climate for the reform of abortion legislation.

Clearly, then, much had to change in order to reach a point where, in 1966–7, more liberal abortion legislation was acceptable to the majority of Members of Parliament. In discussing some of the social and medical factors which led to changes in the law, Brooks has argued that, 'It was not until fertility control was regarded as a widely acceptable social goal, and a necessary part of health care for women, that abortion moved out of the criminal context and into the mainstream of the health services' (1988: i–ii). The acceptability of fertility control was almost certainly a function of new fears of overpopulation, in marked contrast to previous fears of underpopulation, and of an increasingly strong emphasis on the quality rather than the quantity of the population. This emphasis was highlighted by the furore over the effects of an epidemic of

16

measles and of the drug thalidomide on foetal development. Much publicity was given to the difficulties which pregnant women 'at risk' faced in obtaining abortions, and to the considerably greater ease with which better-off women could obtain them.

Although all of these factors were important in creating a favourable climate for changing abortion legislation, two further points deserve special mention. The first is the introduction of the National Health Service in 1948. A major part of its importance for abortion legislation lay in the fact that it provided a means whereby abortion might be carried out on a relatively large scale, but without monetary profit to the operators. It had always been assumed that abortion offered much opportunity for profiteering by those indifferent as to whether the abortion was truly therapeutic. Brooks (1988) has shown that whether a fee had been charged, or how much had been charged, was often an important influence on the outcome of abortion trials. The existence of a non-profit making NHS helped secure the support of both doctors and the public. As we shall see in the next chapters, however, the situation was rather more complex than a simple desire to protect pregnant women from commercial exploitation. It also involved the belief that the NHS would act as a brake on the 'abortion trade' by removing the prospect of financial gain and thereby allowing the objective distinction between deserving and undeserving women who requested abortion.

The second, and closely related, factor which played a crucial role in abortion law reform was the increasing medicalisation of behaviour and experience. By using the term 'unlawful', the 1861 Offences Against the Person Act had implied that abortion might sometimes be lawful and some doctors had interpreted this to mean that abortion might be permitted to save a woman's life. In the early decades of this century, however, there was increasing discussion about the lawfulness of abortion for mental rather than physical reasons. The acquittal of Dr Aleck Bourne, who was prosecuted in 1938 for carrying out an abortion on a 14-year-old 'decent' girl who had been raped, suggested to some that a woman's mental state was as important as her physical state in abortion decisions. The nineteenth and early twentieth centuries, however, lacked an accepted system of thought which allowed the incorporation of a wide range of behaviour and psychological experiences into the notion of health. There was, too, a lack of trust about doctors' abilities and motivations when making judgements about matters of the mind, particularly when money was involved. For many people, 'psychiatric grounds' represented little more than an excuse for wrongdoing. By the mid-1960s, however, attitudes had changed. The 1959 Mental Health Act marked a high point of public faith in the benevolent power of medicine applied to behaviour. This legislation, and the parliamentary proceedings which accompanied it, were based on three important assumptions. The first was that mental illness is an illness like any other. In other words, the 1959 legislation sought to blur or abolish any distinction between physical ailments and psychological distress or disturbing behaviour. The second assumption was that doctors have the knowledge and skills to make impartial judgements about these matters and that they should be allowed to do so free from public or judicial interference. Finally, it was assumed that the intervention of psychiatry was always therapeutic and in the best interests of the patient. The 1959 Mental Health legislation also encouraged a process which had been apparent for some time: that of widening the range of behaviour and experiences which were seen as falling within the remit of 'mental ill-health'. The judge in the 1938 Bourne trial had felt able to sanction an abortion if the woman might otherwise become a 'mental or physical wreck'; in the 1960s, a much broader interpretation of 'psychological harm' could be made without it appearing, at least to the majority, that the boundaries of medicine were being breached. Public confidence in doctors' ability to make impartial judgements about these matters was almost certainly heightened by the existence of the NHS and the lack of a profit motive. The increasing medicalisation of people's lives and the development of the NHS were thus likely to have been closely related influences in the reform of abortion legislation in Great Britain.

Between 1967 and 1990, around twenty attempts were made to change abortion legislation, most of them in ways which would have made it more restrictive. Only one of these – through an amendment to the 1990 Human Fertilisation and Embryology Bill – was successful, suggesting that the major tenets of the 1967 Act are still acceptable to the majority of parliamentarians.

ABORTION LEGISLATION IN NORTHERN IRELAND AND THE IRISH REPUBLIC

Although Northern Ireland is part of the United Kingdom, the 1967 Abortion Act does not apply there. In both Northern Ireland and the Republic, abortion is governed by the 1861 Offences Against The Person Act which was enacted before the partition of Ireland. In Northern Ireland, abortion is also regulated by the 1945 Criminal Justice (Northern Ireland) Act, equivalent to the 1929 Infant Life Preservation Act. English case law, such as the Bourne judgement, could arguably also apply in Northern Ireland (Lee 1995). Attempts to extend the 1967 Act to Northern Ireland, for example through an amendment to the 1990 Human Fertilisation and Embryology Bill, have been unsuccessful, not least because Northern Irish politicians from opposing parties have put forward similar religiously based arguments against abortion. Access to abortion therefore remains very restricted and it is conservatively estimated that two thousand women (from a population of around 390,000 women aged between 15 and 49) travel from Northern Ireland each year to have abortions in Britain (NIALRA 1989).

In the Republic of Ireland, the restrictions placed on access to abortion by the 1861 Act were intensified by a 1985 amendment to the Constitution which read:

> The State acknowledges the right to life of the unborn and, with due regard to the equal right to life of the mother, guarantees in its laws to

respect, and as far as practicable by its laws to defend and vindicate that right.

(Article 40.3.3, NIALRA 1989)

This amendment was interpreted by the Courts as denying women the right to information on abortion or to travel elsewhere to have a legal abortion. In 1993, the Constitution was again amended, by referendum, to allow women to receive information about abortion and to travel outside the Republic to have abortions. In 1994, 4,592 women from the Irish Republic (from a population of around 870,000 women aged 15–49) were officially recorded as having abortions in England and Wales (ONS 1996a).

ABORTION LEGISLATION IN THE UNITED STATES

The process of developing abortion legislation in the United States is different from that in Britain in at least three important ways. First, state as well as national legislatures may enact legislation, so that a wide variety of abortion legislation may be in operation at any one time. Second, interpretation of the United States' Constitution has been central to much legal debate over abortion and, third, abortion in the United States has been associated with far more intense legal, social and political activity than in Britain. This is at least partly due to the greater visibility and influence of both religious fundamentalism and feminism in the US. Nevertheless, until the early 1970s, abortion law in the United States was very similar to that in Great Britain pre-1967 and was largely derived from English Common and Criminal Law.

As in England, the idea of quickening, and the related theological idea of ensoulment, were central to perceptions of abortion; in the US there was no common law crime of aborting a foetus before quickening. During the early nineteenth century, the newly developed English Criminal Law on abortion began to be adopted by some American states. For example, in 1821, Connecticut adopted that part of Lord Ellenborough's Act which referred to post-quickening abortion, but the death penalty was not imposed. It was not until 1860 that pre-quickening abortion was criminalised in that state. In 1828, New York State passed highly restrictive legislation which nevertheless treated abortion before quickening as a less serious offence, a misdemeanour, as compared to second degree manslaughter for abortion after quickening. This statute, however, introduced the concept of therapeutic abortion by allowing abortion if two physicians advised that it was necessary to save a woman's life. By 1840, only eight states had statutes dealing with abortion, but the number increased in the period following the Civil War. By the late nineteenth century, the quickening distinction had almost disappeared; by the early decades of the twentieth century, the majority of states had banned all abortion except to save the mother's life.

The factors which encouraged the development of highly restrictive abortion legislation in the United States appear to have been rather similar to those operating in Great Britain. Mohr (1978) has highlighted concern over the falling birth rate amongst the middle classes and the medical profession's aspiration to control the practice of abortion. One means of achieving this was to emphasise the gravity of the procedure, both morally and physically, and to argue that abortion should only be carried out for the gravest medical reasons, discernible only to a medical practitioner. In 1967, the American Medical Association restated its position on abortion, when a Committee on Human Reproduction urged the adoption of a policy of opposition to induced abortion except where there was 'documented evidence... of a threat to the health or the life of the mother or that the child may be born with incapacitating physical deformity or that pregnancy resulting from rape might constitute a threat to the mental or physical health of the patient' (cited in Doerr and Prescott 1989: 128). By 1970, however, the American Medical Association presented a less united front and noted the polarisation of the medical profession on abortion. It noted also that the views of some members appeared to have changed considerably since the time of the last statement. At the same time, both legal and public attitudes to abortion were becoming somewhat more supportive of reform of the law.

It was against this background that, in 1973, a woman who had been refused abortion in her home state brought her case to the Supreme Court. In the landmark decision, *Roe* v. *Wade*, the Court found in her favour and ruled that the constitutional right to privacy was broad enough to encompass a woman's decision to terminate her pregnancy. The Court considered that the state's legitimate interest in a pregnancy increased with the length of the pregnancy. This interest was minimal in the first trimester, when abortion was very safe and when 'the attending physician, in consultation with his [*sic*] patient, is free to determine without regulation by the state, that in his medical judgement, the patient's pregnancy should be terminated' (*Roe* v. *Wade* 1973). The state was considered to have a more compelling interest in the second trimester and might more strongly regulate abortion in the interests of the woman's health. In the third trimester, this interest was joined by a legitimate interest in the protection of foetal life. State regulation could therefore be extensive during this period. Although the Supreme Court's ruling referred to a woman's constitutional right to privacy in the abortion decision, it is clear that the Court considered that access to abortion was important because of its implications for women's health. Thus, in both Britain and the United States, abortion was seen as therapeutic for women, even if in the US it also involved the idea of constitutional rights.

As Halva-Neubauer (1993) has pointed out, Roe's jurisprudence offered little guidance as to the precise ways in which states might regulate abortion while adhering to the Supreme Court's ruling. Many states interpreted the ruling very narrowly and the years following *Roe* v. *Wade* saw what Halva-Neubauer has called an 'avalanche of legislation restricting abortion' (ibid.: 168). These state laws did not seek to make abortion illegal; rather, they sought to reduce access to abortion and to regulate it as closely as possible. State legislation was concerned with a number of issues including public funding of abortion, that is: with banning or severely restricting the use of public funding for abortion services; with informed consent, which in this context meant physicians telling women about foetal development and about the possible risks of abortion; parental consent; parental and spousal notification; conscience clauses for physicians who did not wish to perform abortions and insurance restrictions which allowed companies to offer policies which included maternal benefits but not abortion. (For a detailed discussion of state legislation, see Goggin 1993a.)

Developments in US legislation

Although the states were actively involved in abortion legislation in the years following *Roe* v. *Wade* – usually in attempts to restrict the operation of the Supreme Court ruling – state legislative activity existed in a somewhat uneasy relationship with the Supreme Court and a number of state laws were rescinded or enacted in a modified form. This meant that the limits of state power were never quite clear. In 1989, however, the Supreme Court's ruling in *Webster* v. *Reproductive Health Services* not only ratified state powers over abortion legislation, but appeared to grant the states more freedom to place restrictions on the availability of abortion. Goggin (1993b) has suggested that this ruling effectively transferred authority over access to abortion services to state politicians; indeed, as he points out, in the months immediately following the Webster ruling, almost forty bills were introduced in state legislatures. Halva-Neubauer (1993), however, has argued that although there was much debate about abortion at state level following the Webster ruling, there was little new legislative activity. Rather, what *has* been noticeable is an intensification of a process which had begun some time earlier, namely a shift in the language used in the debates, particularly by anti-abortion groups. Halva-Neubauer has highlighted a shift from a language of foetal rights, or a language which explicitly supports restriction of women's choice, to a language emphasising parental rights and family cohesion (in the case of adolescent abortion), taxpayers' rights (in the case of public funding of abortion services), the prevention of foetal pain, informed consent and the banning of 'birth-control' abortions – that is, all abortions not involving threats to the woman's life, gross foetal abnormality, rape or incest. As we shall see in later chapters, there has also been an increasing emphasis on the physical and psychological harm which abortion is said to cause. This redefinition of the grounds of the debate has also been apparent amongst pro-choice groups who have placed less emphasis on 'women's rights' and more on individual choice, with slogans such as 'Who decides, you or the Government?' Goggin (1993b) has in fact argued that the 1989 Webster ruling acted as a catalyst to pro-choice groups in the same way as *Roe* v. *Wade* had done for anti-abortion groups. Certainly, pro-choice groups have recently been proactive in debates at state level, introducing, for example, proposals to outlaw harassment of women seeking abortion; legislation to regulate anti-abortion counselling centres and resolutions condemning clinic violence.

The 1992 election of Bill Clinton as President on a pro-choice platform suggested that the focus of the abortion debate in the United States might move from state legislatures to Congress, particularly, for example, in relation to a proposed Freedom of Choice Act which would codify *Roe* v. *Wade*. President Clinton did restore funds to International Planned Parenthood and to the United Nations Population Fund; he also began a review of the import ban on RU486, a post-coital drug for inducing abortion. At the time of writing, however, proposals for the Freedom of Choice Act have not been brought before Congress; the Republican majority in Congress from 1995 makes it unlikely that they would be successful. In addition, the composition of the Supreme Court in 1973 at the time of the *Roe* v. *Wade* ruling, was a 7–2 Liberal majority. In the 1990s, this has been transformed to a 6–3 Conservative majority.

THE NATURE OF ABORTION LEGISLATION: ABORTION, LAW AND POWER

Two clear trends can be discerned in the development of abortion legislation over the last century or so. The first corresponds to that category of 'bio-power' described by Foucault as a bio-politics of the population. As Brooks has put it, abortion has been transformed 'from an important female-centred form of fertility control into a medical event, closely monitored by the State' (1988: 163). This transformation has, of course, been part of a much larger development of state intervention in many aspects of life, health and death in which the state has positioned itself as having a crucial role in the preservation of life and health. The second, closely related, trend concerns the transformation of abortion from a largely criminal to a largely therapeutic procedure, that is, one which is said to be performed in the interests of preserving or enhancing the health and well-being of the woman or her existing children.

The significance of this second transformation for psychology's relationship to abortion can be better understood by using Bean's (1980) distinction between two very different forms of law: formal law and therapeutic or purposive law. Formal law governs criminal acts such as murder, arson, fraud, assault, and so on, and has a number of important features. First, the state's role in formal law is as accuser and penaliser; there is no suggestion that the law is supposed to benefit the accused. Second, the law is operated and interpreted by the judiciary – by lawyers, magistrates, judges and juries. Third, formal law usually operates in public: we may visit courtrooms or read trial reports and transcripts. Finally, because formal law is not assumed to benefit its recipients, there are extensive provisions against its wrongful operation: the right to a legal defence, the right of appeal, and so on.

Therapeutic or purposive law operates in a very different way and under a different set of assumptions. First, it places a strong emphasis on the state's function of protecting the welfare of its citizens, particularly those who are thought to be vulnerable. The law is thus assumed to operate for the benefit of its recipients, as when someone is compulsorily admitted to a psychiatric hospital in order to be treated for a mental illness. Second, therapeutic law is not operated by the judiciary but by administrators and professionals, because it is assumed that people other than lawyers or judges can best interpret the law. Third, the rules of therapeutic law are explicitly formulated to allow professional discretion in decision-making. Because the stated purpose of therapeutic law is to achieve or maintain the health or welfare of an individual, it is assumed that invoking formal legal rules and precedents may be not simply insufficient but irrelevant in reaching a decision about a particular person. Finally, therapeutic law usually operates in relative privacy and it may be difficult for the public to gain access to its proceedings.

Both formal and therapeutic law claim to be authoritative but, as Bean has pointed out, the claims have different epistemological bases. In formal law, claims to authority derive from adherence to formal procedures, appeals to precedent, to the pronouncements of higher law-making bodies, and so on. By contrast, therapeutic law's claims to authority derive from invoking an esoteric and non-public knowledge about, for example, the diagnosis and treatment of mental illness. This knowledge is assumed to be possessed by certain professionals and to be operated in a neutral, value-free way. It is this claim to authority through science, and public acceptance of the claim, which determines the particular ways in which therapeutic law operates. Interpretation of the law is given over to professionals because they, and not the judiciary, are assumed to have the necessary specialist knowledge. This does not mean that the judiciary is never involved in therapeutic law; but as Bean (1980) and Sheldon (1996) have shown, the courts are often reluctant to question the judgement of professionals or at least of the medical profession. The assumed neutrality of professional knowledge and its application is also crucial to the operation of therapeutic law. It is this neutrality which helps justify the privacy in which the law is applied as well as the relative lack of protection against its wrongful operation.

The extent to which abortion law can be seen as part of the system of therapeutic law varies from country to country. In Ireland, for example, and in many Latin American and African countries, abortion remains largely within criminal law and the extent of professional 'therapeutic' decision-making may be very narrow. Abortion legislation is most obviously part of therapeutic law in those countries where abortion is allowed on a wide range of health and socio-medical grounds. The law may still remain within the criminal statute, and if the courts do become involved (for example, if a doctor is accused of performing an illegal abortion) then the mechanisms of formal law will come into play. When abortion is allowed on socio-medical grounds, however, the large majority of abortions are regulated by the mechanisms of therapeutic law. As I have shown, this kind of legislation is dependent on lawmakers assuming that there exists a body of specialist knowledge whose claims to authority do not come from within the judicial system. In the case of abortion, this knowledge involves assumptions about psychological distress, its recognition and its relationship to particular environments and life-events. The knowledge which is regularly invoked by doctors in making abortion decisions therefore concerns human emotions and behaviour. This is, of course, precisely that area of knowledge identified by Foucault as the source of his second type of 'bio-power' – disciplinary power, whose practices he linked with the development of the human sciences.

We can look at the relationship between the law and disciplinary power in two ways. The first is through the explicit use of specialist knowledge about bodies and minds in therapeutic law; unlike formal law, the operation of therapeutic law is dependent on the assumed existence of this knowledge. The second way of looking at the relationship between disciplinary power and law applies to both formal and therapeutic law and involves the idea that the law operates by constructing 'its own image of the legal subject which it seeks to regulate' (Sheldon 1993: 20). This process is unlikely to be clearly articulated and may be discerned only through an analysis of the development and operation of particular laws. The construction of legal subjects is achieved through both popular and professional discourses which allow, or make seem reasonable, particular legal practices. Smart (1989) and Kennedy (1992), for example, have shown how rape trials, operating through formal law, draw on a range of discourses about masculinity and femininity which construct both victim and accused and which influence legal procedure (e.g. what is admitted as evidence, instructions to the jury) and jury deliberations. Therapeutic law also constructs its legal subjects. Mental health legislation, for example, constructs a subject who lacks the ability to make rational decisions and who can therefore be detained or treated without their consent. The law also constructs and regulates the complementary legal subject of the doctor, who is rational and objective and who acts in the best interests of the patient. The two mechanisms of disciplinary power are, of course, related in the sense that the characteristics of a 'legal subject' who is to be regulated must in some way 'match' the specialist knowledge invoked in therapeutic law. Thus, doctors are assumed to know how to diagnose and treat the forms of mental illness which produce the irrational subject of mental health legislation.

This interdependence of legal and psychiatric–psychological discourses calls into question some aspects of Foucault's analysis of juridical (legal) power and disciplinary power. As I pointed out in the Introduction, Foucault argued that over the last two centuries, juridical modes of power and regulation had been gradually superseded by new modes of disciplinary regulation which operate through the language, theories and practices of the human sciences. Although Foucault did not deny the continuing power of legal regulation, he paid little attention to it. His analysis, however, may have created an artificial separation between juridical and disciplinary power and taken insufficient account of the extent to which the two would become interdependent. Indeed Smart (1989) has argued that far from the power of law diminishing in the face of new modes of disciplinary regulation, it has been strengthened by incorporating the discourses of the human sciences. But it is probably equally the case that the power of psychological and psychiatric discourse is strengthened by its incorporation into the law, particularly if, as Bean has claimed, the dependence of therapeutic law on professional knowledge has allowed formal lawyers to 'abdicate from that part of the legal system...to say with justification that they do not need to understand certain parts of the legal system' (1980: 50). The next two chapters will examine more closely this relationship between juridical and disciplinary power, between psychological and legal discourses, in the development and operation of abortion legislation.

3

THE ABORTION DEBATES
1 Motherhood, morality and the sanctity of life

Debates on abortion take place in many settings, but I am going to focus here mainly on debates which are directly linked to the production of abortion legislation. I shall draw on British parliamentary debates of the 1960s, 1980s and 1990s and, to a lesser extent, on United States debates from 1973 onwards. There are several reasons for this focus on legislative debates. First, these debates offer an exceptionally rich source of data on abortion. What is said is extensively documented, as also are voting patterns on particular aspects of legislation. Second, these debates offer an important means of examining that neglected area of Foucauldian theory: the relationship between disciplinary and juridical power. As I pointed out earlier, disciplinary power is said to operate through the use of discourses or ways of talking about bodies and minds; these discourses exist in a symbiotic relationship to social practices, institutions and regulation. A question of major interest, therefore, is how participants in the abortion debates talk about bodies and minds in order to support particular legislative outcomes which, in turn, become part of the mechanisms of juridical power.

The debates will not be treated as if they were expressions of attitudes held by the participants. Of course participants may be expressing deeply held personal views, but the term 'attitude' suggests that we are talking about psychological attributes which are straightforwardly represented by what people say. The idea of attitude can obscure the variability and contradictions in what people say about particular issues, and it provides no clear mechanism for examining either the meaning of such variability or the functions of particular utterances. Instead of using the idea of attitude, the debates will be presented as a set of accounts in which participants use language in organised ways in order to achieve certain effects. The analysis will be informed by two assumptions which were briefly discussed in Chapter 1. The first is that discourses, or organised ways of speaking, are not deployed in a vacuum. Foucault (1979, 1980) emphasised that any given body of statements, from conversations between friends to accounts of scientific studies in learned journals, depends for its comprehensibility on other unarticulated statements which 'carry deeply entrenched convictions and explanatory schemas fundamental to the dominant form of making sense of the world in any given period' (Sawicki 1991: 104). It is precisely because these convictions and explanatory schemas *are* so fundamental to our way of thinking about the world that relationships amongst discursive practices, and their links to social regulation, may not be obvious. The second assumption underlying this analysis of the abortion debates is that discourse is strategic, that is it is used to achieve certain ends, to provide justification for certain social practices. The analysis is therefore less concerned with whether particular statements are 'true' or are supported by evidence – although this may be an important consideration – than with their utility or consequences in terms of legislation and the social practices which follow from them.

The analysis has three major aims. The first is to examine the ways in which the female 'legal subject' of abortion legislation has been constructed so as to make particular forms of legislation seem appropriate. The second aim is to highlight the ways in which psychological and psychiatric research and theory have been used, directly and indirectly, to support particular representations of women in the debates. Finally, I hope that the analysis will cast some light on the question of why abortion has become such a contentious social issue and why it arouses such strong emotions in both pro-choice and anti-abortion groups.

The approach adopted here offers a *deconstruction* of what at first might seem a straightforward set of arguments for and against various sorts of abortion legislation. Deconstruction offers a means of examining the ways in which language operates below our everyday level of awareness (Hare-Mustin and Marecek 1988). Part of this process involves attending to contradictions and inconsistencies in any 'text'; it also involves paying almost as much attention to what is *not* said as to what is said on any topic. One of the reasons why the areas of silence which surround an issue are so crucial in understanding how it is constructed is because meaning is not absolute but relational; in Western culture the meaning of ideas or 'objects' is built on a series of hierarchical opposites: 'man' gains meaning only by being contrasted with 'woman' (by being *not* woman); sanity is contrasted with madness, reason with emotion, and so on. Derrida (1978) has argued that such oppositions, together with the meanings which surround each 'pole' and the value of one pole over another, are maintained only by obscuring – by keeping silent about – the similarities between the two poles. Another way of looking at it is to say that the opposition between two terms or ideas, such as man and woman, is maintained by attaching only a very limited set of meanings to each and by maintaining a silence on the multiple meanings which might be attached to each term. For example, far more effort has been expended in trying to identify psychological differences between men and women than in trying to find areas of similarity and overlap; there is no topic area called 'sex similarities'. In the case of abortion, then, we would expect that at least some of the ways in which it has been represented in the debates will be maintained only by contrasting abortion with events which are represented in very different but equally limited ways, and by maintaining a silence on the full range of meanings which might be attached both to abortion and its 'opposites'.

With this in mind, the next section will examine the ways in which the

27

construction of abortion in the debates, and in the legislation which was proposed, was dependent on constructions of the contrasting event of motherhood. The following section will show how representations of 'women who have abortions' was similarly dependent on representations of 'mothers'.

ABORTION AND MOTHERHOOD

To seek an abortion is simultaneously to make a statement about motherhood: a woman may already be a mother and not wish to make a further investment in motherhood; women who seek abortions and who are not mothers are either rejecting motherhood on this occasion or rejecting it permanently. Following Derrida, then, we can assume that one important meaning of abortion is 'not motherhood'. It follows that the ways in which abortion is represented in the debates and in legislation, may be dependent on particular constructions of motherhood.

Certainly, one of the most striking aspects of the representation of abortion in the debates is the extreme negativity with which it is portrayed. Those who opposed liberal legislation portrayed the negative aspects of abortion through its presumed effects on women exposed to it. (The effects on men were not often mentioned.) It was claimed, for example, that abortion 'destroys women psychologically and physically' (Official Record, Commons, 24 April 1990: 224); that many women and men had been 'emotionally and psychologically scarred' by abortion (ORC 22 January 1988: 1230) and that (unspecified) research had shown that '82 per cent of women who have had their pregnancy terminated suffer from post-abortion syndrome' (ORC 24 April 1990: 252). Similarly, it was asserted that 'we must challenge the assumption that abortion is either safe or desirable' (ORC 22 January 1988: 1231) and that 'abortion is not an easy operation. Indeed, it is a disaster for everybody involved. Frequently people are psychologically scarred for life' (ORC 21 June 1990: 1148). One participant asked why counsellors advise women to have abortions 'given the psychological and physical consequences to which a woman may be subject' (OCR 22 January 1988: 1231). In the United States, similar assumptions, at least in relation to under-age girls, informed the Supreme Court's 1981 ruling on the privacy of 'immature minors': it was assumed that the decision to have an abortion has 'potentially traumatic consequences' for minors and that 'If the pregnant girl elects to carry the child to term the medical decisions to be made entail few – perhaps none – of the potentially grave emotional and psychological consequences of the decision to abort' (*HL* v. *Matheson*, cited in Melton and Russo 1987).

But abortion was not simply seen as having deleterious effects on individual women or men. A number of participants in the British debates who supported very restrictive legislation argued that making legal abortion easily available had socially deleterious effects. It was claimed, for example, that liberal legislation would 'brutalize our country in the eyes of the world' (ORC 13 July 1967: 1357);

that '[there is] great concern in society in general at the way in which freely available abortion has changed the nature of society' (ORC 22 January 1988: 1261). It is notable that MPs who supported more liberal legislation rarely challenged these claims about the negative effects of abortion. In the USA, psychologists have tried to challenge claims about the negative effects of abortion on individual women; these will be discussed in more detail in later chapters. But the British legislative debates are characterised by a largely unchallenged account of the individual and social dangers of abortion. Debates in both countries are also characterised by a relative silence (greater in Britain than in the US) about the dangers of alternatives to abortion, i.e. motherhood and refused abortion. Derrida's analysis of meaning, of course, would predict just this state of affairs: that a limited and extremely negative construction of abortion can only be achieved by presenting an equally limited construction of its opposites and by maintaining a silence about the negative aspects of motherhood.

This presentation of abortion – in contrast to motherhood – as a deviant and potentially unhealthy, if at times regrettably necessary, option is emphasised by two further arguments which were made in the debates. The first is that abortion should be denied in order to benefit infertile couples. One MP, for example, claimed that 'scarce resources' which 'might go to relieve the anxiety of infertile and childless couples' were being used to provide abortions (ORC 30 April 1990: 254). Other MPs claimed that women could easily give up their babies for adoption rather than have an abortion, and so bring happiness to a childless couple. The second argument is more subtle and involves what, at first glance, seems to be a positive aspect of abortion services: the provision of counselling for women seeking abortion. The strongest statements in support of counselling were made by those who supported restrictive legislation:

> In most civilised countries, there is a requirement before an abortion is permitted that the woman – who in such circumstances will obviously be in a state of great distress – is counselled by a doctor. There is a pause during which she is given the opportunity to consider the situation.
>
> (ORC 24 April 1990: 219)

> I am also concerned about those women who have been neglected in the arguments advanced by the Opposition. I refer to those who receive inadequate counselling and who consequently suffer from post-abortion syndrome.
>
> (ORC 21 June 1990: 1164)

Similarly, in its judgements on adolescent abortion, the US Supreme Court expressed doubt as to whether abortion clinics would provide adequate counselling for young girls seeking abortion, or whether these girls would 'make wise decisions' in their choice of physicians. It is clear from these judgements, and from the parliamentary debates, that counselling is seen as a potential means

29

of *discouraging* women from having abortions. When participants talk of helping the woman 'consider her decision' or 'make the right decision', the aim is to give women as much opportunity as possible to decide *not* to have an abortion. In querying the enthusiasm of some MPs for pre-abortion counselling, it is not a matter of arguing that women who seek abortion should be denied the chance to talk about their decision, or of arguing that some women might not later regret their decision to have an abortion. What is striking is the unspoken assumption that such careful consideration need only be given to the decision *not* to become a mother; that the only 'wrong' decision would be to have an abortion; that it is only over the decision to abort that women are likely to experience regret or worse. Thus, the decision to proceed with pregnancy is implicitly construed as normal, natural and unproblematic, while the decision not to proceed cannot be entrusted to women and requires the most careful thought. Similar assumptions are apparent in the US Supreme Court rulings on the legality of requiring parental notification or consent to abortion for 'immature minors'. These rulings were intended to allow parents or the courts to prevent an 'immature' young girl from having an abortion, not to prevent her from proceeding with her pregnancy.

The extent to which these negative accounts of abortion, in comparison with childbirth, are misleading can be seen from Cates *et al.* (1982) reporting of a seven times greater risk of mortality from childbirth than from abortion. They have suggested, as has Tew (1990), that the health risks of childbirth have been underemphasised and obscured. Similarly, Brewer (1977) found a five to six times greater risk of post-childbirth psychosis than post-abortion psychosis, although it was claimed in the 1967 British debates that the rate of post-abortion psychosis varied from 9 to 59 per cent – the lower figure is three hundred times that found by Brewer. Negative feelings following childbirth are so common as to have earned the colloquial term 'baby blues', while more serious psychological distress has been reported in around 20 per cent of women in the first year following childbirth (Hopkins *et al.* 1984). This figure is higher than those reported from women who have had abortions (Brewer 1977; Adler 1982; Cates *et al.* 1982; Lazarus 1985; Adler and Dolcini 1986; Adler *et al.* 1992). In addition, research on women who did not have abortions, but who gave their child up for adoption, suggests that this option also can have negative psychological effects (Sobol and Daly 1992). Similarly, studies of children whose mothers were refused abortion, but who kept the child, suggest that being 'unwanted' can have deleterious effects on children's social and psychological development (Watters 1980; David and Matejcek 1981; David 1992). And, in the light of claims about women suffering from post-abortion syndrome, it is interesting to note Niven's (1988) report that 15 per cent of a group of women followed up for four years post-childbirth reported experiences associated with the birth and said to be symptoms of post-traumatic stress disorder, including intrusive thoughts, nightmares and flash-backs.

Clearly, then, the very negative ways in which abortion is represented in the debates – from something which the woman might at the very least come to regret, to something which could cause the downfall of a whole society – are at least partly achieved by maintaining a silence about negative aspects of motherhood and other alternatives to abortion, and by implying that the decision to become a mother will have no negative consequences. But this silence, apparent amongst many pro-choice –as well as anti-abortion participants – is not specific to the abortion debates. On the contrary, the silence in the debates is made possible, is not 'heard' or challenged, by a social context in which motherhood and the desire for motherhood are seen as part of the natural order, rather than as socially constructed. That motherhood *is* socially constructed has been argued strongly by, for example, Rich (1976), Badinter (1981), Urwin (1985) and Phoenix *et al.* (1991). These writers have demonstrated that the meanings and values which are attached to motherhood are historically and culturally variable. Urwin (1985) has also shown how particular constructions of motherhood have been presented as 'natural' at various times so that their social origins have been obscured. It is this naturalisation of a strongly positive construction of motherhood in the twentieth century which largely allowed the negative aspects of motherhood to be so muted in the abortion debates and which, in turn, allowed such a negative construction of abortion.

Positive discourses surrounding motherhood and negative discourses surrounding its alternatives have been crucial in achieving the idealisation and naturalisation of motherhood. For example, popular discourse provides only negative and derogatory ways of talking about adult women who are not mothers and men who are not fathers – childless, childfree (with its implications of lack of responsibility), sterile, barren, infertile, and so on. Women who try to ensure that they will not conceive are helped by 'Family Planning Clinics' or by the 'Planned Parenthood Federation'; both titles imply that parenthood is inevitable. Women, as Hafner (1994: 145) puts it, are 'inundated...with traditional ideas of motherhood'. Women's magazines, he suggests, are a powerful force in the reinforcement of these ideas. Marshall (1991) has highlighted another popular source of the idealisation of motherhood: childcare and parenting manuals, in which the experience of childbirth and motherhood are described in exalted, at times almost mystical, ways, and where only minor deviations from a positive account may be allowed.

As would be expected from Foucault's analysis of the operation of disciplinary power, psychological and psychiatric theory and practice have played an important role in normalising motherhood and in creating or reinforcing negative discourses around 'not motherhood'. Indeed, it is unlikely that the constructions of abortion and motherhood, which are apparent in the abortion debates, could have been sustained had they not drawn, even if implicitly, on a range of 'expert' knowledge and discourses. Morell (1994), for example, has argued that psychology has helped to normalise motherhood by failing to study women who do not have children unless they are seeking help with conceiving.

Similarly, many theories of life development simply assume that adults are parents or parents-in-waiting and fail to develop theoretical accounts of those who are not. Morell has also suggested that ironically, feminist theory has contributed to the idealisation and naturalisation of motherhood through its emphasis on putative female qualities of caring and relatedness (see, for example, Chodorow 1978; Chodorow and Contratto 1982; Ruddick 1989). The relationship between the content of the abortion debates and psychological theory, however, can be seen more directly through participants' use of arguments derived from the ideas of maternal instinct and the centrality of the mother.

Maternal instinct and the centrality of the mother

The idea of maternal instinct refers to a complex set of psychological and biological theories about women (and, by opposition, about men) developed during the late nineteenth and early twentieth centuries. The development and dissemination of these theories need to be seen against a background in which eighteenth- and nineteenth-century Western states had made a variety of efforts of varying success to persuade women to welcome motherhood. Badinter (1981) has described some of the efforts made by the French state. First, links were made between women's present lack of interest in mothering and the decline and fall of the Roman Empire. Not surprisingly, Frenchwomen did not prove particularly amenable to this argument. Second, an attempt was made to induce guilt by pointing out that animals and women from 'primitive' societies provided a higher standard of mothering than the average Frenchwoman. This argument, too, had little success. The third set of arguments emphasised women's biologically based desire to have and to nurture children *and* the psychological fulfilment which would result from doing so. Had these arguments simply been advanced by the state, it is unlikely that they would have been any more successful than previous attempts. Women knew, after all, that they did not always want to have or to nurture children, as witness the large number of illegal abortions and the common practice amongst upper- and middle-class women of 'boarding out' their children. Women knew also that raising children was not always a joyful and fulfilling experience. Several reasons can be suggested for the greater success of arguments which idealised and naturalised motherhood – and which contradicted many women's experiences. These arguments did not originate in the state – although they were enthusiastically endorsed by it – but in the new disciplines of psychology and psychiatry. Women were thus at an immediate disadvantage in that the arguments were presented as irrefutable scientific fact. In addition, their links with Darwin's evolutionary theories made them seem to be merely descriptions of the natural order, and therefore beyond dispute. McDougall's theory of human instincts, for example, (McDougall 1913, 1923) drew on Darwin's distinction between 'complex' emotions, restricted to the human species, and 'simple' emotions, with no intellectual component and which could be observed in all animals. McDougall's instinct comprised both cognitive and affective components, both of which were innate. In labelling the maternal instinct as primary (simple), McDougall both reinforced the ancient and pervasive alliance of women with nature and made this alliance inevitable. And the human maternal instinct was primary not simply in its suggested commonality with animals; as Shields (1984: 225) has emphasised... 'the maternal instinct was not, for the scientist of the late nineteenth and early twentieth centuries, just one of a constellation of female personality attributes but was *the* attribute' (emphasis in original).

The psychoanalytic theory of motherhood was more complex than instinct theory, but no less strong in its message that motherhood was both an ideal and a natural state for women. In these theories, motherhood was seen as part of women's journey to psychosexual maturity and as motivated by unconscious drives. Shields (1984) and Woollett and Phoenix (1991) have suggested that instinct and psychoanalytic theories of motherhood have been updated by more recent theories which stress 'bonding' and 'attachment' between mothers and infants: 'Because motherhood is seen as almost entirely instinctual, it is considered natural for mothers to love and to "bond" with their infants and such emotions are viewed as the central core of women's experiences of motherhood... attachment and bonding are seen as key concepts for explaining how children's needs are met and how mothers come to love and feel responsible for their children's care and to behave sensitively' (Woollett and Phoenix 1991: 41).

These 'scientific' ideas about motherhood have been widely disseminated to women – and men – through the Child Guidance and Parent Education movements (Contratto 1984; Ehrenreich and English 1979), through pregnancy and parenting manuals (Marshall 1991), and through the mass media. It is not simply their claimed scientific status which has made these theories so powerful; psychoanalytic theories in particular contained elaborate mechanisms for invalidating women who disagreed. If the acceptance of motherhood was part of a woman's journey to psychosexual maturity and if women were unconsciously 'driven' towards motherhood, it followed that a woman who rejected motherhood was, at best, out of touch with her 'real' feelings and, at worst, an immature victim of penis envy. Certainly, there is no mechanism in either instinct or psychoanalytic theory for the temporary or permanent rejection of motherhood to be seen as a mature and positive decision.

But the power of these pro-natalist theories derives also from their acceptance by women themselves. Part of this acceptance may stem from the fact that attempts by both the state and human scientists to idealise motherhood have been most intense during times when women have sought autonomy and a higher profile in public life. The vilification to which women have been subjected when they have sought independence from men (see, for example, Jeffreys 1985; Kent 1990) has made the idealised image of motherhood as an area where women are uniquely powerful and important, all the more attractive. Taken together, these factors – the scientific validation of motherhood as a natural ideal, the use of scientific theory to construct non-mothers as deviant, and women's own endorsement of the idealisation of motherhood – may help account for the striking silence in the abortion debates over the difficulties, challenges and health risks of motherhood except under the most adverse circumstances.

It is notable, however, that it was not only the idealisation of motherhood which was prominent in the abortion debates, but its naturalisation. Although these two aspects of the construction of motherhood coexisted in psychoanalytic and instinct theories, the idealisation of motherhood presented a problem for anti-abortionists because it is provisional: it does not extend to unmarried mothers or to very young women (Phoenix 1991; Spensky 1992). The naturalisation of motherhood, or at least childbirth, can, however, comfortably accommodate all categories of women, even if their pregnancies are sometimes problematic. Indeed, for some participants in the abortion debates, it was as if motherhood was so much part of being female that women scarcely noticed when it happened to them, even if the child had to be given away, or was handicapped, or was foisted on them without their consent:

> Surely it would be more reasonable to have the odd malformed child than to take the risk of killing a normal foetus?
>
> (ORC 29 June 1967: 1065)

> I had the privilege to give occasional parties for physically and mentally handicapped children. About 400 or 500 parents attended and ... when asked they immediately refuted any idea that they were under any strain because their children were abnormal.
>
> (ORC 29 June 1967: 1066)

> I do not think the solution [of the grandmother claiming the child as her youngest] is practised as much as it should be, but it is the humane and good solution in all these cases.
>
> (ORLords 22 February 1966: 545)

> According to the colonial reports, 10 per cent of the women, after they had received abortion, were very sorry they had received it. They regretted losing their babies ... I think that if this were put to these women, that they could take a choice of having a baby and having it adopted, a large percentage, especially of the 'old ladies who live in a shoe' or some of the tougher of the sweaty palmed girls [awaiting consultation for abortion] would take it.
>
> (ORL 28 February 1966: 564, quotation marks in original)

> Of course it is a tragedy that little girls should have babies when they are only 12, 13 or 14 – or even 11. But is it morally right to destroy one child

to help another, and is having an abortion all that much better than having a baby which, after all, if the mother wants, will quite easily be adopted?

(ORC 22 July 1966: 1103)

There is seldom any difficulty about adoption [in the case of under-age girls who become pregnant]. The girl may be none the worse for the experience.

(ORC 22 July 1966: 1121)

My Hon. Friend says that such children are unwanted, but this is not so. Many childless couples in this country would love to adopt them. Surely it is much better to do the honourable thing and give birth to one's child, even if one cannot bring it up oneself?

(ORC 22 July 1991: 897)

Similarly, the US Supreme Court rulings which allow judicial veto of an abortion decision when made by an 'immature minor', also seem to be based on the naturalisation of motherhood. The ruling in the case of *HL* v. *Matheson*, quoted earlier, emphasises this:

if the pregnant girl elects to carry her child to term the medical decisions to be made entail few – perhaps none – of the potentially grave emotional and psychological consequences of the decision to abort.

(Cited in Melton and Russo 1987: 70)

It is mainly supporters of restrictive legislation who have explicitly used the idea that childbirth and motherhood are a natural part of women's and girls' lives. But supporters of more liberal legislation, and some opponents of it who wished to specify when abortion *might* be available, have drawn on a related set of discourses which keep intact the motherhood ideal. These accounts acknowledge that motherhood is not an unmitigated blessing, or an event which women can simply take in their stride. Instead, the accounts suggest that a woman should only be expected to take so much motherhood in order to preserve her central role in the family:

Such a [pregnant] woman [with several children in poor housing] is in total misery and could be precipitated into a depression deep and lasting. What happens to that woman when she gets depressed? She is incapable of looking after those children.

(ORC 22 July 1966: 114–15)

Nevertheless [the social clause] is, I think, of some importance, because without it many women who are far from anxious to escape the responsibilities of motherhood, but rather wish to discharge their existing ones more effectively, would be denied relief.

(ORC 22 July 1966: 1114)

35

[under adverse conditions] it becomes quite impossible for [a woman] to fulfil her real function, her worthwhile function as a mother of holding together the family unit.

(ORC 22 July 1966: 1098)

I believe that, if it comes to a choice between the mother's life or the baby's, the mother is very much more important; she has ties and responsibilities to her husband and children.

(ORC 22 July 1966: 1104)

Does the Hon. Gentleman agree that it is because mothers are concerned about the quality of life for their whole families that they have abortions? . . . They risked their lives and the freedom of those who helped them [have illegal abortions] because of their desire to maintain the quality of life for their families.

(ORC 24 April 1990: 209)

These accounts are reflected in psychological theory and practice which represent mothers as central to the family and fathers as invisible or marginal. This representation is achieved both directly and indirectly. For example, Bowlby's theory of maternal deprivation (Bowlby 1973) and the closely related attachment theory (e.g. Ainsworth 1974) explicitly depict mothers as virtually the only important figures in their children's lives. Less directly, the same impression is created by research which has concentrated on the relationship between mothers and children, and which has implicitly assigned to mothers whatever work psychologists considered necessary in facilitating children's development, from providing the correct stimulation at each developmental stage (in the 1930s) to correctly interpreting babies' earliest attempts at communication (in the 1980s and 1990s) (Woollett and Phoenix 1991). The central role of mothers has also been constructed in clinical theory and practice through what Caplan (1989) has called 'mother blaming', which involves, for example, collecting information about child problems only from the mother, not involving fathers in any intervention, and focusing on the mother–child interaction in attempting to formulate the problem.

In the accounts quoted from the abortion debates, we can detect the fear of serious negative consequences if the mother is unable to devote all of her energies to the task of servicing her children – and husband. More than that, the accounts depict women as ultimately dedicated to motherhood and family. These women, it is implied, are not seeking abortion selfishly in order to pursue their own goals, but for the greater good of their families. The fact that both supporters and opponents of liberal abortion legislation draw on discourses which conflate 'woman' and 'mother', and the fact that both groups are virtually silent about the risks, challenges and difficulties of motherhood except under the most adverse circumstances, is testament to the power of normalising discourses which surround motherhood. This focus on women as mothers, and the imbalance in the discussion of the risks of abortion and of its alternatives, seriously restrict the ways in which women may construct their desire for and reactions to abortion. These aspects of the debate help construct abortion as a deviant and unnatural act, sought in desperation and, unlike motherhood, likely to be regretted. And, as we shall see in the next section, they also normalise the involvement of doctors in the abortion decision.

THE CHARACTERISTICS OF WOMEN WHO SEEK ABORTION

I suggested in the last section that construing abortion as 'not motherhood' offers a useful means of furthering our understanding of the content of the abortion debates and, in turn, the content of legislation. It follows, however, that if abortion is 'not motherhood', then women who seek abortion are 'not mothers' or 'mothers subject to certain limitations'. In this section, I shall explore the extent to which the representation of women who seek abortions is derived from and dependent on cultural and theoretical representations of 'mother'. This is particularly important given the extent to which motherhood dominates cultural representations of women and the extent to which 'woman' and 'mother' have been conflated.

The process of idealising and naturalising motherhood involved professionals assigning particular characteristics to women-as-mothers. Of course, because of the conflation of woman and mother, these characteristics turned out to be synonymous with woman herself. For example, Hafner (1994: 144) suggests that men created images of women-as-mothers as 'endlessly patient and caring; women who put their own needs second to those of their children; women who willingly retreated from the world and abandoned their own pleasures and interests to devote themselves wholeheartedly and exclusively to the welfare of their children'. Similarly, French (1986: 205) has described the mother (and wife), as constructed in the nineteenth and twentieth centuries, as 'a ministering semi-deity who never raised her voice, who was sweet, gentle, submissive and happy in self-sacrifice. Indeed, self-sacrifice was the core of her nature, the fate she was born for'. The saintly, almost mystical aura which surrounds this 'icon of feminine goodness' (Gilligan 1993) was summed up in Coventry Patmore's phrase 'the Angel in the House'; as Gilligan puts it 'the woman who acts and speaks only for others'. The extremes to which this role could be taken are well-illustrated by the Catholic theologian Bernard Haring. If, he suggested 'it were to become an accepted principle of moral teaching on motherhood to permit a [pregnant woman] whose life was endangered simply to sacrifice the life of her child in order to save her own, motherhood would no longer mean absolute dedication to each and every child' (cited in Callahan 1970: 421).

These depictions of 'mother' as combining the virtues of an ideal domestic servant with those of a saint were both promulgated and supported by the psychological theories outlined earlier. Instinct, and the related attachment

37

theory, suggested that selfless devotion of a mother to her children was a natural characteristic. Psychoanalytic theory not only insisted that true femininity was attained through sacrifice, particularly of 'masculine' desires, it suggested that this process of self-denial, culminating in the acceptance of motherhood, provided women with true emotional fulfilment. But what of those women who reject impending motherhood by seeking abortion? As we might expect, they risk being constructed within a set of discourses which are the reverse of those which surround the mother ideal.

Abortion, selfishness and women's moral inferiority

In her study of women who had chosen not to have children, Morell (1994) identified three themes prominent both in the literature on 'not mothers' and in cultural representations of them: compensation, regret and derogation. The first of these depicts women without children as sublimating their natural desire to nurture children into other activities, as in the classic example where pets are seen as child substitutes. The second theme, regret, is, as we have seen, prominent in the abortion debates. It is often referred to directly; it underlies much of the discussion on the necessity for counselling prior to abortion, as well as attempts by some US states to enforce waiting periods between a doctor's agreement to carry out an abortion and the procedure itself. It is the third theme, of derogation, which is of particular interest here: if 'mother' places the welfare of others before her own, if she is nurturant, self-denying and self-sacrificing, it seems to follow that 'not mother' or 'not mother on this occasion' is self-absorbed, self-interested or, more bluntly, simply selfish.

In the abortion debates, one of the major ways of representing the selfishness of women who reject impending motherhood has been to present women's reasons for having abortions in a derogatory way. It is difficult to over-emphasise the strength and persistence of this theme amongst supporters of restrictive legislation throughout the abortion debates. In 1929, for example, the *British Medical Journal* declared that abortion had become a 'fashion', implying, one supposes, that its meaning for women was synonymous with the acquisition of a new hat (BMJ 1929: 203). The same journal, in 1937, encouraged doctors to educate women that abortion was not 'a trivial event for gossip with their neighbours' (BMJ 1937: 1192). Around the same time, in 1932, Professor Sydney Smith put forward his views on 'the modern woman', who, he claimed 'had her own point of view and that was that she had control of her own body, and if she was not inclined to go through the trouble and *inconvenience* of childbearing there was no moral right to compel her to do so' (cited in Brooks 1988: 15, my italics). In 1959, a BBC programme 'Life Line' declared that it was unlikely that doctors would want to associate themselves with a law which would put them 'on to the slippery slope of deciding more readily that they could end one life for the convenience rather than the salvation of another' (ibid.: 149).

The idea that women have abortions for their 'convenience' has proved remarkably persistent. In debates in the 1990s, for example, one MP claimed that 'the *de facto* grounds for abortion in the great mass of cases is now that of serious inconvenience to the mother' (ORC 24 April 1990: 252), while another spoke of 'the lives of unborn children [being] taken away merely because they happen to be a social inconvenience' (ORC 22 July 1991: 894). Similar arguments were put forward by others:

> Abortions for the most trifling reasons are granted on one ground or another.
>
> (ORC 21 June 1990: 1144)

> [Abortion on demand] will allow abortion on all sorts of specious grounds.
>
> (ORC 21 June 1990: 1152)

> Abortion is undertaken too lightly by many women.
>
> (ORC 24 April 1990: 252)

Interestingly, these speakers did not elaborate on what 'trifling' or 'specious' reasons motivate women to have abortions, although a national newspaper was not so reticent: commenting on a reported fall in the Italian birth rate, the *Daily Mail* spoke of 'figure conscious women who put work before children' (31 August 1993).

The idea that women have abortions for 'trifling' reasons, for 'mere convenience', not only suggests selfishness and a preoccupation with trivia, it also implies that aspirations which women might have are of no value beside the opportunity to become a mother on any number of occasions. But the choice of language to describe women's reasons for having abortions suggests much more than this. It implies a moral deficiency in women who, it appears, are unable to understand that acceptance of a pregnancy has a higher moral value than a woman's other, selfish, concerns. One speaker in the debates made this quite explicit when he spoke of 'amoral social convenience' as a motivation for abortion (ORC 24 April 1990: 251). Similarly, Petchesky (1984) has highlighted the practice in some US clinics of informing abortion patients that 'the unborn child is a human life from the moment of conception', thus implying that women are likely to overlook certain crucial factors in making moral judgements. This practice was proscribed by the Supreme Court in 1983, but because it 'intruded on the discretion of the pregnant woman's physician' rather than because it might be insulting to the woman herself.

Women were presented in the debates not only as morally deficient, but also as morally devious. Brooks (1988), for example, cites a professor of medicine who wrote to the Abortion Law Reform Association claiming that the 1861 Act was working satisfactorily, and that reform of the law might encourage doctors who were 'prepared to accept the patient's story at face value without adequate investigation'. What is implied here, of course, is that women would lie about their life circumstances if abortion were to be allowed other than on strict health grounds. One specific aspect of their circumstances about which women were assumed to be potential liars concerned rape. As we shall see, pregnancy following rape has always presented problems for abortion legislators, and rape as grounds for abortion has never been specifically mentioned in British legislation. There are several reasons for this, but an important one is that MPs were able to draw on the widespread cultural belief that women's accounts of rape were not to be trusted (see, for example, Lees 1995): women would lie about having been raped in order to secure an abortion, as witness the 'well-known' fact that women already made false accusations of rape.

In constructing women as morally deficient and morally devious, participants in the abortion debates were able to draw on a closely interrelated set of cultural, legal and psychological ideas about women's morality. In Judeo-Christian mythology, woman's status as a moral agent is exemplified by her role as temptress, inclined to lead men into sin: woman's moral nature, within this tradition, has for millennia been defined in opposition to her carnal nature. And it is probably not accidental that in abortion debates, women's morality is being questioned in relation to events where her carnal nature has clearly been involved. The perceived balance between women's carnal and moral natures has, however, varied in different cultural contexts. In the nineteenth century, for example, the balance changed from one of women as predominantly sexual creatures to one in which they were less lustful than men. Cott (1978) has argued that this ascendancy of woman's moral nature over her carnal nature originated in evangelical protestantism: faced with declining male congregations, pastors made women the targets of attempts to uphold Christian values (and congregations) in a world of extraordinary social and industrial change. It was hoped that women would 'provide a haven of peace and security, a repository of moral values' in an increasingly disorderly world (Kent 1990: 33). But this idealisation of women's moral virtues, like the idealisation of motherhood, was provisional. For example, working-class women and prostitutes were usually exempt. And when women were seen as virtuous, it was a very different kind of virtue from men's: female morality was depicted as affective, rather than cognitive, and manifested itself in the domestic sphere, in the care of husband and children. It did not extend to an understanding of abstract concepts like justice or the public good (Shields 1984). The limitations on female morality were theoretically justified by the idea of maternal instinct. To postulate human instincts was obviously to acknowledge links between humans and animals. Writers such as Darwin, Herbert Spencer and McDougall, in keeping with a long cultural tradition, seemed much more prepared to do this in relation to women than to men and the idea of maternal instinct provided an excellent vehicle for the comparison. McDougall, for example, claimed that the maternal instinct 'which impels the mother to protect and cherish her young is common to almost all higher species of animals' (1913: 68). When he addressed the National Congress of Mothers in 1905, G. Stanley Hall refrained from making direct comparisons between his audience and animals; these were, perhaps, better made at a distance and in writing. Hall, however, did the next best thing by comparing women with children: 'The body and soul of womanhood, which is larger and more typical, more generic, as I said, than that of man, is nearer the child and shares more of its divinity than does the far more highly specialised and narrowed organism of the man' (1905: 27, cited in Contratto 1984: 233). This idea finds a modern echo in the remarks of two British judges:

It is well-known that women in particular and small boys are liable to be untruthful and invent stories.

Human experience has shown that girls and women do sometimes tell an entirely false story which is very easy to fabricate but extremely difficult to refute. Such stories are fabricated for a variety of reasons ... and sometimes for no reason at all.

(cited in Smart 1989: 35)

Women have thus been assigned a moral nature which has been simultaneously lauded and derided. Certainly, women have consistently been positioned as morally *different* from men and this difference interpreted as deficiency. Psychological theory has provided apparently scientific support for the idea of women as morally different and deficient. Freud's view of female morality was derived from his theory of the relationship between male castration anxiety, resolution of the Oedipal complex and superego formation; it turns out to be surprisingly similar to the views of instinct theorists:

I cannot evade the notion (though I hesitate to give it expression) that for women the level of what is ethically normal is different from what it is in men. Their superego is never so inexorable, so impersonal, so independent of its emotional origins as we require it to be in men. Character traits which critics of every epoch have brought against women – that they show less sense of justice than men, that they are less ready to submit to the great exigencies of life, that they are more often influenced in their judgements by their feelings of affection or hostility – all these would be amply accounted for in the modification of the formation of their superego. We must not allow ourselves to be deflected from such conclusions by the denial of the feminists, who are anxious to force us to regard the two sexes as completely equal in position and worth.

(Freud 1977: 342)

Freud did go on to comment that he was talking about theoretical constructs and not about actual male and female characteristics. We might be forgiven for displaying some scepticism about this but even if it were the case, Freud's theory still places 'woman' as a class in an inferior moral position, as an inevitable consequence of the conditions of female development.

Freud's major assumption was that women's morality is more flexible (or perhaps fickle) than men's, more likely to be determined by momentary personal concerns and less dependent on abstract and transcendent notions of justice. This assumption has been updated, and lent apparent empirical support within

41

mainstream psychology by Piaget (1965) and Kohlberg (1976, 1981). From his studies of game playing, which he saw as the focus of the development of a sense of morality, Piaget suggested that girls and boys have different attitudes to rules. Girls were said to adopt a more 'pragmatic' or flexible attitude to rules 'regarding a rule as good as long as the game repaid it' (1965: 83). Boys, by contrast, were said to have more respect for rules and to be less likely to make exceptions. It is clear that Piaget regarded boys' moral style as superior: he considered a rule-bound legal sense to be essential to moral development. This sense, however, was 'far less developed in little girls than in boys' (ibid.: 77).

Kohlberg, following Piaget, proposed a stage model of moral development in which children were said to progress through a number of stages in which they typically made particular kinds of moral judgement. His model proposed three levels and six stages of moral development: level one (stages one and two) involves morality based on fear of punishment or on what will satisfy the self. At level two (stages three and four) moral judgements involve attention to others' intentions, rather than deeds, and a willingness to do one's duty to win respect rather than affection. At the highest level (stages five and six), morality invokes shared standards of rights and duties, based on principles. At stage five these could be, for example, the legalistic principles of a contract; at stage six, morality involves judgement and action according to universal principles such as 'justice' or 'human rights'.

Kohlberg's theory, like Freud's and Piaget's, is not simply an attempt to describe cognitive and social development; it is a hierarchy of values, where stage six is seen as embodying the highest form of moral judgement. The model involves movement from a form of morality which is primarily egocentric to one which makes virtually no reference to the self or to relationships. Gilligan (1982) has pointed out that the research on which Kohlberg based his theory involved no female participants. When his moral reasoning scale was later applied to females, their reasoning was found often to exemplify stage three, where moral judgements involve acknowledgement of particular relationships. And, since Kohlberg's model is prescriptive, women were therefore morally inferior. Kohlberg's theory, like Freud's and Piaget's, is in fact remarkably similar to instinct theory in which women's morality, like their maternal instinct, was seen as affectively rather than intellectually based, as concerned with the concrete and particular, rather than the abstract and universal. This recalls the point I made earlier, that women have been assigned a moral nature which is both lauded and derided: it is those qualities which have traditionally defined female goodness and virtue, such as concern for particular others and fulfilment in serving and pleasing the family, which also mark woman as ultimately and inevitably morally deficient. In other words, female morality has been constructed as inseparable from female nature. Participants from different sides in the abortion debates were able to draw on this theoretical unity, this connection between woman's morality and her nature, to put forward what seemed on the surface to be very different arguments, with different legislative outcomes, but which actually drew on the same set of theories about female characteristics. I have already discussed the arguments used by legislators who questioned women's moral judgement and who favoured restrictive legislation. The next section will examine the arguments used by legislators who did not directly question women's moral judgement but who also supported restrictive legislation, and, finally, the arguments of those who supported more liberal legislation and who took an apparently sympathetic attitude to women with unwanted pregnancies.

Abortion, women's emotionality and vulnerability

Before I discuss the arguments about women's emotionality in relation to abortion, it is worth summarising the theories of woman's morality, her psyche and her reproductive system, which were implicitly drawn on by all sides in the abortion debates. Woman's child-bearing capacity, with its attendant visible bodily cycles, positioned her closer to nature; men, lacking this capacity, were allied with culture. Women, being thus closer to animal life, were lower on the evolutionary scale, as witness the primacy of the maternal instinct and its obvious parallels in animals. Psychologically, therefore, women were more favourably endowed with the lower mental processes – perception and emotion – whereas men excelled in intellect and cognition. Women were therefore more sensitive (perceptive) to the needs of others and more likely to focus on the immediate and affective aspects of any situation, rather than on abstract ideas. Women might therefore be appalled by the ugly and brutal, but fail to see beyond this to a set of justifying principles. Woman's bias towards the lower mental processes was accentuated by the fact that her brain and uterus vied for her body's limited energy and resources. It followed that woman's intellect would be least in evidence when her reproductive system was in the ascendant (Ortner 1974; Smith 1981; Shields 1984; Showalter 1987; Ussher 1989). These ideas depicted women as genteel, rather childlike, often irrational and irresponsible, and as subject to physical and psychic weakness as a result of the action of their reproductive systems.

Women's lack of moral judgement, their emotionality and their psychic and physical delicacy were therefore part of a unified system of thought in which woman's 'body' was – and is – a signifier of the negative (right-hand) poles of culture–nature, reason–emotion, strength–weakness, active–passive. It was this theoretical unity which enabled many participants in the abortion debates to by-pass the sensitive issue of women's status as moral agents, but nevertheless to remain within a construction of woman as weak and as not to be trusted with the abortion decision. A number of participants, for example, argued that in early pregnancy women were too emotional to make reasoned judgements or to know what they 'really' wanted. As these arguments also involved the conflation of woman and mother, it was assumed that what women really wanted was *not* to have an abortion. It was never suggested that this same lack of judgement might cause a woman to think she wanted a child when in fact she 'really' wanted an abortion:

[The intentions of this Bill] are apparently humane, but most of these women who appear harassed and disturbed [by their social conditions] in the early stages of their pregnancy... come to terms with it later. After the birth of their child, the baby is precious to them.

(ORC 29 June 1967: 949)[1]

The phase of rejection is short-lived in most and is hardly in evidence after the fourth month and many have written to express their gratitude to us for our refusal to terminate. This has some bearing on recommending abortion... for the state of not wanting is generally a temporary one, while to abort is a permanent and final act.

(ORC 22 July 1966: 102)[1]

That brings me to the point doctors have made to me, that in the first three months many women are feeling perfectly 'seasick' the whole time and will do anything. But after that their maternal instinct takes over and they do not want to be aborted.

(ORL 12 July 1967, quotation marks in original)

These speakers, like those who questioned women's moral judgement, wanted to restrict women's access to abortion. Those speakers who wanted to widen access, however, could hardly draw on women's moral deficiencies, or their mistaken beliefs that they wanted an abortion. Instead, they drew on closely related but apparently less derogatory discourses of women's general psychic weakness and vulnerability, their emotionality and desperation in the face of an unwanted pregnancy. Thus, many accounts were given of women terrified to reveal their pregnancy; of women abandoned by their partners; of women unable to bear the burden of another child; of women who would – and did – go to any lengths, swallowing ground glass or bleach, using knitting needles and coat-hangers, in attempts to secure an abortion. This emphasis on women's suffering and vulnerability was also apparent in the Lane Committee's 1971 Report on the operation of the 1967 Act: the Act was said to have relieved a 'vast amount of individual suffering'. Similarly, the 1973 US Supreme Court ruling *Roe* v. *Wade*, claimed that abortion should be available to women, otherwise 'psychological harm may be imminent' (*Roe* v. *Wade* 1973: 727).

Arguments which stressed women's weakness and vulnerability were sympathetically received in the abortion debates and were almost certainly very influential in the liberalisation of British abortion law. It is not that these arguments were false. Women did go to horrific lengths, often resulting in severe injury, to secure abortions. They did feel desperate in the face of an unwanted pregnancy. But the arguments presented abortion, and women in relation to abortion, in ways which were not necessarily as helpful to women as they appeared. First, in focusing on women's suffering and vulnerability, the

---

1 Speakers quoting correspondence from doctors.

arguments obscured women's strength and resourcefulness in the face of unwanted pregnancy. There was, for example, no mention of the strong and efficient self-help networks, such as the factory insurance scheme mentioned in Chapter 2, which women had organised to facilitate access to abortion. It is not that these made legal abortion unnecessary, but they presented a very different picture of women in relation to unwanted pregnancy from that presented in the debates. A second consequence of the focus on vulnerability was to individualise and pathologise abortion and women in relation to it. Abortion was presented, to quote the Lane Committee, as a form of relief for *individual* suffering – a form of therapy – and not as a social and political issue. Thus, legal abortion was said to be necessary in the face of women's psychological and physical suffering, not, for example, because compulsory motherhood is an extremely effective means of maintaining women's economic dependence on men and limiting their opportunities for other achievements. In the debates in the 1990s, a few MPs argued from this social perspective, but it was never more than very marginal to the discussions. And, in associating unwanted pregnancy with mental distress, the debates continued the long tradition of pathologising women's reproductive processes and constructing women as intrinsically weak in relation to them (cf. Ussher 1989). Finally, the prominence given to women's suffering and distress supported legislation in which the medical profession played a central role in the abortion decision and which required women to approach abortion from a position of weakness.

There is no one answer to the question of why arguments involving women's suffering should have been so prominent in the British debates. A straightforward answer, of course, is that women did suffer under restrictive legislation and, as was frequently pointed out, the risk to health and welfare was much greater for poor women. It could also be argued that appeals to the alleviation of suffering offered the best defence to arguments which depicted women as seeking abortions for frivolous reasons and that these were the only arguments available in a context which lacked – and still lacks – positive discourses for women's rejection of motherhood. Nevertheless, the emphasis on women's suffering helped ensure that the debates and the legislation remained within the familiar discourse of female weakness and reproductive pathology; this emphasis also re-created a traditional relationship between male and female: she is in distress and awaits rescue by a more powerful male figure. The overwhelmingly male legislators may well have felt more comfortable within that framework than within one which emphasised the political, social and personal implications of women's reproductive autonomy.

ABORTION AND THE SANCTITY OF LIFE

Arguments about women's nature and about the effects of having or not having abortions, were very prominent in the legislative debates. Another set of arguments, however, about the need to respect human life, were equally prominent at least amongst supporters of restrictive abortion legislation. This apparent concern for 'life' is reflected in the label 'pro-life' which many anti-abortionists use to describe themselves; in Britain, an all-party group of MPs who oppose the present legislation refers to itself as the 'pro-life Committee'. The centrality of a pro-life commitment has been apparent in many speeches in the debates. The Bill which preceded the 1967 Act, for example, was said to undermine 'respect for the sanctity of human life, which is fundamental to British Law' (ORC 22 July 1966: 1080); if passed, it would 'reverse the trends we have tried painfully to build up in this and other countries for respecting all human life as something sacred in itself' (ORC 22 July 1966: 1087). The Bill was said to rest 'upon denial of the sacred character and value of human life' (ORC 22 July 1966: 1155). David Alton's 1987 Bill, which attempted to reduce the time limit on all abortions, was said to be about the 'right to life of the unborn' (ORC 6 May 1988: 1195), while the debate on amendments to the 1990 Human Fertilisation and Embryology Bill, concerning time limits for abortion, was said to be 'very much...about the sanctity of life' (ORC 24 April 1990: 254) and about the 'saving of lives' (ORC 24 April 1990: 216). MPs were told that 'we in the House have a great duty, whatever our personal beliefs, to recognise that there is nothing more sacred than life' (ORC 24 April 1990: 211). Similarly, a 1990 US Supreme Court ruling accepted a state's right to legislate on abortion during the first six months of pregnancy to protect 'potential life'.

As well as arguing that abortion debates are about the sanctity of life, participants argued that disregard for life, as evidenced by liberal abortion legislation – was responsible for many of society's ills:

I am suggesting that, unwittingly, the [1967] Act has helped to create a climate in which people do not have so great a regard for the sanctity of human life.

(ORC 24 April 1990: 209)

Sadly, we live in an aggressive and violent society. We meet aggression every day of the week. We see it on the tube. We experience it among drivers. There is no longer respect for humanity. This is highlighted by what the House has done since 1967.

(ORC 24 April 1990: 255)

Disregard for the sanctity of life and the rights of the unborn child has had a bad effect on our society.

(ORC 21 June 1990: 1151)

Arguments which link abortion with a lack of respect for the sanctity of life clearly depend on the assumption that human 'life' begins at or shortly after conception. Yet there is not and never has been agreement on when human life should be thought to have begun or on what criteria should be used to make this judgement. Various points made in the British debates illustrate this lack of consensus:

46

I am told that three weeks after conception, the embryo has a heart that beats. This seems to be as clear a case of the existence of an independent human life as is possible to have.

(ORC 22 July 1966: 1087)

Modern microbiology has confirmed that human life is fully present from the moment of conception and there is no qualitative difference between the embryo and the born child.

(ORC 22 July 1966: 1156)

We do not know when human life begins.

(ORL 12 July 1967: 277)

Similarly, a 1990 opinion poll showed that 45 per cent of a British sample believed that human life begins at conception; 25 per cent believed it begins at birth, while 10 per cent claimed not to know. This lack of consensus is also clear from cross-cultural analyses. As Morgan (1989) has pointed out, we tend to assume that the products of human conception will be human, but cross-cultural data show wide variation in such beliefs. In some societies, for example, very premature babies are not considered to have any human attributes; in others, judgements about whether the foetus is human may be reserved until its biological attributes can be empirically verified at birth. But even if it were possible to reach a consensus on when human life begins, this would not, as Petchesky (1984: 37) reminds us 'move us one step toward knowing what *value* to give the foetus, what *rights* it has or whether to regard it as a person in the moral and legal sense' (emphasis in original). The question of the value which should be placed on the foetus can have no absolute answer, but it can be clarified by considering a distinction rarely made in the abortion debates, between 'human' and 'person'. A number of writers (e.g. Petchesky 1984; Flower 1989; Minturn 1989; Morgan 1989) have pointed out that the abortion debates have often been conducted in a cultural vacuum, where insufficient attention has been paid to the implications of this distinction and to the fact that 'personhood is not a "natural" category or a universal right of human beings, but a culturally constructed assemblage of behaviors, knowledges and practices' (Morgan 1989: 105, quotation marks in original). That this is the case can be inferred from the wide range of practices by which 'personhood' is conferred and which may take place at birth or up to several years later. During this transition period between biological birth, the latest point at which human status is usually conferred, and social birth, where personhood is bestowed, the infant/child does not have the same value as other members of the social group and infanticide is not regarded as murder. Western groups are unusual in making virtually no distinction between biological and social birth; Minturn has argued that Western maternity services, with their emphasis on the immediate, if unofficial, recording of births, have played an important part in the blurring of this distinction. Medical practices such as amniocentesis, which reveal the sex of the foetus, and ultrasound scanning, which

47

provides a 'picture' of the foetus, which the parent(s) may be encouraged to take home, are likely to blur this distinction still further.

It is possible, then, to argue that those who regard the foetus unequivocally as 'life', and to be protected as such, are merely being culturally and philosophically naive; that they are regarding as absolute what is in fact provisional, a cultural construction. This may well be the case, although participants in the abortion debates who invoke the sanctity of life could argue that there is nothing wrong with moral absolutes; that regardless of other social practices, Western society can still adopt the position that human life is sacred, or is to be valued, from the moment of conception. The links between opposition to abortion and respect for the sanctity of life, however, are much more complex than this. I mentioned earlier that one of the major characteristics of a deconstructionist approach to the study of discourse is its focus on areas of silence and inconsistency in linguistic accounts. These, it is argued, can highlight unarticulated assumptions which underlie particular accounts as well as revealing the strategic function of these assumptions and the mechanisms of power which they imply. The following sections will use this method of examining gaps and inconsistencies, in order to explore the 'hidden' relationship between pro-life arguments and assumptions about women's nature and social roles. I will do this first in relation to abortion and rape, and second in relation to the construction of abortion as 'killing'.

Abortion, rape and female sexuality

The idea that women who conceive as a result of rape should have a right to abortion has a long history and continues to be popular even among those most strongly opposed to liberal legislation. The Select Committee which reported prior to the 1929 Infant Life (Preservation) Act stated that they would not wish to see any impediment to abortion for victims of rape and incest. The British Medical Association's report on abortion in 1936 listed 'rape of a girl under 16 years old' as a proper indication for 'therapeutic' abortion (Brooks 1988). It is therefore probably not coincidental that the two abortion cases which have received the greatest publicity this century – the case which led to the prosecution of Dr Aleck Bourne in 1938 and the case of a girl who was subject to the rulings of the Irish High Court and Supreme Court in 1992 – both involved 14-year-olds who had been raped and both upheld the right to abortion in the face of highly restrictive legislation.

Various statements made during the British debates illustrate support for abortion in cases of rape (all of these statements were made by opponents of liberal legislation):

> We all agree about the horror of bearing a child as a result of sexual assault. Many Hon. Members who oppose most of the provisions in the Bill agree that an abortion would be justified in those circumstances.
>
> (ORC 13 July 1967: 1174)

48

I [regard] these circumstances as meriting special consideration. I want to see rape spelled out as a particular reason for abortion.

(ORC 13 July 1967: 1181)

The minute a lady takes part in a sexual act, other than by force, she loses the right to control what happens to her body because at the time of conception there is the beginning of another life inside her.

(ORC 22 January 1988: 1283)

We pledged that we would make an exception to the time limits for cases involving rape and incest.

(ORC 24 April 1990: 198)

There can be no debate about cases arising from rape and incest.

(ORC 24 April 1990: 207)

In the United States, many attempts by states to restrict access to abortion have excepted pregnancy as a result of rape. Some states, for example, have attempted to ban what anti-abortionists have called 'birth control abortions', defined as all abortions except those necessary to save the mother's life and in cases of rape, incest and gross foetal abnormality (Halva-Neubauer 1993). Similarly, proposals to restrict abortion which were passed by the Idaho legislature in 1990 – and which, if put into effect, would have become the most restrictive abortion legislation in any US state – made exceptions for pregnancy as a result of rape, provided the rape was reported to the authorities within seven days.

It is obvious that facilitating access to abortion for women who have been raped places some strain on the pro-life dictum that the foetus should be treated as having human rights, including the right to life. It might be argued that those who declared themselves to be pro-life, yet supported abortion in cases of rape, were merely doing so to gain support for restrictive legislation out of political necessity. This may be so in some cases. For example, the amendment to David Alton's 1987 Bill allowing later abortions in cases of rape of girls under eighteen, was added at a late stage in the proceedings. This explanation, however, does not seem wholly to reflect the content of the debates or the force of the arguments which were put forward. But even if it did, we would still have to explain why those who develop legislation think it is politically expedient to add rape clauses to restrictive legislation; why they think it will encourage others to support them.

It is difficult to explain this situation without focusing on what appears to be the only relevant difference in the cases of a pregnant woman who has been raped and one who has not, which is whether she is thought to have consented to the sexual activity which led to her pregnancy. The woman who is not held responsible for her pregnancy is to be relieved of her burden with no further questions asked; the woman who is held responsible is not. Indeed, according to the 'pro-life' argument, she is to be *forbidden* access to an otherwise legally available procedure as a means of resolving her situation. As Radcliffe-Richards

49

(1982) has pointed out, the only circumstances in which we forbid people to evade the consequences of their actions is when we want the consequences to act as a punishment. This point was in fact alluded to by one opponent of the 1967 Act: 'One needs to think before one removes all the consequences of folly from people. One does at least need to think what the implications are' (ORC 22 July 1966: 1121).

It might be argued that it is not a matter of making women face the consequences of their behaviour, but of not sacrificing a foetus without grave reason. But what is this reason? It cannot be the relief of human suffering because it has never been suggested that the relative suffering of raped and unraped pregnant women be assessed, or that if the suffering of an unraped woman is as great as that of any raped woman then she too should have an automatic right to abortion. It was, in fact, simply assumed that a woman pregnant as a result of rape *would* be in great psychological distress and this argument was used to support the claim that rape clauses were unnecessary in British legislation. But as we cannot assume *a priori* that the suffering of a woman seeking abortion as a result of rape is always greater than that of a woman unwillingly pregnant after consensual intercourse, then the only justifying factor for granting one and not the other an automatic right to abortion, is whether the sexual activity was voluntary. It is very difficult to avoid the conclusion reached by Radcliffe-Richards: that restrictive legislation which includes a rape clause makes it possible to punish women who consent to sex but not motherhood by forcing them to bear an unwanted child. We can add another conclusion to this: we force people to face the consequences of their actions not only to punish them but also to act as a deterrent to others. The unwanted child may thus serve as an instrument of both punishment and deterrence for women who consent to intercourse but reject pregnancy and motherhood. And it seems reasonable to suppose that these direct and vicarious learning experiences are aimed mainly at women, who have so much more to lose than men if access to abortion is restricted.

It is difficult to demonstrate directly that support for rape clauses in restrictive legislation is linked to the desire to control female sexuality because there has been so little direct discussion of sex in the legislative debates. Further evidence, however, of a strong relationship between support for restrictive abortion legislation and support for restrictions on sexuality and gender roles comes from a number of sources. Prescott and Wallace (1978), for example, examined voting patterns in the Pennsylvania House of Representatives concerning restrictions on state funding for abortion and proposals to reinstate 'fornication and adultery' into the criminal code. There was a striking relationship amongst voting patterns on the abortion and the sexuality proposals such that those who supported restrictions on sexual behaviour were highly likely to support restrictions on funding for abortion ($p < 0.00000005$). Granberg (1978), using National Opinion Research Center survey data, found a relationship between opposition to abortion and a conservative approach to morality as reflected in, for example, disapproval of premarital sex, support for restrictive divorce laws, opposition to sex education in schools and to the wide dissemination of information about contraception. More recent studies (e.g. Jelen 1984; Luker 1984; Guth *et al.* 1993; Schnell 1993) provide further support for this relationship between conservative attitudes to sexuality and gender roles, and support for restrictive abortion legislation.

Abortion as socially sanctioned killing

McKenna has argued that abortion cannot now be discussed 'in plain English'; that we do not confront the fact that abortion is a 'killing process' (1995: 52, 53). Certainly, supporters of liberal legislation have carefully avoided the language of killing, murder or destruction of life, whereas those opposed to abortion have used it extensively. But if abortion *is* a form of socially sanctioned killing, it is reasonable to expect that those who insist on this definition of abortion will show some consistency in the way they approach abortion and in the way they approach other forms of socially sanctioned killing. And, if this is not the case, then we are entitled to assume that opposition to abortion on the basis of a 'pro-life' ideology means something other than it appears.

I have already questioned the consistency of the anti-abortion/pro-life ideology in relation to abortion in cases of rape. Further evidence that concern for the sanctity of life amongst anti-abortionists is highly provisional comes from a number of sources. In a study of voting patterns in the US Senate, Prescott (1978) found a strong positive relationship between opposition to abortion, support for capital punishment ($p < 0.0009$) and support for the continued funding of the Vietnam War ($p < 0.0002$). He also found a strong positive relationship between opposition to abortion and opposition to gun control legislation ($p < 0.0006$). A similarly striking positive relationship between support for restrictive abortion legislation and support for capital punishment for certain military offences ($p < 0.00001$) was found in the UK Parliament (Boyle 1993a).

These data suggest that legislators do not simply treat abortion and other forms of socially sanctioned killing as separate issues, with the law on each to be decided on its merits. On the contrary, the data suggest that there is a considerable overlap between the group who oppose what they think of as one form of socially sanctioned killing – abortion – and the group who support other forms of sanctioned killing, such as capital punishment and war, or the wide availability of the means to kill, such as guns. In the UK study, for example, I found that 88 per cent of MPs who voted for the most restrictive amendments on abortion in the 1990 debates, also voted, in 1991, to reinstate the death penalty for certain military offences, whereas 90 per cent of MPs who voted for the least restrictive amendments voted against the death penalty for these same offences.

A similar picture emerges outside legislative settings. Smeal (1995) has commented on the militaristic pretensions of some anti-abortion groups. One of the founders of the group 'Missionaries for the Preborn', for example, told an audience of the US Taxpayers Society: 'This Christmas, I want you to do the most loving thing, I want you to buy each of your children an SKS rifle and five hundred rounds of ammunition.' Prescott (1978) used standard anthropological data on the social practices of pre-industrial societies to examine the relationship between abortion and a range of other social practices including infanticide, slavery and torture, and mutilation and killing of enemies captured in war. Prescott found no relationship between restrictive and permissive abortion practices and infanticide, but he did find a significant relationship between restrictive attitudes to abortion and the practices of slavery, torture, mutilation and killing of enemies captured in war. These findings are ironic in the light of claims made in the UK debates that adoption of liberal legislation would lead us to resemble Nazi Germany, with its lack of respect for human life. Abortion was, in fact, severely restricted in Nazi Germany, at least for Aryans, and was punishable by death.

Hafner (1994: 141) has drawn attention to a closely related issue: the historical connection between attempts to encourage motherhood and support for sanctioned killing through war. He cites Napoleon's dictum that 'the fewer children who die at an early age, the more soldiers at twenty'. In 1943, during the Second World War, the Prime Minister, Winston Churchill, made a rather similar statement: if Great Britain were 'to maintain its leadership of the world and survive as a great power that can hold its own against external pressure, our people must be encouraged, by every means to have larger families' (cited in Brooks 1988: 134). One of these means, of course, was restrictive abortion laws. The same reasoning lies behind a judge's summing up during an abortion trial in 1920. Noting that the circumstances of the First World War had led to an increase in abortion, and that the public conscience was 'dead with regard to it', Mr Justice Darling asserted that:

> a country which permits its population to be dealt with in this way is bound to decay. Those who have as many enemies as the British Empire must for their own safety have plenty of children to meet these enemies at the gate. We have many gates to defend; therefore it is that the law for that and other reasons makes [abortion] penal and awards a heavy punishment for [it].
>
> (cited in Brooks 1988: 30, parenthesis added)

And, although the abortionist in this case was not sentenced to death, the judge declared that hanging would have been an appropriate punishment. In other words, the state would be justified in killing a man because he had destroyed a foetus which, fully grown, could have been dispatched to kill in the service of the state.

The striking lack of consistency in the 'pro-life' ideology can perhaps partly be explained by the fact that if anti-abortionists have urged us to define abortion as premeditated killing, then Western cultures as a whole have assiduously avoided construing other forms of state killing, such as 'capital punishment' and most especially war, in this way. Indeed, one reads some of the pronouncements of those who espouse a pro-life ideology with a sense of bemusement, wondering if they suffer from a form of selective amnesia which prevents them recalling that in this century alone, around one hundred million people have been killed in war, the majority in wars which have been sanctioned by Britain and/or the United States:[2]

> We are . . . making clear our belief that the destruction of a human being is wrong in any circumstances.
>
> (ORC 24 April 1990: 256)

> It now seems, in our society, that human life is to have value only under certain conditions and [proposed] new Clause 1 [abortion on request in the first trimester] . . . highlights just how much society has drifted towards abortion on demand and towards the view that human life is disposable.
>
> (ORC 21 June 1990: 1152)

> We in the House have a great duty, whatever our personal beliefs, to recognise that there is nothing more sacred than life . . . nothing more precious than life.
>
> (ORC 24 April 1990: 211)

> No issue raises more agonies of doubt and consciences than abortion. On the one side there is the natural revulsion at the destruction of life and on the other side the certain tragedies of desperate women. There is no more reactionary deed because abortion turns life into death.
>
> (ORC 24 April 1990: 251)

This last statement recalls the summing up of the judge I mentioned earlier, who, shortly after the First World War, declared that 'the public conscience was dead with respect to abortion' and that 'a country which permitted its population to be dealt with in this way is bound to decay'. The judge did not seem to consider that a war in which at least ten million people had been killed, and which had apparently led to an increase in illegal abortion, might also indicate a problem with conscience or that allowing a population to be dealt with in *that* way might also lead to social decay. And the MP who, seventy years later, declared that 'doctors who do not agree with abortion will be targeted mercilessly. . . they will be targeted in a most vicious, wicked and un-British way' (ORC 21 June 1990: 1163) seemed to have forgotten that twentieth-century British law has sanctioned the imprisonment and execution of men who refused to participate in war.

These speakers, of course, are not unaware of the fact that war involves killing; nor would it be appropriate to suggest that all of them *support* war while

---

2 None of these speakers voted against capital punishment in a debate in 1991.

condemning abortion. But their silence on the killing which war involves, and the fact that they do not readily explain how this destruction of life is different from abortion, is testament to the extent to which we are encouraged to construe war in such a way that its relationship to the premeditated killing of adults and children is muted. For example, we often use the passive voice ('lives were lost') or opaque language ('heavy casualties', the 'high costs of war', 'collateral damage') which suggests that death is an unfortunate by-product, rather than a planned outcome, of war. Similarly, the innocuous sounding names given to two of the early atomic bombs, including one dropped on Hiroshima in 1945 – 'Little Boy' and 'Fat Man' – deflect attention from the bombs' true destructive potential. Pilger (1995) has drawn attention to the policy followed by the Independent Television news service in reporting the Falklands War in 1982: 'A nightly offering of interesting, positive and heartwarming stories of achievement and collaboration born out of a sense of national purpose'. And the BBC claimed to have followed a policy of suiting 'the emotional sensibilities of the public'. Pilger also notes that during the Gulf War much publicity was given to the supposed 'surgical strikes' of US bombers and little to the civilian deaths and injuries (*Guardian*, 31 March 1995).

But it is not simply that our gaze is persistently turned away from the deliberate slaughter of war. It is that war itself is transformed – at least in the official version – into something so different from large-scale killing that the enterprise becomes scarcely recognisable as involving it. I discussed earlier Foucault's analysis of the profound changes which have occurred in the mechanisms of power in the nineteenth and twentieth centuries: the major form of power, that of deduction, the power to take away, to impose injury or death, has been supplemented by power 'bent on generating forces' (1979: 136). As we have seen, this 'bio-power', ostensibly benign, is concerned with the regulation of birth, health, welfare and well-being; with life-enhancement rather than life-detraction. Foucault, however, has pointed to the paradox in this development:

> Yet wars were never so bloody as they have been since the nineteenth century, and all things being equal, never before did regimes visit such holocausts on their own populations.
>
> (1979: 136)

Foucault has argued that if we are to maintain the stated ideals of bio-power, but without relinquishing war, then war must somehow be integrated into the idea of life-enhancement:

> Wars are no longer fought on behalf of a sovereign who must be defended; they are waged on behalf of the existence of everyone; entire populations are mobilized for the purpose of wholesale slaughter in the name of life necessity: massacres have become vital. It is as managers of life and survival, of bodies and the race, that so many regimes have been able to

wage so many wars causing so many men [*sic*] to be killed... The principle underlying the tactics of battle – that one has to be capable of killing in order to go on living – has become the principle that defines the strategy of states.

(1979: 136–7)

President Clinton provided a striking illustration of Foucault's analysis during the fifty-year commemorations of the 1944 D-Day landings when he declared that, 'We are the children of these men's sacrifice'. This is a modern echo of Winston Churchill's comment during the Second World War that 'without victory there is no survival'. But although the discourse of life has become part of the discourse of war, the term 'life' is not always used literally. Instead, 'life' has come to mean 'life under conditions we take to be life-enhancing'. In the Falklands War, for example, it was scarcely suggested that the islanders' lives were under threat from Argentina; instead, as is evident from parliamentary debates at the time, the war was ostensibly fought on behalf of their *conditions* of life, on behalf of freedom, sovereignty and democracy.

Foucault's analysis of the modern discourse of war in relation to changing mechanisms of power is extremely valuable. It is, however, limited in that it does not explain why this discursive shift should have been so necessary during the nineteenth and twentieth centuries. Nor does it adequately account for the striking relationship which has been found between opposition to abortion and support for measures which allow state killing or facilitate illegal killing. Perhaps it is those who oppose abortion as life-detracting who most strongly espouse the life-enhancement discourse of war, but Foucault provides no way of understanding why this should be so. In the next section I shall extend the discussion of abortion as state-sanctioned killing by considering the issue most strikingly absent from Foucault's analysis, that of gender.

Abortion, war and gender

Sanctioned killing of adults and children is an overwhelmingly male activity. This does not mean that women have been uninvolved in the enterprise; far from it. Although women have rarely played a formal role in state executions, their contribution has always been essential to the conduct of war. Their major role historically, however, has been to support and service men, as mothers and wives, as prostitutes, nurses, replacement workers, and as military service workers. A letter written in 1945 by the Chief of Combined Operations to the Commandos who had fought in the Second World War, illustrates women's subordinate role:

Your country is proud of you and I... am deeply honoured to have been associated with you... I hope that you will not hesitate to apply for advice and help, if you need them, to the Women's Committee of the Commandos' benevolent fund whose desire it is to serve you to the best of their ability.

55

More recently, women have been allowed limited combat roles, although the British, US and Israeli armies exclude women from front-line combat. Muir (1991), however, has argued that women's increasing visibility in the Western military has less to do with a wish to promote women as the military equivalent of men, than with the necessity to secure recruits of a reasonable standard, following the abolition of conscription and the draft.

But whether or not women undertake combat roles, their voices remain muted in public discussions of the planning or conduct of war. In the Second World War, Winston Churchill used members of the Women's Royal Naval Service to record his summit meetings with Roosevelt and Stalin. Later, he thanked the women as 'chickens, for laying so well without clucking' (cited in Ellworthy 1996: 62). Even today, it is still unusual for the media to consult women on the planning and conduct of war. A notable exception, of course, was Prime Minister Margaret Thatcher during the Falklands War. But as if to emphasise how exceptional this was, other women MPs are not recorded as saying a single word in four separate parliamentary debates on the war, during March, April and May 1982.

Explanations for women's exclusion from the 'real' business of war have included: their gentility and distaste for brutality; the fact that pregnancy might prevent them from carrying out military duties; that women are needed at home as mothers and wives; and that the public would not tolerate the deaths of women, especially mothers, as they have tolerated the deaths of men. War is thus constructed at least partly as a kind of chivalric enterprise which men undertake on behalf of women and others who are less fitted to the task or who are needed elsewhere. But what is omitted from these accounts and, indeed, is invisible in most public discussion of war, is the interdependence amongst militarism, patriarchy and the ideal of masculinity. Livingston and Rankin (1986) and Enloe (1983) have argued that the silence which surrounds this relationship, and in which women participate, is essential to the construction of militarism as an integral part of civilised society and, they might have added, to its construction as a force for life-enhancement.

The links between militarism and patriarchy are evident, for example, in the tradition of representing families not simply by the male name, but also by the military insignia (coat of arms) traditionally worn by males. Connell (1994: 159) has characterised the military as dedicated to the deliberate cultivation of a 'dominance-oriented masculinity' through the rigours of basic training. French (1986), Miles (1992) and Hafner (1994) have also highlighted the close affinity between values inculcated in the military and conventional masculinist values. Similarly, McCarthy, reviewing studies of males' own constructions of masculinity, argues that 'masculine role prescriptions continue to emphasise qualities which are little more than slightly diluted versions of warrior values' (1994: 118). These role prescriptions include aggressiveness, energy and physical and moral courage. Conventional wisdom might suggest that these qualities are simply those needed in warfare and that, as women become more visible in the military, they will attach to both men and women. The problem with this argument becomes apparent when we consider a further quality common to both to lay constructions of masculinity and to the military ideal: the avoidance of femininity or womanness (French 1986; Connell 1994; Hafner 1994; McCarthy 1994). It is this which makes the construction of particular forms of masculinity not 'an incidental effect of [the operation of military affairs] but a vital pre-condition of them' (Connell 1994: 159). The importance to the military of the avoidance of femininity can be understood by considering French's (1986) view of patriarchy as a system which positions males as superior to and more important than females, and in which social structures are designed to reflect and reproduce this hierarchical arrangement. Patriarchy is thus dependent on the *separation* of males and females, both physically and psychologically. Historically, the highest status has been accorded those men who achieved the greatest degree of separation from women and womanly values. The high status which has consistently attached to warriors (McCarthy 1994), is dependent on this. Thus, the values most publicly associated with warriors – courage, endurance, strength, skill and honour (McCarthy 1994), are precisely those which signify men's *transcendence* over the realm of nature to which they have assigned women (Ortner 1974; French 1986; Miles 1992). It is not surprising, therefore, that we should find evidence from a wide variety of sources of strongly negative attitudes to women amongst groups and cultures where warrior values are esteemed. In discussion of pre-industrial cultures, Hafner (1994) and McCarthy (1994) have emphasised the extent to which rigid separation of the sexes during adolescence and adulthood, and denigration of supposed feminine qualities, is associated with rituals designed to render boys and men as unfeminine as possible and to inculcate the transcendent attributes of warriors, including the ability to kill without remorse. As Hafner notes, these rituals are remarkably similar to aspects of military training in which, as one commentator put it, 'the basic process is the breakdown of the former self so that the more brutal self will emerge...the whole issue of maleness, of macho, is crucial to the process' (BBC Radio 4, 23 May 1995). The importance of male segregation is also suggested by a recent (1995) legal case in which a woman barred from admission to a South Carolina Military Academy took her case to law (BBC Radio 4, 7 August 1995). Perhaps in anticipation of defeat, the state suggested spending $3.4 million to provide 'a similar but separate' course. Yet South Carolina funded only ten abortions in 1990 (Meier and McFarlane 1993) and in the mid-1980s, that state had the lowest of all state scores on the National Organisation of Women's Index of State Policy on Women's Rights Legislation (Hansen 1993).

Smith (1993) has used an unusual source of data – a song and notebook written by members of a US Fighter Squadron and 'mistakenly' made public – to illustrate the links between militarism and the sexual denigration of women. Her analysis highlighted the conjunction of sexual and aggressive imagery, in which conquest of 'the enemy' was depicted in sexual language, while sexualised women were aligned with the enemy or with death. The association of militarism and women's sexual denigration is further illustrated by Brownmiller's (1976) analysis of the pervasiveness of rape in war. In the Vietnam War, for example, rape was said by one veteran to be 'pretty SOP' (standard operating procedure) for the US troops. As Brownmiller shows, rape has been construed as an inevitable, if regrettable, by-product of war in which access to women's bodies has been variously seen as a reward, as a necessity, or as a way of 'keeping the boys happy' (ibid.: 96). Brownmiller argues, however, that rape is integral to war, is part of the technology of war, and that through its association with conquest, subordination and control, it derives from the same value system as militarism itself:

> War provides men with the perfect psychological backdrop to give vent to their contempt for women. The very maleness of the military – the brute power of weaponry exclusive to their hands, the spiritual bonding of men at arms, the manly discipline of orders given and orders obeyed, the simple logic of the hierarchical command – confirms for men what they long suspect, that women are peripheral, irrelevant to the world that counts, passive spectators to the action in the center ring.
>
> (ibid.: 32)

The construction of war as a highly gendered activity which serves important functions in patriarchal societies assists the analysis of the abortion debates in at least three ways. First, it clarifies certain aspects of the debates which would otherwise be paradoxical or muted. Second, by highlighting some of the 'hidden' ways in which abortion threatens traditional gender relations, the analysis may cast some light on why the issue of abortion raises such strong feelings. Finally, constructing war as a gendered activity helps make understandable the very different ways in which some people have talked about the destruction of life, depending on whether it is initiated by women or men.

The separation of male and female in terms of social roles, physical space and psychological attributes which characterises patriarchal systems is crucial to these first two points. The separation may be more or less extensive and may be supported by highly visible or very subtle forms of regulation. As we have seen, this physical and psychological separation is fundamental to military activity and thus to the legitimation of men as socially sanctioned killers. Women's pursuit of abortion and in particular their desire for so-called abortion on demand, offers a considerable threat to those men and women with a strong investment in social structures which emphasise the differences between, and the separation of, men and women. If women, too, become killers on a large scale – even if only of 'potential life' – then the separation of male and female becomes more difficult to sustain. The threat, of course, is more complex than this. Women's traditional position in relation to war is in supporting 'fighting men' – or, we might say, 'killing men'. The visible aspect of this role involves civilian employment of various sorts, voluntary work and military service roles. The less visible aspect involves women as the providers of psychological support to men damaged by war. The letter I quoted earlier to commandos of the Second World War, alluded to this: 'If you (need) advice and help... apply to the Women's Committee of the Commandos Benevolent Fund'. Women have also traditionally provided men with a haven from, and a contrast to, the horrors of war through the feminine roles of homemaker, mother and receptive lover. Hafner (1994) has suggested a further, even more hidden, role for women in relation to men's role as legalised killers: as a repository for the guilt and shame which men feel about participating in war. The idea that those who participate in legalised killing need a mechanism of expiation has ancient roots. Maccoby (1982), for example, has suggested that the biblical story of Cain is in fact a story of a man made to bear the burden of the group's shame over carrying out socially sanctioned killing (human sacrifice). Cain is therefore expelled from the group, but in recognition of his role is protected by God during his exile. In modern warfare, however, it is extremely difficult to identify such a visible mechanism. On the contrary, those who plan and participate in war are glorified by their dominant social groups and, while regret may be expressed at the 'loss of life', public expressions of shame and guilt are rare. What Hafner is suggesting is an unconscious or at least unarticulated, mechanism of projection whereby men's guilt and shame is projected onto women, who come to be seen as guilty for male aggression. In peacetime, men's warrior role becomes metaphorical, most obviously in relation to work and sport, but women's traditional role remains that of support worker who provides both a haven from, and a contrast to, the aggressive masculine world of work and play.

Given all of this, it is not difficult to understand why the perceived outcome of liberal abortion legislation – the creation of woman as destroyer of life, as sexually autonomous and as 'not mother' – should be so threatening to those who strongly support patriarchal structures. And this group does not just include men. Luker (1984) noted that women anti-abortion activists were likely to have made mothering and the family the centre of their lives. And Ginsburg (1984), French (1986) and Kent (1990) have argued that women who oppose measures which seem to give women greater independence from men, consistently show very negative attitudes towards men and believe that patriarchal structures, with their public emphasis on the family and on men's duty to protect and care for women, offer women their best chance of protection from male brutality. If women step outside these structures, if they reject motherhood and take on men's role as legalised killers, then the consequences for all women will be a highly competitive sexual market place and a vulnerability to, at best, male exploitation and, at worst, male violence. The woman who has been raped and seeks abortion does not, of course, pose quite the same threat to either men or women. She can therefore be treated differently, and attempts in Britain and the US to restrict rape clauses to girls under sixteen or eighteen suggests that it is indeed the woman's perceived 'innocence' which is of concern here. Similarly, women who seek abortion for foetal abnormality may also be treated sympathetically because they have not explicitly rejected their sexual and social roles.

I suggested, finally, that highlighting the gendered nature of war could help in understanding the contrasting discourses of militarism and abortion, particularly amongst anti-abortionists. Although both abortion and war have been constructed in very negative ways, the negative presentation of war is often overshadowed by a highly positive language of heroism, courage and glory. And, as we have seen, attributes assigned to successful warriors have consistently been culturally valued. More specifically, we can contrast in two major ways the discourses which construct 'war' and 'abortion'. The first concerns the perceived effects of engaging in the destruction of life. Anti-abortionists have claimed that abortion is highly detrimental to women's psychological health and for that reason ought to be proscribed. And, although they have not directly supported such claims, supporters of liberal legislation have not rushed to deny them. By contrast, one of the major aims of military training is to teach men to destroy life without remorse or other apparent psychological damage (Hafner 1994). War is therefore not constructed as necessarily harmful to those who participate, although the effort expended in producing warriors suggests that this construction is rather tenuous. Of course, it is accepted that some men will react very negatively in war, but this is often seen as an individual failing to be remedied by selection and training, rather than as a reasonable response to the demands of war (Rose 1989). Zahave *et al.* (1986), for example, discuss tests which identify those men 'suited for combat', i.e. those who will not become psychologically 'disturbed'.

The second contrast between the discourses of war and abortion concerns the putative reasons for destroying life. In the case of abortion, as we have seen, the reasons have been depicted as selfish, trivial or specious, or as involving an individual woman's weakness or vulnerability. By contrast, war is waged and life destroyed for noble reasons – at least from the point of view of the participants. It is waged, as Foucault pointed out, for the purpose of life-enhancement on a grand scale, for freedom, democracy and in defence of human rights. The contrast between these two sets of reasons mirrors exactly the contrasting moralities which have been attributed to men and women by nineteenth- and twentieth-century psychological theory. While women's morality has been depicted as based on the personal, the interpersonal and the emotional, men's is based on rationally derived universal principles. But, if the destruction of adults and children through war can be justified by recourse to principles of freedom, justice, or even economic prosperity, then it is difficult not to argue that the destruction of foetuses can also be justified by recourse to another set of principles involving women's right to reproductive autonomy, with its profound implications for their social status relative to men.

It is not a matter of arguing here that some forms of socially sanctioned killing are 'wrong' and others 'right', or of attempting to construct moral arguments to justify abortion. What is clear, however, is that if we adopt a definition of abortion which accepts that it destroys life, then we uncover a set of silences and inconsistencies which are very difficult to reconcile with anti-abortionists' stated concern for the sanctity of life but which become understandable when we consider the possible implications of abortion for women's social roles.

CONCLUSION

In this analysis of the abortion debates, I have argued that the debates themselves, and abortion legislation, are strongly dependent on a set of discourses about 'woman' and 'man', about 'masculinity' and 'femininity', and that they are less concerned than they seem to be with gender-neutral issues of health or life. It is this 'hidden' agenda which can help account for the very strong emotions engendered by abortion. In line with Foucault's thesis on disciplinary power, I have also argued that the disciplines of psychology and psychiatry have played an important role in both producing and supporting the gender-based discourses which have been prominent in the debates. The next chapter will extend the analysis of the debates and of abortion legislation by examining the role of the medical profession in abortion. As we shall see, its role is both complex and crucially important, not least in that it has provided legislators with a discursive resource which has simultaneously allowed the construction of arguments about 'woman' *and* arguments about health and well-being which have served to obscure the gendered nature of abortion.

4

THE ABORTION DEBATES
2 The medical profession and abortion

A woman may decide that she wants an abortion, but it is doctors who decide whether she may have it. The 1967 Act and its 1990 amendment give the woman no role in this decision; the extent to which her lack of involvement may be tolerated is illustrated by a 1995 legal case (*Regina* v. *Dixon*) in which a gynaecologist who carried out an abortion on a woman who did not know she was pregnant, was found to have acted within the law (for details of this case and some of the controversy surrounding it, see Sheldon 1996). The strength of British legislative opinion on medical involvement in abortion decisions can be gauged from the fact that a proposed amendment to the 1990 Human Fertilisation and Embryology Bill, allowing abortion on request up to twelve weeks of pregnancy, received so little informal support that it was discarded before voting could take place. Another amendment, allowing all abortion up to twelve weeks with the agreement of only one doctor, was defeated in a free vote. In Northern Ireland, where abortion is illegal under the 1861 Offences Against the Person Act, case law has established the right of doctors to make abortion decisions where the woman's life or health is believed to be at serious risk.

By contrast, the 1973 US Supreme Court ruling, *Roe* v. *Wade*, might at first glance seem to leave the abortion decision to the woman herself. Careful reading, however, shows that it is the *doctor*, 'in consultation with his [*sic*] patient' who is to be free 'to determine, without regulation by the State, that in his medical judgement, the pregnancy should be terminated' (*Roe* v. *Wade*: 131). The point is emphasised later: 'The abortion decision and its effectuation must be left to the medical judgement of the pregnant woman's attending physician' (*Roe* v. *Wade*: 183). A recent study by Francome (1994) suggests that if United Kingdom law similarly spoke of the abortion decision's being made 'in consultation between the woman and her doctor', this would be interpreted by doctors to mean that the decision should actually be made by them.

Although some doctors have campaigned against it,[1] this decision-making

---

1 For example, 'Doctors for a Woman's Choice on Abortion' is a British organisation which campaigns for legal changes to allow the woman herself to decide whether to have an abortion.

power has not generally been contested by the medical profession; on the contrary, it has been persistently sought. Yet the abortion decision clearly involves factors beyond the medical. Radcliffe-Richards (1982) has argued that granting or refusing an abortion conflates two quite separate types of decision. The first concerns the likely outcome of terminating or not terminating the pregnancy. The second is about whether the predicted outcomes justify the sacrifice of a foetus. Even if we allow for a moment that the first of these decisions is purely descriptive, the second clearly is not. It might be argued that parliament and not doctors has decided on the matter of when a foetus should be sacrificed and that doctors are merely engaged in the technical task of deciding whether those conditions apply in a particular case. This argument is unsatisfactory for two reasons. First, it overlooks the fact that decisions about 'mental health' or 'handicap' always involve subjective judgement and reference to social norms about appropriate behaviour or achievement in particular contexts. Second, the law gives no indication of how great the benefits of termination need to be to justify the sacrifice of a foetus. Indeed, as Bean (1980) has emphasised, in therapeutic law the rules are explicitly formulated so as to allow professional discretion.

How has this state of affairs come about? How did it happen that a group of people whose expertise is in the workings of the body should be allowed to decide whether a woman must continue with a pregnancy against her wishes or, indeed, whether her pregnancy should be terminated without her consent? We do not, after all, allow nuclear physicists to decide on the deployment of the atomic weapons about which they know so much; nor do we allow engineers to decide when and where, as distinct from how, new roads should be built. It is recognised that these decisions involve matters of value with important social and political implications, and are not simply matters of technical expertise. The first part of this chapter will be concerned with this issue of the assignment of power in abortion decisions. Bearing in mind Foucault's argument that one of the important functions of discourse is to render certain courses of action reasonable and to make alternatives seem inappropriate, I shall focus on the ways in which particular discourses helped to produce legislation in which it seemed reasonable that the medical profession should play such a central role. I shall also examine the issue of the perceived *desirability* of this legislative outcome, on the assumption that the outcome was not an automatic result of available discourse, but was actively sought by legislators. This analysis, of course, also involves looking at the ways in which the 'legal subject' of 'the doctor' was constructed in such a way as to justify legislation in which doctors play such a central role. The second, briefer, part of the chapter will explore some of the practical implications of medical power in relation to abortion: what knowledge are doctors assumed to use in making abortion decisions? Is this knowledge available, and if not, what is used in its place?

GIVING POWER TO DOCTORS: THE DISCOURSE OF MEDICAL DECISIONS

The central involvement of doctors in the abortion decision was justified in the debates primarily by presenting the decision as straightforwardly 'medical'; this presentation, however, was achieved in a number of different ways. For some parliamentarians, the involvement of doctors was so taken for granted as to need no further justification or discussion:

> I suggest to the House that given...the right of doctors to decide the issue.
>
> (ORC 22 July 1966: 1116)

> It seems to me a very big decision and it must always be a medical decision, to declare that a life must be condemned unseen.
>
> (ORC 22 July 1966: 1029)

> While obviously the decision must be a medical one...the decision in the end must be that of the gynaecologist who is to be expected to perform it.
>
> (ORL 22 July 1967: 308)

Other participants, perhaps sensing that some justification might be needed for medical involvement, argued that abortions must only be granted for 'medical reasons'. This presentation had two major advantages. First, it appeared naturally to justify allowing doctors to make the abortion decision; certainly the links between the premise (abortion for medical reasons) and the conclusion (doctors must decide on a woman's behalf whether she continues with an unwanted pregnancy) were taken for granted rather than spelled out. The second advantage was that carrying out abortions 'for medical reasons' about which only doctors could decide, ensured that abortions would only be performed for 'good' reasons and circumvented women's tendency to seek abortions for 'trivial' and 'specious' reasons:

> The amendments to the Bill have satisfied many doctors and certain medical bodies that the main basis of the Bill for abortion is medical. Good ethics in medicine and surgery demand that an operation should not be done unless it is justifiable or indicated for medical reasons. Some surgeons do operations for non-medical reasons, but the main body of surgeons refuse to do so.
>
> (ORC 12 July 1967: 282)

> '[M]edical conscience' should direct him that he should do an abortion only for medical reasons.
>
> (ORC 12 July 1967: 283)

Whatever may be the failings of the Abortion Act 1967, at least it requires good reasons to be given for abortion. It provides some, albeit paltry, recognition of the fact that the unborn child is special and that abortion is special and cannot be equated with a simple operation, such as having a tooth out. If we remove the medical grounds, we remove the minimum recognition of the difference between such operations.

(ORC 21 June 1990: 1164)

I fear abuse because [proposed] new Clause 1 [abortion on request for the first twelve weeks of pregnancy] requires no reason for abortion other than the mother's demand. It will abandon all pretence of medical causes and will open the door to social abortions, abortions of convenience. I suspect that it will allow abortions on all sorts of specious grounds.

(ORC 21 June 1990: 1151)

But the insistence that abortion be performed only for 'medical reasons' was for some participants in conflict with the 'social-clause' in the 1966 Bill (that the woman's actual or foreseeable environment could be taken into account) and with the Bill's use of terms like 'well-being'. The implications of allowing abortions for 'social reasons', including the effects on existing children, were clearly spelt out:

[H]ow can a doctor decide how an abortion or pregnancy will affect existing children? It is not a question for a doctor to decide.

(ORC 12 July 1967: 275)

I think that one of the essential facts to remember is that we are trying to lift the burden from the doctor where he is not qualified to make the decision...there are circumstances in which a psychiatrist or a social worker knows more about the total environment...such a person can examine the situation for the woman who is asking for her pregnancy to be terminated.

(ORC 29 June 1967: 1029)

This potentially difficult situation, where extending the grounds for legal abortion could reduce doctors' involvement in decision-making, was uneasily resolved by arguing that the 'social clause' was not really social but medical: in order to make decisions about mental health – which were assumed obviously to be medical – doctors had to take social factors into account. Thus, physical and mental health held identical status as medical reasons for abortion; it was simply that different factors needed to be taken into account in judging whether these reasons were present in a particular case:

The purpose of the amendment [to delete 'well-being' and to limit the clause to physical and mental health] is merely to make it clear that the decision which two professional medical gentlemen must take is intended to be nothing other than a medical one about only the medical aspect of the problem and that we are not placing upon those in the medical profession the duty of deciding matters which lie outside the scope of their ordinary skill and training... their individual prejudices about what should or should not be done are not exercised, but only their skill, judgement and knowledge as doctors.

(ORC 21 June 1967: 531)

As I pointed out in Chapter 2, it would have been impossible for parliamentarians to have taken such a position had not the medical model of psychological distress and disturbing behaviour already become widely accepted. The medical profession had expended considerable energy in putting forward this model and it had reached a high-point of acceptance in the 1959 Mental Health Act. Thus the redefinition of 'social reasons' as 'medical reasons' and the assumption of equivalence of psychological distress and physical illness were accomplished with relative ease.

But the ease with which legislators were able to satisfy themselves that abortion involved a 'medical decision' taken for 'medical reasons' is called into question, and at the same time put in a wider social context, by Kennedy's (1983) failure to find a satisfactory answer to his query: What *is* a medical decision? Is it a decision made by doctors? Clearly not, because doctors make many decisions – how to vote, whether to accept a pay rise – which no one would call medical. Is it, then, a decision made by a doctor in a medical context? But this begs the question of how we define a medical context: if someone is dying at home, is that a medical context? Kennedy finally suggests that perhaps a medical decision is a decision made by a doctor about health or illness. However, as Kennedy and many others have shown, decisions about health and illness – indeed our definitions of health and illness – are profoundly influenced by social norms and values. In other words, what we think of as medical decisions are not objective and descriptive, but are likely to be decisions 'about what ought to be done in the light of certain values' (Kennedy 1983: 83). In the same way, the idea of 'medical reasons' is also problematic. When we invoke these, what we usually mean is that the outcome of an intervention given by a doctor or health professional is highly valued and that the 'patient' clearly deviates from the desired outcome. For example, a woman with invasive cancer is given radiotherapy because we value the prolongation of life, often above its quality; a teenager with severe acne is given drugs because we value pustule-free skin. On the other hand, to say that a procedure is being carried out for 'non-medical reasons' is to say that a lower value is placed on the outcome, or that there is less consensus about its value, or that the 'patient' does not deviate very much from a desired outcome – for example, having a straight rather than a slightly crooked nose, being wrinkle-free at fifty, or being able to pursue a career rather than become a mother.

Medical involvement in the abortion decision, involving as it does value judgements about the foetus, the woman's wishes and her social and personal circumstances, can therefore be seen as part of a larger context in which doctors, through custom or law, regularly take decisions which involve matters well beyond the 'objective', the physical and the descriptive. The following sections will extend the discussion of why this seems to be so socially acceptable both generally and in relation to abortion, by looking at two issues: first, the relationships amongst medicine, religion and morals and, second, the gendered nature of both medicine and abortion.

MEDICINE, RELIGION AND MORALS

Raymond (1982) has noted that both medicine and religion deal with issues of 'ultimate concern'; she draws a number of parallels between various medical traditions and the sacramental rites of the Roman Catholic Church. Similarly, Turner (1995) has emphasised the extent to which both medicine and religion share a preoccupation with the regulation of the flesh; he notes also that the categories of sin and sickness have only recently and imperfectly become separated. There are certainly very striking similarities in the languages of religion and medicine: both are engaged in the business of salvation, saving souls or saving lives; and terms such as 'malady' or 'malignant' remind us that notions of badness and evil are incorporated into supposed descriptions of bodily states. The power to perform miracles has been attributed to both doctors and deities (a medical miracle; a miracle cure) and the notion of faith is applied to both medicine and religion. Shorter, for example, has argued that the 'art of curing illness' is dependent on patients being able to 'muster the requisite faith that the doctor can cure, that his [*sic*] healing hand and all-knowing gaze will restore' (1985: 259).

These links between medicine and religion, between the care of the body and the care of the soul, have historically allowed doctors to move between statements about bodies and statements about morals without seeming to overreach their sphere of competence. By the mid-nineteenth century, however, this situation was under threat. There was intense competition for the care of the body in an increasingly commercialised market place and medical men could no longer be assured of their privileges in this area. A US physician, Walter Channing, bemoaned this loss of status in an address to the incoming class at Harvard Medical School in 1845 when he recollected that the physician had been held 'in great honor' from Cicero to Dr Johnson and that 'the hospital was a temple in which presided a god...The physician had an important place in society, in the literature and science of the time' (cited in Mohr 1978: 163–4). Channing urged the students to restore this loss of status; in both Britain and the United States, doctors made vigorous attempts to do just that. Two factors played an essential role in the success of this campaign: the eventual creation of a unified medical profession and the promulgation of a system of professional ethics – a code of conduct – which was to apply to all members of the unified profession. Medical men, of course, had long taken the Hippocratic oath, but this hardly amounted to a system for specifying and controlling the conduct of doctors throughout their careers. The new code of conduct constructed doctors as providing a disinterested service entirely in the interests of patients and the community (Witz 1992; Lupton 1994; Turner 1995). Claimed adherence to such a code has a number of advantages for the medical profession. It justifies regulation of the profession by itself, as well as a medical monopoly over substantial aspects of health care. Turner (1995) has argued that the medical code of ethics can also be seen as an 'apologetic' response by the medical profession to the fact that, unlike the clergy, they are well paid for their services to the sick. But such a code is also functional for the public. It is, after all, very comforting to believe that those we approach at our most vulnerable, and who are allowed access to our most private selves, will act only in our best interests.

In the face of strong competition amongst 'health providers', and in order to convince the public of the credibility of a new professional code of conduct, nineteenth-century doctors had to position themselves as professionally trustworthy, as morally above reproach on some of the important issues of the day. Mohr (1978) has suggested that the issue of abortion was 'nearly perfect' for 'regular' doctors' crusade to professionalise and restore the status of medicine. Abortion, in this respect, had four important features. First, it was an area in which the law was regularly flouted. By drawing attention to and condemning this, doctors could present themselves as upholders of the law and as opponents of crime. Second, abortion provided an opportunity for doctors to contrast the greed of commercial abortionists who operated for money, with the higher values of doctors who although obviously obliged to charge a fee, would perform abortions only for the gravest medical reasons. Third, as Mohr has pointed out, abortion, with its obvious social and moral dimensions offered an opportunity for doctors 'to recapture what they considered to be their ancient and rightful place among society's policy makers and savants' (ibid.: 163). Finally, abortion offered an opportunity for the emerging specialty of obstetrics and gynaecology to develop what might be called a unique selling point – social altruism and moral probity – in a particularly competitive market place for women's custom. Brooks (1988) has noted that obstetrics at that time was not defined by any major advances in knowledge or technique over the services offered to women by midwives or other healers; professionalism and trustworthiness therefore offered about the only credible means of gaining ascendancy in the market place.

In the resulting campaign to enforce abortion legislation, to restrict access to abortion and to ensure medical control over abortion decisions, doctors positioned themselves as moral educators to the public:

> It is not sufficient that the medical profession should set up a standard of morality for themselves but the people are to be educated up to it. The profession must become aggressive towards those wrongs and errors which it only can properly expose and successfully oppose.
>
> (Christian 1867, cited in Mohr 1978: 171)

And as I mentioned in the last chapter, the British Medical Journal saw a need to educate women that any miscarriage 'was not a trivial event, for gossip with their neighbours' (BMJ 11 December 1937: 1192). In this educational context, the medical, social and ethical aspects of abortion were so intertwined as not only to seem synonymous but also as naturally to fall within the province of medicine. Abortion, then, was 'A CRIME AGAINST PSYCHOLOGY, A CRIME AGAINST MORALITY and A CRIME AGAINST THE LAW' (Hale 1867; cited in Mohr 1978: 175; emphasis in original). An English gynaecologist, speaking against abortion, claimed that women had created the unemployment problem by taking jobs from men and that by talking of 'equal rights' they sought to deny the importance of the biological differences between men and women (Brooks 1988). A British Medical Association report on abortion in 1936 showed a similar conflation of social and biological issues by suggesting that one of the grounds for abortion should be the rape of a girl under sixteen. The Eugenics Movement also provided opportunities to blend the biological, social and moral and to give the impression that doctors spoke with equal authority on all three. Thus, the same gynaecologist who had claimed that women caused the unemployment problem, expressed the fears of many of his colleagues in Britain and the United States about the increasing number of white married women who were having abortions: the 'stability of the race', he claimed, depended on the 'purity of the family' and the married woman who claimed to 'have sole right over her own body' was a 'biological reject' (Brooks 1988: 63). Other doctors did not trouble to add a biological perspective to their argument. Married women were accused of having no 'shadow of excuse ... for their heartless depravity' in asking for an abortion (Mohr 1978: 87), while 'intellectual women', in refusing to become mothers, were leading Britain to the same downfall as the ancient civilisations of Greece and Rome (Brooks 1988). It is notable that although some doctors and lay people disagreed with these sentiments, virtually no one suggested that many of these issues lay outside the province of medicine or that doctors were no more likely to be expert on them than any other group. It seems then, that in attempting to establish their moral credentials, doctors had a receptive audience. Indeed, Kennedy has argued that we, the public, have 'connived' at this process of enhancement of medical authority into areas well beyond the workings of the body 'whether out of ignorance or trust or even out of choice' (1983: 13). I also suggested earlier that the public have an interest in accepting doctors' moral authority as one means of reducing our vulnerability in medical encounters. Whatever the reasons for this 'collusion', the result was that by the 1960s and 1970s, when abortion legislation was being debated, the conflation of biological, social and moral issues in relation to abortion was so well established as often to be invisible. Not only did it appear reasonable for doctors to make statements and judgements about values, morals and social issues, it appeared that many of these statements were a natural part of the practice of medicine. It is important to emphasise that the conflation was one way only: while doctors were assumed to have authority in matters of value and morals, lay people were not assumed to have authority in medical matters.

If doctors' authority on issues of value was well established by the late 1960s, so too was their professional integrity. Doctors were described in the debates as 'highly skilled and dedicated' (ORC 13 July 1967: 1352) and as belonging to a 'high and proud profession' whose code of ethics was designed to protect not the profession 'but those with whose welfare the profession is concerned. In the case of medicine it is the patient' (ORC 22 July 1966: 1090; ORL 12 July 1967: 284). Another MP, describing Chile's use of medical panels to make abortion decisions, claimed that 'The members of the panel are all medical men of standing and *therefore men of experience and human understanding*' (ORC 2 June 1967: 1030, my italics). A number of speakers, however, seemed to suggest that some doctors were more trustworthy than others and attempts were made to secure legislation stating that only gynaecologists or senior members of the profession could take abortion decisions. Gynaecologists had traditionally been more conservative than other medical specialties in their attitude to abortion and had played a prominent role in attempting to restrict access to abortion. Thus, when one speaker claimed that it was 'too dangerous' to allow the abortion decision 'to two young registered medical practitioners' (ORC 29 June 1967: 942), he was expressing a general fear that junior doctors, and particularly general practitioners, might too easily agree to abortion or be 'taken in' by the woman's account, or have too much sympathy with her to make an objective judgement. In countering such arguments, however, speakers who favoured less restrictive legislation were able to draw on the idea that all doctors were bound by their professional code of conduct and that all were therefore fit to make judgements in these matters. Nevertheless, some misgivings obviously remained, because in 1990 MPs voted against a proposal to make all first trimester abortions legal with the consent of only one doctor. It was argued that this would not provide sufficient safeguard for the woman and that the law would be flouted:

If the signature of only one doctor is needed and abortion becomes immediately and readily available... women will be less likely to receive good counselling and to be given sufficient time to consider what they are doing.

(ORC 21 June 1990: 1164)

everyone knows that under the present system, when two doctors' signatures are required, collusion sometimes occurs. Abortions for the most trifling reasons are granted on one ground or another... If only one doctor's signature is now to be required it is inevitable that the situation will get worse.

(ORC 21 June 1990: 1144)

It is notable, however, that the answer to these doubts about doctors' professional integrity was seen as more, and not less, medical involvement in the abortion decision.

I began this discussion of medicine and morals by asking how legislation which grants doctors authority in the abortion decision should have been seen as reasonable and appropriate. At least two factors seem to have been important in this process. The first involved a willingness on all sides to subsume many different kinds of judgement under the heading 'medical' and to assume, further, that such decisions naturally belonged to the medical profession. Although there were some limits to this process, these had been set very widely indeed by the extension of medical authority to many aspects of behaviour and experience under the flexible concept of mental health. The second factor, even allowing for the reservations expressed by some speakers, was the joint construction of the medical profession, by the legislators and by the profession itself, as professionally and ethically trustworthy. Doctors were portrayed as a group whose training enabled them to take judgements in the best interests of patients, even if patients disagreed. Moreover, this moral authority had been developed over decades in relation to abortion. In the next sections, I will consider another set of factors which served further to enhance the apparent appropriateness and the desirability of medical involvement in the abortion decision: the gendered nature of both abortion and medicine.

GENDER, ABORTION AND THE MEDICAL PROFESSION

Abortion legislation enables doctors to take decisions on their patients' behalf. The patient, however, is always female and has been constructed in the debates as possessing characteristics which serve to emphasise the appropriateness of depriving her of the right to make decisions on her own behalf. As we have seen, many of those who argued for less restrictive legislation portrayed unwillingly pregnant women as vulnerable and desperate, as deserving of abortion, but also as natural patients, in no fit state to take rational decisions. Those who favoured restrictive legislation portrayed women as devious and irresponsible, equally unfit to take such an important decision themselves.

If women's characteristics helped justify doctors' decision-making power, so too did the assumption that doctors possessed knowledge about the female psyche, by virtue of its supposedly close association with female reproductive processes. One MP, for example, himself a doctor, declared that 'The reproductive cycle of women is intimately linked with her psyche' (ORC 22 July 1966: 1113); similarly, a contemporary article in a journal of obstetrics and gynaecology stated that 'As evidence has accumulated linking pelvic function and psychological factors, the obstetrician-gynaecologist has tended to undertake a broader role in the management of the total patient' (1967, cited in Ehrenreich and English 1979).

Arguments like these, together with arguments about doctors' professional standing and about abortions being performed only for medical reasons, contributed to the apparent appropriateness of doctors' power in the abortion decision. In other words, they functioned to make one course of action seem reasonable and proper, and alternatives seem unreasonable or even perhaps unthinkable. It can be argued, however, that giving doctors the right to make abortion decisions on women's behalf was also seen as desirable. Even if many value judgements are almost unthinkingly portrayed as medical decisions, it seems unlikely that legislators would have so readily argued for medical power in the abortion decision had this outcome not been seen as desirable as well as reasonable. Indeed, we might go so far as to argue that it was precisely because this outcome was so desirable to the legislature that it had to be made to look so reasonable. Three factors seem important in understanding this issue. The first brings us back to the gender of the patient in the abortion decision – she is always female. One important consequence of the insistence that abortions only be carried out for 'medical reasons', in the UK at least, is that every abortion is officially justified on the grounds that the woman, her foetus or her existing children are suffering from, or vulnerable to, physical or mental illness or handicap. In practice, the vast majority of abortions – over 90 per cent – are performed because the woman herself is said to be suffering from or vulnerable to mental disorder, usually neurotic or depressive disorder (ONS). Thus abortion legislation which relies on health grounds produces weak and vulnerable women. Clearly these images of mass female weakness, and the impossibility of having an abortion from a position of strength, were acceptable to the overwhelmingly male legislature; they can be seen as one means of reducing the potential threat posed by female reproductive choice. The second factor, which may relate to the desirability of medical involvement in the abortion decision, concerns threats to the autonomy of the medical profession. Fears were expressed that if women made reproductive decisions, doctors would be reduced to mere technicians rather than, as had been claimed, members of a 'high and proud profession':

> Where does the medical profession stand if women in certain instances could claim abortion of right? ... This is an important consideration to which [the Royal Medico-Psychological Association] made an important reference when it mentioned the possibility of the psychiatrist or doctor becoming a mere technician if people could demand this as a right.
>
> (ORC 22 July 1966: 1127)

> The medical profession has never recognised that patients have a right to give its members such orders ... as they might order their plumber to disconnect the supply pipe from their bath.
>
> (1935, cited in Brooks 1988: 59)

> The doctor's position will be made ambiguous by the new clause [to allow abortion on request in the first twelve weeks].
>
> (ORC 21 June 1990: 1151)

The prospective loss of professional autonomy was doubly threatening. Autonomy had, after all, been granted by the state partly in exchange for doctors undertaking to abide by a code of conduct, which in turn reinforced claims to moral integrity. If autonomy were removed in this important instance then what assumptions could we make about doctors' future ethical conduct? As well as this, however, it is important to bear in mind that in the case of abortion, and in spite of references to 'people', we are talking here about women. And if doctors do not take orders but give them ('doctor's orders'), then they certainly would not take them from a group historically constructed as childlike, irrational and irresponsible. Indeed, it is striking how often in the debates the threat of 'abortion on demand', with its implication of women giving orders to doctors, is used to oppose changes in the law, as if the mere phrase itself constituted an argument or justification.

Nevertheless, in seeking to avoid depriving doctors of their professional autonomy, legislators had to be confident that doctors would not simply accede to women's requests for abortion. Throughout the debates, concerns had been expressed over women making the 'wrong' decision, over the health services being overwhelmed by the demand for abortion, and over the need to grant abortion only to 'deserving' cases and for 'good' reasons. The argument that doctors would abide by their code of ethics provided one means of instilling confidence; another means, which was never explicitly discussed in the debates, and is the third factor important in understanding the desirability of medical involvement in decision-making, is the gendered nature of the medical profession.

Gender and the medical profession

We can look at the relationship between gender and medicine in a number of ways. Most obviously, medicine is numerically dominated by men, particularly at the senior levels of the profession. I mentioned in Chapter 1 that around 80 per cent of gynaecologists and 75 per cent of general practitioners in England and Wales are male; in Northern Ireland, around 95 per cent of gynaecologists are male (Francome 1994). By contrast, other groups involved with patient care but traditionally subservient to medicine, tend to have much higher female representation. As Witz points out, this link between gender and health professions has long been acknowledged, but has been explained in rather static ways 'which take the gender of the practitioner as "already given" and resort to untheorised notions of supposed gender-specific attributes, attitudes and "problems" which women "bring to" professional employment' (1992: 2).

An alternative way of looking at the relationship of gender to medicine is through an analysis of medicine as a profession and of its process of professionalisation. Traditional theories of the professions have emphasised their benevolent and altruistic role within Western society, as well as the distinctive attributes which allow professional groups to claim particular powers and privileges. These theories have also examined what aspiring professional groups have to achieve in order to have their claim to professional status publicly endorsed. Such accounts, however, have been strongly criticised as merely holding a mirror to the established professions' idealised image of themselves (Freidson 1970; Johnson 1972; Witz 1992; Turner 1995). An alternative account sees a profession not as an occupation whose members have particular attributes or values, but as an institutionalised means of controlling occupational activities.

Within this framework, Witz (1992: 64) describes the process of professionalisa-tion as involving 'strategies of occupational closure which seek to establish a monopoly over the provision of skills and competencies in a market for services'. Thus, professionals and aspiring professionals seek to build and maintain clear lines of demarcation between themselves and related groups through, for example, exclusionary entry criteria and rules about occupational activities. Although these more critical accounts of the professions have emphasised the dominance and subordination implicit in professional relationships, they have not, as Witz notes, provided a detailed account of the ways in which gender relates to strategies of occupational closure and exclusion.

This process of occupational closure and its links to gender, can be examined in relation to the medical profession by looking at three factors which Larson (1977) and Witz (1992) have highlighted as crucial in the process of professionalisation. The first is the standardisation of both producer and product. The second is the establishment of links between occupation and education such that those without particular qualifications cannot lay claim to membership of an occupational group. Finally, competitors must either be controlled or eliminated in order to secure and maintain a monopoly of substantial aspects of service provision. The unification of some health providers into one occupational group (medical practitioners) in the mid-nineteenth century, was a necessary development in securing a standardised producer and product. The 1858 Medical (Registration) Act did not restrict medical practice to men; it spoke of 'persons' who could register as medical practitioners. The initial exclusion of women from medicine was achieved indirectly by the fact that only male-dominated groups were included in the unification process; midwives were excluded. The exclusion of women was also achieved directly by the refusal of universities, medical schools, the Royal colleges and the British Medical Association to admit women as students, graduates or members. The BMA did not accept women for membership until 1892 and the Royal College of Surgeons until 1908, against the wishes of a large number of its members. Thus, the links between occupation and education in medicine were explicitly developed in such a way as originally to create a male-dominated profession.

The third factor considered important in the process of professionalisation was the control or elimination of competitors in order to secure a monopoly of substantial aspects of service provision. Before the creation of the modern medical profession, health care was provided by a variety of people: healers, midwives, wise women, herbalists, and so on. Witz (1992: 75) has argued that the elimination or deskilling of these and the control of newly emergent healers were processes 'at the core of medicine's modern evolution'. The group which offered the greatest challenge to the creation of a male medical monopoly were the female midwives. Midwives were well established as 'health providers' by the nineteenth century; indeed they had attempted to form a Royal College in the seventeenth century. It is not surprising, then, that the regulation of the male medical specialty of gynaecology was seen as an important part of the organisation of medical practice as a whole (Moscucci 1990). Two arguments used by medical men in their attempts to control female midwives are of particular interest in relation to abortion. The first sought to link midwives with crime by accusing them of acting as abortionists. In 1870, the Obstetrical and Gynaecological Society proposed a scheme for the control of midwives in an attempt to 'suppress practice by persons likely to engage in criminal activities ranging from abortion to murder' (cited in Brooks 1988: 73). And a remark by a US physician suggests that the opposition to gynaecologists was seen as being 'woman' rather than simply a rival health provider: 'Almost every neighbour-hood or small village has its old woman *of one sex or another* who is known for her ability and willingness [to break the law] for a pecuniary consideration' (1874, cited in Mohr 1978: 161, my italics). Arguments like these enabled male doctors to claim the moral high ground in relation to the organisation of health services.

The second argument used to control female midwives, and which is relevant to abortion, was more subtle. Medical men made a distinction between *assisting* and *intervening* in childbirth which drew on the emerging and prestigious discourse of scientific medicine in two ways. The first was by the obvious association of specialist academic and technical knowledge with 'intervention', which was to be the province of doctors. The second was through the less obvious association between 'assistance' and 'co-operation with nature' and between 'intervention' and 'conquering nature'. As early as the seventeenth century, men-midwives had asserted that female midwives' duty was 'but to attend and wait on Nature' and that female midwives should know 'that they be Nature's servants' (Witz 1992: 106), carrying out, according to one account 'that portion of attendance which is suitable to a mere woman' (HMSO 1892, cited in Witz 1992: 110–111). By contrast, scientific medicine positioned (male) scientists as 'nature's masters' (Harding 1986; Hollway 1989). It is notable that the construction of female midwives by doctors attempting to exclude them from medical practice, drew on discourses similar to those used in constructing 'woman' in the abortion debates: she is potentially immoral; will have or carry out abortions for specious reasons; is allied to nature and is in need of guidance from the medical profession.

It seems unlikely that the largely male legislature which has debated abortion legislation would have been completely unaware of the medical profession's attempts to exclude and regulate women, or of the fact that the profession was not known for its championship of female independence. Certainly, doctors were almost always referred to in the debates as 'he' and the MP who 'applauded' the work of gynaecologists 'to keep our homes and our families and country right' (ORC 2 June 1967: 501) was not only aware of, but clearly approved, the medical profession's role in the regulation of women. And doctors, of course, had helped to provide those constructions of woman which dominated the debates and which appeared to justify medical involvement in the abortion decision. This is not to argue that all legislators were consciously aware of these issues or could have articulated them, or that some did not sincerely believe they were acting in women's best interests. But, given the content of the debates, it is difficult to imagine that a male-dominated legislature would so willingly have given women into the care of a female-dominated medical profession which had consistently supported women's autonomy. Even those MPs who believed that doctors were much too sympathetic to women's requests for abortion still saw medical involvement as an important barrier to the threat of 'abortion on demand'.

MEDICAL KNOWLEDGE AND THE ABORTION DECISION

Therapeutic law assumes not only that doctors will always act in their patients' best interests, but also that doctors possess special knowledge which enables them to make decisions on their patients' behalf. In spite of the importance of this latter assumption to the development of therapeutic law, very little attention was paid in the abortion debates to the nature of this 'special knowledge' and to whether doctors could reasonably be expected to possess it. One doctor argued that the woman herself was not in the best position to make the abortion decision because she was 'not fully aware of all the factors involved' (Chesser 1950, cited in Brooks 1988: 146) but he did not clarify what these factors were or why doctors, but not women, should be aware of them. I mentioned earlier that several MPs had argued that 'well-being' and 'social factors' fell outside the province of doctors and that this was resolved by deleting references to 'well-being' in the Abortion Act and by arguing that social factors were relevant to (medical) decisions about mental health. Again, however, doctors' knowledge was assumed rather than described or demonstrated:

> We are not placing upon those in the medical profession the duty of deciding matters which lie outside the scope of their ordinary skill and training... their individual prejudices about whether something should or should not be done are not to be exercised, but only their skill, judgement and knowledge as doctors.
>
> (ORC 29 June 1967: 531)

Similarly, in the 1990 debates medical involvement of only one doctor was justified by non-specific reference to medical education:

> When the Abortion Act was passed in 1967 there were disparities in the training of medical practitioners, general practitioners and consultant practitioners in hospitals. That was recognised by the fact that two signatures were required – that of the GP for the initial referral and that of the consultant to specify that he agreed. Medical practice has moved on since that Act was passed and general practitioners are given full and rigorous training before being allowed to take up their position. They are adequately trained and informed to make that judgement without it being subjected to that of a second party.
>
> (ORC 21 June 1990: 1163)

76

This vagueness over what exactly doctors are trained to do or to know in relation to the abortion decision may be partly attributed to the need, both public and professional, to maintain an indeterminate medical knowledge base. A number of writers (e.g. Freidson 1970; Jamous and Pelloile 1970; Lupton 1994; Turner 1995) have emphasised the fact that medical decision-making is portrayed as not merely based on facts and figures, but as an intuitive process based on 'clinical experience'. This stance is essential to the maintenance of professional status because, as Freidson (1970) and Lupton (1994) have pointed out, it does not require rational justification of medical decisions and ensures that the claimed knowledge base remains esoteric. Similarly, Jamous and Peloille (1970) and Turner (1995) have argued that an evident reliance on knowledge easily described to lay people could lead to the routinisation of decision-making and its possible delegation to technicians, or even machines. These writers have argued that claims to an indeterminate knowledge base act as a protection against this threat to professional status: 'the knowledge of the professional has to have a distinctive mystique which suggests that there is a certain professional attitude and competence which cannot be reduced merely to systematic and routinized knowledge' (Turner 1995: 133). The belief that medical knowledge is indeterminate and is not easily available to non-doctors, together with the need to maintain a professional mystique, a need arguably shared by the public and the profession, may help to account for the fact that there was so little discussion of the knowledge base which would underlie abortion decision-making. But we are still entitled to ask about this knowledge and about its use in the decision-making process.

What knowledge is assumed by abortion legislation?

The 1973 US Supreme Court ruling which legalised abortion did not make any specific statements about the knowledge which would guide doctors' 'medical judgement' that 'the patient's pregnancy should be terminated', although reference was made to the 'protection of the woman's health'. British legislation is more specific and requires doctors to assess and compare the likely outcomes, in terms of physical and mental health, of termination or continuation of pregnancy for the woman and/or her existing children; in cases of suspected foetal abnormality, the doctor must assess the likely outcome in terms of serious handicap.

We can look first at the knowledge base necessary for a legal abortion decision by considering data relevant to the outcomes for the woman of termination or continuation of pregnancy. The available evidence suggests that the risks to women's physical and psychological health from childbirth are greater than the risks from elective legal abortion and, further, that the physical and psychological risks from abortion are low (Brewer 1977; Cates *et al.* 1982; WHO 1978; Lazarus 1985; Adler *et al.* 1990, 1992; Wilmoth 1992; Clare and Tyrrell 1994). Only one (Scandinavian) study drew a different conclusion about the comparative psychological risks of abortion and childbirth: David *et al.* (1981) found that the rate of admission to psychiatric hospital of divorced, separated or widowed women who had had abortions was significantly greater than the rate for a similar group of women who had given birth. Hospital admission, however, is a problematic measure of comparative psychological outcomes because there may be a reluctance to admit mothers of very young children. There is also another factor to be taken into account here. If a woman is refused an abortion, she does not simply continue with the pregnancy. Assuming she does not obtain an abortion elsewhere, she may continue the pregnancy against her wishes. We therefore also need to consider data on outcomes for women who are refused abortions. The few studies which have examined this issue suggest that the psychological outcome of refused abortion may be more negative than that of abortion itself (Watters 1980; Clare and Tyrrell 1994). These findings are particularly striking when we consider that women may be refused abortion because they are considered to be mentally healthier than those women granted terminations.

These data, of course, come from studies of varying methodological rigour (Posavac and Miller 1990). They are, however, what is available to doctors in predicting the outcomes of granting or refusing abortion, and they consistently suggest that if a woman requests an abortion, she will be at lower psychological and physical risk if her request is granted. Three objections might be raised to this conclusion that the relevant knowledge base supports abortion on request. The first is that because these data may be subject to methodological criticism, doctors are entitled to ignore them and to rely instead on their own experience. This is, of course, the indeterminate knowledge argument I mentioned earlier. The argument is, however, deeply problematic because there is no evidence that doctors are less biased than lay people in making 'intuitive' judgements from clinical or statistical information; indeed, under some circumstances, they may be more biased (Chapman and Chapman 1982; Eddy 1982; Bennett 1983). The second objection is more serious, and is that population statistics are general statements which do not necessarily apply to each woman about whom doctors have to make an abortion decision. Doctors, then, would be entitled to draw on data relevant to outcomes in individual women; some of these data might justify refusing abortion. This argument, however, is also problematic because of the lack of data on which to base predictions about individual women that would be more valid than those based on population statistics. Hopkins *et al.* (1984), for example, could find no individual variable which was reliably related to a later diagnosis of post-natal depression. But even if such data existed, they would have to be applied in conjunction with data on the individual outcomes of refused abortion. And, although some population figures are available for such outcomes, there are no data on which factors account for individual differences in outcome. Data on individual factors associated with the outcome of having an abortion are also relevant here, but are not much more helpful. Adler *et al.* (1990), reviewing studies of reactions to abortion, noted that women's dissatisfaction with their decision, their initial emotional response to the pregnancy and partner support, accounted for almost 40 per cent of the variance in measures of psychological response two to three weeks after the abortion. But this still leaves most of the variance unaccounted for. These data also cannot tell us how women who react negatively to abortion – perhaps ambivalent about their pregnancy and lacking partner support – would have reacted to childbirth, so that using these factors to predict the responses of other women would be very problematic.

Finally, it might be objected that a woman's decision to have an abortion could have been made under pressure or that she would prefer to continue the pregnancy if some practical help could be offered. In this case, it would clearly be against the woman's interests to base the legal decision on population figures. There are two problems with this argument. The first is that many participants in the abortion debates seemed to find it very difficult to accept that when women request an abortion they 'really' mean it. Women might therefore be disadvantaged by a decision-making procedure which emphasises the potential 'wrongness' of their own decision. The second problem is that even if we accept the idea that some women do not actually want to have an abortion, and would benefit from having their request refused, there is no reason to suppose that *medical* knowledge and training is needed to identify such women.

It would be tempting to assume that the situation was more clear-cut in the case of individual, rather than population, predictions of medical outcomes, but there is little evidence that this is the case (Callahan 1970). Since Callahan drew this conclusion, there have, of course, been considerable advances in the prediction of foetal abnormality. The law, however, refers to the child's being 'seriously handicapped' rather than to its suffering from a specific abnormality. But handicap is a social, as well as a medical, judgement and the degree of handicap will be influenced by the environment in which the child is raised. Medical knowledge therefore cannot offer all that is necessary to make such judgements. In the case of abortion decisions based on predicted effects on existing children (and very few abortions are carried out solely on these grounds), there are virtually no data to guide decision-making. A few studies have examined the development of children born to women who were denied abortion for that pregnancy (see e.g. Forssman and Thuwe 1966; Watters 1980; David *et al.* 1988; David 1992). While these suggest various negative outcomes for the children, it would be hazardous to generalise to the 'existing children' specified in the legislation.

The knowledge base assumed by abortion legislation is clearly not so straightforwardly available as was implied in the debates. With this in mind, the next section will consider how doctors have in practice made abortion decisions.

Doctors and abortion decision-making

Doctors are not obliged to keep records of refusals to grant abortions or of their reasons for doing so. There are therefore no official data on refusals to terminate to compare with the data on abortions carried out. These data, of course, give little indication of the actual reason why abortion was granted, but consist only of what is legally necessary. Since 1982, the information required on British abortion notification forms has been limited to the main *medical* condition said to justify the abortion and makes no reference to the woman's 'actual or reasonably foreseeable environment'. As we have seen, the vast majority of abortions are officially granted because the women concerned are said to be suffering from, or vulnerable to, mental disorder. I will focus here on that area of decision-making; decisions about potentially handicapped foetuses will be looked at in more detail in Chapter 6.

In the decade following the 1967 Abortion Act, a number of studies examined the characteristics which differentiated women who were granted or refused abortion on 'psychiatric grounds'. Kenyon (1969) and Hamill and Ingram (1974) reported that married women were more likely to be granted terminations than were single women; McCance and McCance (1970) found that marital status had no effect on decision-making. The latter authors also found that terminations were more likely to be granted to women who had a previous psychiatric history, while in Kenyon's sample this was irrelevant. Both Hamill and Ingram and McCance and McCance reported that older women were more likely to be offered terminations; in a sample studied by Clarke *et al.* (1968) it was younger women. The potential role of value judgements in the decision-making process is illustrated by Kenyon's suggestion that in reaching decisions about abortion, doctors should ask themselves whether 'this is a case of a narcissistic woman for whom a child is a social inconvenience which would curtail her activities and spoil her body'. They are also urged to take into account 'the degree of emotional maturity, intelligence, promiscuity and sensible use of contraceptives' (Kenyon 1969: 244). Similarly, Allen (1981) noted that some women who had not been using contraception at the time of their pregnancy experienced more difficulty in obtaining abortion that those who had.

Clare and Tyrrell (1994) have suggested that few requests for abortion are now refused, at least in Western countries. (They were presumably referring to those Western countries where abortion is legal.) If this is the case, it was not always so. McCance *et al.* (1977), in a study of 300 women who had requested abortion, reported that 40 per cent had been refused. The suggestion that few women are now refused abortion is difficult to interpret in terms of doctors' decision-making, and we cannot conclude that it shows a shift to the consistent use of specialist knowledge. Instead, it may reflect the 'channelling' of women into services likely to grant their request. General practitioners who support abortion requests are unlikely to refer women to gynaecologists known frequently to refuse them. Similarly, private or charitable abortion services now advertise widely and are many women's entry point to the abortion services. The idea that selective referral might at least partly explain the low refusal rate in some countries is supported by unopposed claims about disparities in the availability of abortion made during the 1990 parliamentary debates. It was claimed, for example, that 95 per cent of abortions in one health district were performed on the National Health Service, while 99 per cent of abortions in another district were performed outside the NHS (ORC 21 June 1990: 1138). It was also claimed that in 1987, a consultant gynaecologist in a third health district had told a 'Life' conference that it was 'impossible – or almost impossible – to obtain an NHS abortion in his district' (ORC 21 June 1990: 1158). There are also, of course, considerable disparities in the number of publicly funded abortions carried out in different American states (Goggin 1993a). In Britain, however, where publicly funded health care is the standard, large disparities in the apparent availability of NHS abortions are difficult to explain without some reference to inconsistent decision-making practices amongst doctors. Francome (1994) also found what he described as 'a great deal of inconsistency' amongst gynaecologists in Northern Ireland in relation to abortion decisions.

None of these results is surprising given the lack of empirical data, apart from population figures on the outcomes of abortion and its alternatives, on which doctors might base abortion decisions, and given the potential role of value judgements in the decision. The problem is compounded by the fact that doctors may be reluctant publicly to rely on the population figures on the outcomes of abortion, refused abortion and childbirth because they risk precipitating the routinisation and demystification of medical decision-making. In addition, public reference to these figures draws attention to the potential risks of childbirth, an issue which many participants in the debates were at pains to avoid.

CONCLUSION

The question addressed in this chapter was that of how medical power in abortion decisions came to be seen as both appropriate and desirable. The answer is clearly complex: medical involvement is justified discursively by the language of medical decisions taken for medical reasons; this in turn is supported by cultural practices which conflate prescriptive and descriptive judgements and which endorse medical authority on matters of value as well as of bodily functioning. The appropriateness of medical involvement is further enhanced by the construction in the debates of two contrasting and complementary legal subjects: the (female) patient is emotional and vulnerable, or irresponsible and immoral; the (male) doctor is knowledgeable and objective and is bound by high standards of ethical conduct. But granting doctors the right to make abortion decisions is also highly functional for both the profession and the legislature: it protects medical autonomy and supports the gendered regulation of reproductive decisions which are clearly seen as having profound social and moral as well as medical implications.

5

CONTRACEPTION AND ABORTION

When a woman requests an abortion, she is indirectly saying something about contraception: that it was not used when conception happened, that it was used inefficiently, or that the method failed in spite of 'proper' use. In that sense, at least, the relationship between contraception and abortion is obvious. It is precisely because of this obvious relationship – that both are methods of fertility control – that contraception, like abortion, has historically been treated as a social and moral issue. Yet the relationship between the birth control movement and the abortion law reform movement in the early decades of this century was often hostile (Brooks 1988). This was partly because many supporters of contraception opposed abortion on principle, seeing it as having a quite different moral status. Even those who supported abortion, however, were often reluctant to voice this because they feared that the association between contraception and (criminal) abortion would undermine their campaign to increase access to contraception. Nevertheless, similar arguments were often used to oppose access to both contraception and abortion. Until at least the 1950s, for example, it was feared that widely available contraception would deplete the population at a time when the state was concerned about the falling birth rate, particularly amongst the white middle classes. It was also assumed that contraception would encourage moral laxity by allowing intercourse without thought for the consequences, particularly outside of marriage. The consequences, of course, were more serious for women and many saw contraception as an important step in women's emancipation. Not all women shared this view. Feminists and anti-feminists alike opposed birth control as encouraging men to evade their responsibilities and as denying women their most effective means – fear of pregnancy – of refusing male sexual demands. Not surprisingly, then, vigorous attempts were made to control access to contraception. For example, in 1924 the Ministry of Health issued a memo to welfare centres instructing them not to give contraceptive information under any circumstances (Brooks 1988). Earlier, the US Comstock Laws of 1873 made it a criminal offence to provide either contraceptive information or devices; it was not until 1958 that the US Government abandoned its attempts to ban contraceptive shipments through the postal system (Lewin 1984). But, as with abortion, health arguments have often

82

been deployed in support of contraception and some doctors advocated its use under medical surveillance for women whose health would be seriously impaired by further childbirth. It was not until worries about a low birth rate had receded, and fertility control was seen as a desirable social goal, that governments could regard with equanimity the idea of less restricted access to both contraception and abortion. Wider access to contraception, however, was still accompanied by moral strictures: many early birth control clinics officially accepted only married women and, even in the 1970s, women attending the renamed family planning clinics were routinely asked the date of their wedding.

It might be assumed that the increased availability of contraception and decreased sanctions for its use would lead to a gradual reduction in the rate of abortion – certainly this was anticipated by supporters of birth control – but the opposite seems to be the case: demographers have repeatedly observed a positive correlation between the use of contraception and the use of abortion (Mohr 1978). This apparent paradox has been explained by the theory that use of contraceptives is associated with a commitment to fertility control, but that lack of experience with them results in unplanned pregnancies which are subsequently aborted. Although contraceptive use and resort to abortion clearly do suggest a commitment to fertility control, lack of experience with contraceptive methods is likely to provide only a partial account of contraceptive 'failure' and later resort to abortion. This chapter will examine a range of social and psychological factors which seem to be related to the use – and non-use – of contraception amongst men and women who are apparently committed to fertility control. I will look first at contraceptive use immediately prior to a request for abortion and then consider some of the explanations put forward for the non-use of contraception. Finally, the adequacy of these accounts will be discussed by looking at some of the ways in which contraception highlights the operation of gendered power in heterosexual relationships.

CONTRACEPTIVE USE PRIOR TO ABORTION

It is not easy to establish patterns of contraceptive use before an abortion request. The most usual research method is to ask women seeking abortion about their use of contraception in the weeks preceding conception. These women, however, are in a difficult position. As we have seen, women seek abortion in the role of supplicant and may fear that non-use of contraception will prejudice their case. And they are right to do so, given the negative remarks made in the abortion debates about women who do not make 'sensible' use of contraception or who allegedly use abortion as a form of birth control. It is therefore not surprising that Griffiths (1990) should report that many of the women in his study who initially reported using contraception should later 'with careful questioning', and after their request for abortion had been agreed, report that the method had not been used at the time of conception.

This reticence to report accurately on contraceptive use, together with a number of other factors, suggests that many figures for contraceptive use prior to abortion are likely to underestimate the extent of non-use or inefficient use of contraception. For example, studies may report whether contraception was used in the month of conception rather than whether it was used efficiently every time a couple had intercourse. Yet there is good evidence that the phrase 'using contraception' covers a variety of practices. Maxwell and Boyle (1995), for example, found that women who said they relied on condoms for contraception often discarded them at 'safe' times of the month or started intercourse without a condom, but used it before ejaculation. Similarly, women may miss one or two contraceptive pills, or delay taking them when timing of the dose is important, without using a 'back-up' method. Researchers may also include very different practices under 'method failure' which can obscure the extent of inefficient contraceptive use. Griffiths (1990), for example, included in this category cases where pregnancy had occurred with an intrauterine device still in place *and* cases in which contraception was used in what the woman believed to be the correct way, even if this included ways which would reduce the efficacy of the method.

Bearing in mind these difficulties of interpretation, however, research clearly suggests that in a considerable number of cases where abortion is requested, contraception either was not used or was used inefficiently.[1] Figures collected by the British Pregnancy Advisory Service (personal communication) suggest that around one-third of women seeking abortion report that no method of contraception was used at the time of conception. Griffiths' (1990) figures are similar: 32 per cent of a sample of women seeking abortion reported not using contraception; 30 per cent used it inefficiently. The remaining pregnancies were attributed to 'method failure'. Duncan *et al.* (1990) provide a higher figure – 43.2 per cent – of women requesting abortion who reported that no contraception was used in the conception cycle. One of the highest figures for non-use of contraception comes from a Scandinavian study. Seventy per cent of Holmgren's (1994) sample of women seeking abortion reported that contraception had not been used at the likely time of conception. These studies, and others, also suggest that reported contraceptive 'risk-taking' is higher amongst males than females,[2] amongst younger people, and amongst those who are not in long-term relationships (Krishnamoorthy *et al.* 1983; Metson 1988; Griffiths 1990; Ingelhammer *et al.* 1994).

There has been little serious attempt in the abortion debates to understand why so many people who apparently do not want pregnancy should nevertheless fail to protect themselves adequately against it. Instead, the impression is sometimes given of women (and it is usually women who are criticised) who are

---

1 The problem of non-use or inefficient use of contraception is not confined to pregnancies where the woman has an abortion. Research (e.g. Metson 1988; Fleissig 1991) suggests that at least a third of pregnancies are unplanned or unintended and that only a minority of these are terminated.

2 This apparently paradoxical result reflects the fact that men more often claim to have intercourse without contraception than do women; it may be that men give this response in cases where they do not know if the woman is using any contraception.

wilfully negligent and who perhaps ought to be 'taught a lesson' by having access to abortion made difficult:

> [The 1967 Act] was not introduced in the spirit that abortion could become a convenient form of birth control.
>
> (ORC 21 June 1990: 1158)

> A mother can make a decision. A woman can speak. She makes a choice about the sexual act that may bring about conception. She makes a further choice of whether to conceive a child.
>
> (ORC 24 April 1990: 235)

> [Medical involvement in the abortion decision is necessary] solely so society can satisfy itself that she is not using the medical profession as a source of late contraception.
>
> (ORC 24 April 1990: 250)

Similarly, Allen (1981: 77) quoted the views of one doctor, which were apparently typical of many:

> They don't get pregnant twice unless they're hopeless. You're always left with the hard-core who think they understand [contraception] but it still goes wrong.

Fortunately, researchers have tried to develop more complex and constructive theories of contraceptive use. Because the concern here is with the relationship between contraception and abortion, the focus will inevitably be on the non-use or inefficient use of contraception and the factors which seem to influence it.

WHAT INFLUENCES CONTRACEPTIVE USE?

A number of factors have consistently emerged as important influences on contraceptive use, and as contributing to our understanding of why people who do not seek pregnancy should have unprotected intercourse. Four of these will be discussed in this section: knowledge of contraception and reproduction; the desire for trust and commitment; social and interpersonal costs of contraception; and the experience of side effects.

Knowledge of contraception and reproduction

It has long been assumed that if only people had adequate knowledge of contraception, then unwanted pregnancies would be a very much rarer occurrence. In 1916, for example, evidence to the National Birthrate Commission from the Malthusian League stated that a 'universal knowledge of hygienic and reliable contraceptive devices is the only possible method of eliminating [induced abortion]' (cited in Brooks 1988: 64). Similarly, in 1949 the Royal Commission on Population Report claimed that evidence of 'faulty knowledge' was 'most glaringly apparent' in the prevalence of criminal abortion (Brooks 1988: 64, 135).

It is certainly the case that failure to use contraception effectively is associated with a lack of knowledge of both conception and contraception. A number of researchers, for example, have noted that the belief that pregnancy will not happen is frequently offered as a reason for not using contraception (e.g. Washington *et al.* 1983; Morrison 1985). This belief may be related to ideas such as 'fertility does not begin with menstruation', or 'if a girl truly doesn't want a baby she won't get pregnant', or 'pregnancy doesn't happen the first time a woman has intercourse', or 'pregnancy doesn't happen for a while after you start having sex' (Kantner and Zelnick 1972; Sorensen 1973; Allen 1981; Cvetkovich and Grote 1983). Morrison (1985) also noted that attendance at sex education classes was only a weak predictor of adolescents' knowledge of conception and reproduction. In samples which included both younger and older women, Griffiths (1990) and Bromham and Cartmill (1993) noted that knowledge of the 'morning after pill' or 'post-coital contraception' was extremely limited. They noted also that some women had not been told about or did not remember factors likely to reduce the efficacy of oral contraceptives, such as gastro-intestinal disorders and certain drug interactions. Some women were also unaware of the need for secondary contraception under these circumstances.

It would be relatively easy to reduce the number of unwanted pregnancies if knowledge of contraception and conception were all that was necessary. Unfortunately, there is good evidence that possession of knowledge does not automatically lead to changes in behaviour (Azjen and Fishbein 1980). The following factors highlight some of the reasons why this might be the case in relation to contraception.

The desire for trust and commitment

Hollway (1989) has provided two case studies of 'making love without contraception' which illustrate the importance of its meaning for the couple involved. In neither case was pregnancy unambiguously desired; indeed, in the couple where the woman did conceive, the pregnancy was terminated. In both cases, making love without contraception symbolized closeness, trust and commitment in a 'suppressed' way, in circumstances where the people involved were unsure of their partner's commitment to the relationship, and where such uncertainties were difficult to discuss. One of the participants records her disappointment when her partner eventually took responsibility for contraception during one sexual encounter because 'that meant maybe he wasn't so committed to our relationship after all' (ibid.: 48).

The importance of trust in relation to contraception is further emphasised by studies of condom use. Abandoning condoms is widely seen as highly symbolic in a relationship: it signifies that the relationship is no longer casual, that some degree of commitment has been established (Holland *et al.* 1990; Maxwell and Boyle 1995). If the couple then use another reliable method of contraception, pregnancy is unlikely; it is when this does not happen or when condoms may need to be reintroduced that problems arise. In the last ten years or so, the meaning of condoms has changed because of their widely publicised role in preventing transmission of HIV and other genito-urinary infections. Using condoms can then signify not only the desire to avoid pregnancy, but also the belief that one or both partners might transmit infection. Conversely, abandoning condoms is a way of saying that the partner is now to be trusted. But reintroducing condoms could then be problematic because of the implicit message that trust has been violated. Maxwell and Boyle (1995) found that women would be very unlikely to reintroduce condoms into a long-term relationship even if they or their partner had had an affair and risked infection. Yet condoms are the most widely suggested 'back-up' method of contraception when the efficacy of the pill has been compromised. In some relationships, of course, their use would not present any problems. In others, where there are uncertainties about trust, or where the woman fears being accused of having an affair, then taking a risk over pregnancy might seem the least risky option for the relationship.

Interpersonal and social costs of contraception

Luker (1975) has suggested that many researchers assume that the benefits of using contraception outweigh the costs and that the costs of non-use outweigh the benefits. This model constructs contraceptive use as a rational act and positions those who have unprotected intercourse as deviant. As we have already seen, this way of looking at contraceptive use is problematic, but it is the model adopted by some participants in the abortion debates, sometimes with the added suggestion that such 'irrational' women might be taught rationality by being forced to bear an unwanted child. Looked at in another way, however, the costs of contraceptive use may be very high and greater than the anticipated costs of non-use or inefficient use. It is important to bear in mind that the costs of using contraception can be immediate and obvious. The benefits are in the future (when it becomes clear that pregnancy has not happened) and uncertain (pregnancy might not have happened anyway or might even have happened with contraception). It is exactly under these conditions that we would expect inconsistent and inefficient use of contraception.

One of the most obvious costs of contraception is that it is a signifier of actual or anticipated sexual activity. It is difficult for anyone to obtain or use contraception without facing the fact that they are at least willing to consider having intercourse. Of course, it is also difficult to have intercourse while denying that you are; but we can draw on a range of discourses (getting carried away; overwhelmed by passion; couldn't stop, etc.) to help separate our volitional selves from our behaviour. There are few popular discourses surrounding contraception which allow us to separate its purchase or use from the anticipation of intercourse; the claim that women can take oral contraceptives to 'correct menstrual irregularities' is one of very few examples. No doubt it is easier to achieve this separation of contraception and intercourse when the contraceptive method is distant in purchase and use from intercourse itself; the popularity of the pill, in spite of other costs associated with it, is likely to be partly attributable to this. Conversely, methods such as the condom, which are less easy to distance from intercourse, may involve considerable costs. Problems with condom use will be discussed in more detail later, but it is worth noting Holland *et al.*'s comment that they 'found embarrassment at every stage of condom use' (1990: 22).

It is not surprising, then, that researchers should have found such a consistent relationship between negative feelings about sex and difficulties in using contraception. Bruch and Hayes (1987), for example, found that anxiety about heterosexual relationships correlated negatively with the use of effective contraception at first intercourse. Similarly, Morrison (1985) notes the 'unanimous conclusion' that 'high sex guilt' is associated with less use of contraception. As Gerrard *et al.* (1993) point out, negative emotional responses to sex may well prevent any sexual activity; but when they do not, they are likely to create difficulties in planning for the consequences of intercourse, in terms of finding out about, obtaining and using contraception. It would be simplistic and misleading, however, to see 'negative emotional responses to sex' as possibly pathological attributes of the individual which then direct behaviour, although they are often presented in this way by researchers. Emotional responses to sex are developed in a social context which strongly supports certain types of sexual activity and relationships and strongly sanctions others. Such sanctions may help to explain the often found relationship between unwanted pregnancy, subsequent requests for abortion, and unplanned sexual activity. People who do not belong to groups where regular intercourse is 'approved', by their family, their peers or by the wider social community may be reluctant to be seen to be anticipating sexual encounters by obtaining and using contraception.

Anticipation of disapproval over contraception was very evident in Allen's (1981) interviews with women seeking abortion. Those aged under twenty had made far less use of family planning clinics than had the older women. The younger women reported that they had been too shy, afraid of being turned away or lectured at, or fearful of lack of privacy, to use these services. Other studies confirm that assurances of confidentiality are an important factor for young women in deciding whether to use these clinics (Torres *et al.* 1980; Zabin and Clark 1983; APA 1987) For those women who do use these services, there are additional costs. While some women find clinics welcoming, others are dismayed by the medical examinations, long waiting times and lack of privacy. Indeed, Allen (1981) reports that a substantial number of the women in her sample were nervous or even terrified before their first visit and that some found the experience so aversive that they never returned.

Side effects and health concerns

It is ironic that those methods associated with the fewest unwanted pregnancies – the contraceptive pill and the intrauterine device – are also those associated with the most negative side effects and health risks. The experience of negative side effects and worries about health risks have consistently emerged as amongst the most important factors in the non-use of the pill and the IUD in sexually active women (Washington *et al.* 1983; Metson 1988; Ingelhammer *et al.* 1994). Women using these methods are also exposed to periodic reports of long-term health risks, but often in ways which make it difficult for them to judge the risk to themselves.

If women chose not to use the contraceptive pill or an IUD, then clearly the information they receive on other methods is crucial. Allen (1981), however, found that many women who obtain contraceptive services from their GPs are only offered the pill and do not receive advice on a range of methods. Metson (1988) also noted that women advised by their GPs were less well informed about post-coital contraception than women attending specialist clinics. Finally, a number of the younger women in Allen's (1981) sample of women seeking abortion reported that they were reluctant to use the pill because of its side effects; but they saw other methods as unreliable and therefore used no method at all.

THE SOCIAL CONTEXT OF CONTRACEPTIVE USE

Some of the research described in the last sections has acknowledged that decision-making about contraception takes place in a social context which can discourage rather than facilitate its use. But much traditional psychological research on contraception either overlooks this aspect or makes only limited reference to it. Two aspects of the context of contraceptive decision-making have received very little attention from psychologists, although there are good reasons to suppose that they are very important to our understanding of contraceptive decision-making. The first is the fact that contraception is only necessary in heterosexual relationships. Of course, some contraceptive methods are now used in homosexual relationships to prevent infection, but their use for the prevention of pregnancy is obviously only necessary amongst heterosexuals. We need, then, to consider whether males and females are positioned differently – by discourse, by social practices, by consequences – in relation to sexual encounters and, if so, how this might influence contraceptive use. The second issue concerns intercourse: contraception need not be used in all heterosexual encounters where pregnancy is possible but unwanted; it is only necessary if the couple have intercourse. The extent to which this simple fact, or at least its implications, has been overlooked in the traditional literature is very striking. The literature has generally conflated 'sex' and 'heterosexual intercourse', making it look as if contraception is an inevitable part of heterosexual relationships where pregnancy is unwanted. These factors will be examined through discussion of the role of gender and power in contraceptive decision-making.

Gender, power and contraception

Ramazanoğlu and Holland (1993: 243) have suggested that their discussions with young women and men about sexuality and safer sex provide support for Foucault's contention that 'the body is a site where the large-scale organisation of power is connected to the most minute and local practices'. Thus, what is constructed as a natural and private act – sexual intercourse – is, in an important sense, highly constrained and public. Similarly, some points made by Ramazanoğlu and Holland about safer sex apply equally to contraception: contraceptive use is not a neutral and rational response to the risk of unwanted pregnancy, in which methods are chosen for personal convenience and safety, but a highly gendered activity in which male–female power relations construct and constrain choices and decisions. The ways in which gendered power relations operate in relation to contraception will be examined, first, by looking at women's responsibility for contraception and, second, through an analysis of the construction of male and female sexuality.

Women's responsibility for contraception

A number of writers have noted that the burden of responsibility for contraception is both given to and taken up by women (Schinke 1984; Chilman 1985; Pollack 1985; Wight 1992). The implicit belief that women are more responsible than men for contraception shows itself in many different ways. For example, the majority of the psychological literature on contraception is concerned with women; indeed Schinke (1984) claimed that males 'are forgotten' in most research on the prevention of unwanted pregnancy. If this is an exaggeration, men are certainly not very visible: in fourteen studies reviewed by Beck and Davies (1987), aimed at encouraging teenagers to use contraception, seven were aimed exclusively at females and only one exclusively at males. The media can show a similar bias. A 1995 advertisement for the charity 'Population Concern' stated that:

> Millions of women want to plan their families and safeguard their reproductive health but 10,000 will die this week because they don't have the chance . . . with your help, many more young women can plan their families and safeguard their reproductive health.

There is no suggestion here that men are in any way involved in 'family planning' or that contributions will be used to change their reproductive behaviour. Nor was there any mention of men in a discussion of 'family planning' in Bangladesh (BBC Radio 4, 'Today', 12 July 1994), where it was reported that birth control programmes had reduced the population by 40 per cent in one decade. Research on men's relationship to contraception suggests some possible effects – or causes – of this bias: males are less knowledgeable about contraception; less concerned about it; more likely to say that they 'take risks' with contraception; and less likely to play an active role in contraceptive use (Krishnamoorthy *et al.* 1983; Zellman and Goodchilds 1983; Marecek 1987). As Chilman (1985) has pointed out, however, this situation can create difficulties for males who do want to take their share of responsibility for contraception.

As well as bearing more responsibility for contraception, it seems that women are also expected to tolerate a high level of inconvenience – or worse – in using contraception. This point will be discussed in more detail later in relation to sexual pleasure, but women who participated in the discussion I mentioned earlier of family planning in Bangladesh, reported being strongly encouraged to continue using oral contraceptives in spite of aversive side effects; one woman reported medical refusal to remove an intrauterine device when she was in pain. Methods used by women also often involve close medical supervision which, as Allen (1981) showed, many women find embarrassing, intrusive, time-consuming and inconvenient.

If women are expected to take most of the responsibility for contraception, and expected to endure more in using it, they are also held more responsible when contraception fails. The GP in Allen's (1981) study who considered that only 'hopeless' women had two unwanted pregnancies, had nothing to say about the men who helped create such pregnancies. Similarly, in comparison with the amount of criticism levelled at women in the abortion debates, whether for creating an unwanted pregnancy or seeking an abortion, males were let off very lightly indeed. And even when it is male methods of contraception which are being discussed, their 'failure' may be transferred to women. Griffiths (1990: 16), for example, claimed that condom failure was highest in 'younger single women'. Indeed, women may take on themselves responsibility for men's failure to use contraception, as is illustrated by the woman in Holland *et al.*'s study who reported saying to herself during unprotected intercourse '*I'm* not using a condom here' (1990: 24, my italics). It is difficult to imagine a man in the same situation saying to himself 'I'm not using a cap here'.

Why should women carry such a disproportionate responsibility for contraception? The obvious answer is that it is they who get pregnant. But we do not apply this kind of reasoning to other situations: householders are expected to protect themselves from burglary; pedestrians to take care on busy roads, yet we still recognise the responsibility of the 'other party' and do not suggest, for example, that pedestrians should take more care than drivers. Two related reasons can be suggested as to why this reasoning does not seem to be applied to contraception. The first is that female sexual and reproductive behaviour has traditionally been subjected to far greater scrutiny and censure than has male. Most of the scrutineers have been male, so that scrutinising female behaviour has served to protect their own behaviour from examination and evaluation. Placing most of the responsibility for contraception on women can therefore be seen as a means of controlling women's sexual and reproductive behaviour through medical surveillance and moral censure. That these two aspects of control have historically been closely associated is illustrated by a suggestion from an obstetrician to the Birkett Committee in 1937: he suggested that birth control clinics should be established at women's hospitals, especially maternity hospitals, in order to limit the dissemination of contraceptive information and also in order that staff could exert 'a certain amount of moral control over patients' (cited in Brooks 1988: 115). A second possible reason why women have disproportionate responsibility for contraception is that traditionally the idea of 'woman' has been conflated with 'sex' and 'reproduction' to an extent never applied to 'man' (Ussher 1989; Kent 1990). Thus, the association of pregnancy and women is conceptual in a way which goes well beyond what might be expected from the material fact of pregnancy occurring in women's bodies. It is this conceptual link which helps foster the idea that women are primarily responsible for all aspects of pregnancy, including its prevention, as distinct from simply being the group who 'become pregnant'.

Contraception and the construction of heterosexuality

Women and men occupy very different social and psychological positions in relation to heterosexual encounters, and have access to very different sexual discourses for communicating and interpreting feelings and behaviour. It is ironic, then, that women should bear the major responsibility for contraception when heterosexual relationships can be seen as a site of inequality where women in general have less power than men to control the progress and content of an encounter. This difference in power is manifested in a number of related ways. Historically, heterosexual sex has been defined from a male viewpoint. In ecclesiastical writings, the 'sex act' was defined as the male capacity to 'erect, enter and emit' (Darmon 1985) and, as a number of writers have shown, this framework has been highly influential in the writings of modern sexologists (Stock 1988; Jeffreys 1990; Boyle 1993b, 1994; Ussher 1993). One consequence or corollary of this androcentric view is that both sexologists and lay people have seen male pleasure as paramount in sexual encounters. It is not that female pleasure is assumed to be absent, but it is subordinated to male pleasure and may be defined in terms of male-centred activities, as in the pathologising of women who do not orgasm during intercourse. Maxwell and Boyle (1995), in a study of older women's attitudes to safer sex, noted that many of their participants seemed to see their entire sexual experience as a site of struggle against the centrality of male pleasure, with many feeling that female sexual satisfaction was almost a by-product of male pleasure. As two of the women put it:

> The most important thing was to make sure that he had his . . . he got what he needed, you know, that male pleasure was very important.

... it's this thing around the way you're brought up that in every aspect that men are supposed to have the best, enjoy the best with your body.

(ibid.: 282)

It is in this context, where male sexual pleasure typically takes precedence over female, that sexual intercourse has been portrayed not simply as one amongst many sexual acts, but as *the* sex act, to the point where 'sex' and 'intercourse' may be treated as synonymous, at least by heterosexuals. Like the idea that male pleasure is paramount in sexual encounters, this conflation has been shown to be pervasive amongst both sexologists and lay people (Hite 1981a; Jeffreys 1990; Boyle 1994; Maxwell and Boyle 1995). It is well illustrated by the responses of two participants in Holland *et al.*'s study in which young women were asked what sex meant for them:

Q   You only count it as a sexual relationship if you actually...?
A1   Having sex, I think.
A2   When anyone ever said sex before, all I ever thought was sexual intercourse. That's what it is, isn't it?

(1990: 8)

Yet intercourse has different meanings for males and females and its conflation with sex has different consequences for them. There is, for example, good evidence that women do not reliably orgasm during intercourse and that men do (Hite 1981a, b; Quilliam 1994); intercourse has also been construed as a means of male dominance over women and as a means of female fulfilment through subordination (Jeffreys 1985, 1990; Stock 1988; Boyle 1994). One consequence of the conflation of sex and intercourse is therefore to naturalise and make seemingly essential to any 'proper' sexual encounter, an activity more reliably associated with male than with female sexual pleasure, more associated with male dominance than with sexual equality and, for many women, likely to result in pregnancy unless some form of contraception is used.

The conflation of sex and heterosexual intercourse is a discursive practice which appears to be shared by men and women and to apply equally to both; other discourses, however, apply differentially to males and females. Three of these discourses are particularly important in relation to contraception. The first is that of the male as the active agent in sexual encounters, with the female playing a receptive role. Masters and Johnson even projected these social roles onto sexual organs:

Full penile erection is, for the male, obvious physiological evidence of a psychological *demand* for intromission. In exact parallel, full vaginal lubrication for the female is obvious physiological evidence of a psychological *invitation* for penetration.

(1970: 195, my italics)

93

Similarly, in a feature entitled 'Sex and the assertive woman', Glenn Wilson warned of the dangers posed to men by assertive women, claiming that men have to feel some degree of dominance 'in order to fulfil their sexual function' (*Daily Mail*, April 30 1992). This positioning of males and females is so entrenched it has even been extended to accounts of the 'behaviour' of sperm and ova (Martin 1991). It is not that women are denied power in these sexual scenarios; their power, however, lies in their ability to arouse men by their appearance or manner, and to make men desire them. This construction is strongly evident in popular literature and the media (Coward 1984; Holland *et al.* 1991) and contrasts with the paucity of depictions of women who, as Holland *et al.* put it, are both 'acceptably feminine and in control of their sexuality' (1991: 3).

The second discourse which divides men and women, and has implications for contraception, is that of the 'natural' male sex drive (Hollway 1989). Male sexuality has consistently been depicted as more pressing, more straightforward and less concerned with situational or emotional factors than female. Comfort (1987: 34), for example, claimed that the male sexual response was 'far brisker, more automatic than the female', while Kaplan (1974: 345) asserted that 'as compared to the female response, the sexual response of many males...is relatively insensitive to psychological influences'. And in an article aimed at women, Michael Crowe declared that men's desire for sex tends to be dictated more than women's by biological urges which lead to their '*requiring* sex at certain times' (*Cosmopolitan*, May 1990, my italics). These professional statements are reflected in lay accounts of sexuality: Marecek (1987) noted that surveys of young people's beliefs about sex suggested that many believed that men have a greater innate need for sex than women and that some believed that it is physically or psychologically dangerous not to satisfy men's needs.

The third discourse by which men and women are positioned differently in heterosexuality relates to social judgements of sexual behaviour through which men and women derive very different reputations from the same sexual practices (Ramazanoğlu and Holland 1993). English is rich in derogatory language to describe sexually active women (e.g. slut, slag, whore, nympho) and has no clearly positive term for them. By contrast, there are few, if any, very derogatory terms for sexually active males, but a choice of positive or at least non-condemnatory ones (e.g. Romeo, Casanova, Lothario, sowing wild oats, bit of a lad) (Spender 1985; Lees 1986; Mills 1991).

The potential importance of these discourses can be seen in terms of Foucault's suggestion of a link between the operation of disciplinary power and discursive practices which produce self-regulating subjects. Ramazanoğlu and Holland (1993) have suggested that for women, this involves disciplining their bodies, not to take care of themselves, but to express their femininity in meeting men's needs even if this means not using contraception. This process is illustrated by two women in Maxwell and Boyle's study talking of how male pleasure had priority in their sexual relationships:

94

I've always sort of fell madly in love...and that was it...all I ever wanted to do was to please them.

I don't think that now...I don't think I'm ever coerced by my partner, but I think I might coerce myself on his behalf...in a very subtle, almost unconscious sort of way.

(1995: 283)

Similarly, as Ramazanoğlu and Holland have emphasised, men are able to dominate women without wanting or intending to, so that both parties may feel they are simply 'doing what comes naturally'.

But an intellectual awareness of these problems may not be sufficient to transform sexual encounters or to encourage efficient use of contraception. This will be discussed in more detail in the next section, but one reason for this failure is that heterosexual relations are constituted not only by disciplinary or discursive power, but by other forms of more overtly coercive power. Holland *et al.* (1991: 21) reported that almost 25 per cent of their sample of young women had had unwanted sexual intercourse in response to pressure from men, which included threats, physical assault and rape. One woman put it succinctly:

Q Were you able to say what you wanted, that you didn't want to have sex?
A If I didn't want to have sex there would have been violence.

The two forms of power, however, are closely related in that milder forms of male aggression are portrayed as a normal part of heterosexuality and eroticised as such (Jeffreys 1990). Comfort's remark in his sex manual 'The Joy of Sex', that male strength is an 'obvious' turn-on for women, is part of this process; so too is the widely available discourse of romance as is clear from Heyn's account of the guidelines for authors of a best-selling series of romantic novels:

[The hero is] eight to twelve years older than the heroine. He is self-assured, masterful, hot-tempered, capable of violence, passion and tenderness...
[the heroine is] young (19–29)...basically an ingénue, and wears modest make-up and clothes.

(*Cosmopolitan*, December 1993)

Both men and women are therefore placed in a power structure which not only normalises, but eroticises, male dominance and female subordination in heterosexual relationships. This structure, as Ramazanoğlu and Holland (1993) have emphasised, is both embraced and resisted in the negotiation of heterosexual encounters. It is against this background that we need to consider some of the difficulties faced by both women and men in relation to contraception.

Gender, power and contraceptive decision-making

Some of the problems faced by women and men in negotiating contraceptive use are well illustrated by accounts of the use of one particular contraceptive – condoms. As Holland *et al.* (1990) have pointed out, the analysis of these accounts needs to acknowledge the weight of meanings carried by condoms and the social character of sexual relations. From this perspective, condoms, or indeed any form of contraception, cannot be seen as a straightforward and practical way of dealing rationally with risk. Rather, their use or non-use is the outcome of negotiation between partners who are conceptually, as well as materially, very differently placed in relation to sexual encounters. The study of condom use is particularly important because their use directly confronts two of the major factors which structure power relations in heterosexual encounters: the pre-eminence of male sexual pleasure and assumptions about the male sex drive.

One corollary of the focus on male pleasure in sexual encounters is the apparent expectation that contraception should not unduly interfere with it. Reading *et al.* (1982), for example, commented on the far greater concern surrounding the effect of male chemical contraception on sex drive than was ever the case during the development of female oral contraceptives, in spite of women's reports that they could reduce sex drive. Similarly, a report on trials of the female condom (*Observer*, 12 February 1988) did not mention any effect it might have on female pleasure, but noted only that 'men whose partners have tried the device... reported that sensation was much less reduced than with a conventional condom'. This concern over a reduction in their own pleasure is one of the major reasons given by men for disliking condoms (Pleck *et al.* 1990; Wilton and Aggleton 1991). What is interesting is that women use similar language to men in describing some of *their* reasons for disliking condoms. Participants in Maxwell and Boyle's (1995) and in Holland *et al.*'s (1990) studies used phrases such as 'holding hands with gloves on', 'washing your feet with your socks on', 'eating a toffee with the wrapper on' to describe what intercourse was like with a condom. The fragility of women's accounts, however, was illustrated in several ways. Holland *et al.*, for example, noted that one young woman who had claimed that intercourse with a condom was like having a bath with your clothes on, later revealed that for her the most positive aspect of her limited experience of intercourse was that it had now 'stopped hurting'. Maxwell and Boyle noted that some of the women's accounts of the effect of condoms on sexual sensation were challenged during group discussions by participants who claimed to notice no difference in sensation. In the face of these challenges, women became rather confused about what they *did* dislike about condoms, particularly in the face of the researchers' question:

> If condoms improved the sensation for men and decreased it for women, would women use them more?

Maxwell and Boyle note that the question was generally met with a confused silence or a change of topic. The general view, however, was that women *would* make more use of such condoms:

> I bet we would...Cos I mean pleasure quite often isn't a major, um, consideration for women in sex...I don't...I mean it isn't is it...you know.

> Without a doubt...I mean it would be easier for them to put it on, they'd be happier wearing it.

> Are we really that dumb? Wouldn't it reverse the whole thing that we'd be the ones who'd be pressurizing not to use them...We would be that dumb! I'd never really thought about it till you asked.
>
> (Maxwell and Boyle 1995: 284–5)

What seems to be happening here is that women have taken on some men's reasons for disliking condoms and repeat them as if they applied equally to women. The fact that these accounts are more male- than female-centred can make it difficult for women to develop their own ways of speaking or even thinking about what condom use means to them.

As well as confronting the focus on male sexual pleasure in sexual encounters, condom use also confronts the idea of a male sex drive which, as Holland *et al.* put it 'cannot be interrupted or diverted' (1990: 9). The ideas mentioned earlier – that the male sex drive is more insistent than the female, more automatic and more impervious to personal or situational factors, are variations on the same theme. It is not surprising, then, that women should report that considerable assertiveness is sometimes needed to secure men's co-operation in using condoms:

> I mean you really do...well, in my experience you really do have to insist on it and say 'look, I'm not prepared to have sex with you unless you wear a condom'.
>
> (Maxwell and Boyle 1995: 282)

> He really hates using them so I used to say to him 'look, right, I have no intention of getting pregnant again and you have no intention to become a father, so you can put one of these on.' And he starts whingeing. He goes 'Oh, no, do I have to?' I say 'look...do it or you know...'.
>
> (Holland *et al.* 1990: 12)

Other accounts show women's concern with interfering with male pleasure and suggest that women may end up having unprotected intercourse in the face of difficulties in securing condom use:

> It's difficult to ask them...to do something they may not like.
>
> (Maxwell and Boyle 1995: 283)

> I think that's what it is, you don't want to hurt his feelings.
>
> (Holland *et al.* 1990: 16)

97

About two weeks ago, I ended up not asking him [to use a condom] and had to go and get the morning after pill. I wouldn't say anything, and kept thinking I'd say something in a minute, it's just so difficult . . . and then it was too late.

(ibid.: 20–1)

The last two guys . . . I said something I think, and one of them said 'Oh you're not going to make me wear one of those, are you?' And I could have said – I should have said 'yes' . . . but I wanted sex as much as he did and I didn't want any aggro.

(ibid.: 23)

When I got pregnant, I thought to myself, I'm not using anything, but I just couldn't say 'Look, you know . . .' and then the consequences were disastrous.

(ibid.: 24)

These accounts illustrate not only women's reluctance to assert themselves by interrupting sexual encounters, but also the extent to which they take responsibility for condom use: 'I ended up not asking him to use a condom'; 'I'm not using anything'; 'I should have said . . .'. They illustrate, too, the extent to which women may have to step outside their culturally prescribed feminine role and become dominant in sexual encounters in order to protect themselves from pregnancy.

Many men, of course, are not reluctant to use condoms and take the initiative in their use. Pleck *et al.* (1990), for example, found that men's intention to use condoms was significantly related to the belief that men should take some responsibility for contraception and to the belief that a reduction in sensation was a small cost compared to the benefit of their partner's appreciation. And Holland *et al.* (1990) reported that 32 per cent of their sample of young women had partners who liked or preferred using condoms. Nor is it the case that male reluctance to use condoms can be wholly attributed to concern for their own sexual pleasure. Many males, particularly since the introduction of female oral contraceptives, are unsure how to use condoms and may not have access to popular knowledge on the subject. Men also know that the reality of their sexual functioning does not match the popular stereotype and that it may all too easily be affected by situational and personal factors, including worry about using condoms correctly. But there is no acceptable popular language with which men can express their sexual fears or ignorance, or with which women can confront them. Men do, however, have access to a 'legitimate' discourse of male pleasure and its importance which they can use to reject condoms, without revealing their embarrassment and fears. But there is no popular discourse which women can use to talk about or talk to men who refuse to wear condoms, or who seem to put their own sexual pleasure before the risk of unwanted pregnancy.

The problems of using condoms are compounded, as I mentioned earlier, by the additional meanings carried by condoms since the advent of HIV and AIDS.

These new meanings have been added to an existing set of negative associations between condoms, casual sex and 'one-night stands'. Indeed, so frequently are condoms discarded when a relationship becomes established that many of the participants in Maxwell and Boyle's (1995) study, when asked if they used condoms every time they had intercourse, assumed they were being asked about the start of the relationship. Many accounts of giving up condoms stress the importance of trust and commitment. Given the difficulties discussed earlier, however, it may be that the alacrity with which condoms are discarded is also influenced by women's reluctance to press for their use on a long-term basis. As one woman put it:

> You can't meet somebody and start, first time say, 'I know, let's use condoms, I'm not on the pill... and then a week later, still be saying 'let's use condoms' and the week after that still be saying 'let's use condoms'.

> Q You don't think you could do that long term?

> A You couldn't do that, no.

(Holland *et al.* 1990: 18)

Some couples, of course, continue to use condoms as their main form of contraception. For them, commitment might be demonstrated by sharing the cost or by both taking responsibility for purchase. But for other couples who initially use condoms, there is a speedy transition to female-controlled forms of contraception which do not 'interrupt' the sexual encounter. If the new method is used efficiently, then there may be few problems as far as unwanted pregnancy and abortion are concerned. The problem is that the transition may be made for *social* reasons, to avoid the negative connotations of condom use, rather than because the new method positively 'suits' the couple. As Holland *et al.* (1991) have pointed out, the pill (and the IUD) allow women to meet the cultural demand to focus on male sexual pleasure, without challenging the power dimension of the situation. The power imbalance is emphasised by the fact that the transition is often to methods which, even if they do not intrude on the sexual encounter, do intrude on the woman's body. It is these methods which are most frequently associated with health 'scares' and with complaints of side effects. Thus, women may continue using these methods not because they positively 'suit' them, but because they do not involve confronting the power imbalance inherent – whether the couple intends it or not – in heterosexual encounters. Women may also use oral contraceptives inefficiently if they experience side effects or health' scares', but without the couple using a 'back-up' method. For example, in the first quarter of 1996 there was a 6.2 per cent increase in abortions over the same period in 1995 (ONS 1996b) following a widely publicised report of a possible link between some brands of the pill and thrombosis. Although the figures cannot necessarily be interpreted as a straightforward result of the 'health scare', it appears that some women simply stopped using the contraceptive pill when the story was publicised, but without them or their partners adopting another contraceptive method.

Finally, one extremely efficient method of reducing the risk of unwanted pregnancy is not to have vaginal intercourse. But, as I emphasised earlier, heterosexual intercourse is culturally constructed not simply as a sexual act, but as *the* sexual act whose absence can be taken to mean that 'sex' did not happen. Heterosexual intercourse can also serve as both a symbol and an act of male dominance and female subordination. More positively, both men and women see heterosexual intercourse as an important way of achieving intimacy and emotional closeness (Hite 1981a, b). And the cultural conflation of 'sex' and 'intercourse' functions for both men and women as a way of allowing a variety of sexual activities outside a major relationship, without the person feeling that they have been technically unfaithful (Maxwell and Boyle 1995). The avoidance of intercourse as a means of contraception, even if used only occasionally, is therefore fraught with difficulties, one of which may be conceptual: the conflation of 'sex' and 'intercourse' is so strong that it may simply not occur to heterosexual couples that sex without intercourse is an option. Indeed, Holland *et al.* (1991) have suggested that young women's knowledge of and access to contraception may effectively structure what is thought of as 'sex'. For example, a 1996 advertisement for a device which measures women's hormone levels and converts them into information about fertility, claimed that 'if there's a red light showing you can either avoid sex or use a barrier method'. Similarly, messages which urge young people always to use contraception when they have sex, deny the possibility that sex without mechanical contraception can effectively avoid the risk of pregnancy. Other problems are less abstract. In heterosexual encounters where intercourse is clearly an option, avoiding it involves confronting its role as the central source of male pleasure:

> For me as a woman it doesn't bother me if his willy comes in, for my own pleasure, but for the thought of... as many men think sex is penetrative only... um in my mind I would be feeling it's not as fulfilling for him because he feels he's got to come into me.
>
> (Participant, Maxwell and Boyle 1995: 286)

Both men and women also have access to a derogatory discourse about women who want to 'stop short' of intercourse:

> Actually, seeing as you asked me earlier, 'Did you find it enjoyable or pleasurable?' I find everything enjoyable and pleasurable except for the actual penetration so I mean, why bother? I think really if you're with a guy and you are going to do everything but, it's obviously a big tease.
>
> (Participant, Holland *et al.* 1990: 9)

On the other hand, there is little positive popular discourse about male heterosexuality which does not involve intercourse. On the contrary, as Marecek (1987) has pointed out, having intercourse with women may define male heterosexuality, in the sense that it appears to confirm that the man is not homosexual. For both men and women, then, there is little cultural support for

100

non-penetrative sex if the opportunity for intercourse is available. And for some women, there is the added concern that they would be forced to have intercourse whether they wanted to or not:

> I mean how can you say you are now going to have non-penetrative sex . . . I mean especially with a man that's easily turned into something else without you being able to control it at all, I think . . . You could end up in a potentially rape situation.
>
> (Participant, Maxwell and Boyle 1995: 286)

This account of the difficulties which women and men face in relation to the avoidance of unwanted pregnancy presents a far more complex picture than was apparent in either the parliamentary debates ('a woman can speak, she makes a choice') or in the remarks of some doctors ('they don't get pregnant twice unless they're hopeless'). Remarks like these support Ramazanoğlu and Holland's (1993) suggestion that the difficulties faced by many women seeking to resist male power in sexual situations is seriously underestimated. The remarks, and others quoted earlier, also illustrate the extent to which the abortion debates have rendered men, and the difficulties they face in preventing unwanted pregnancy, virtually invisible. The debates, however, did briefly acknowledge that contraceptive services might play an important role in limiting the number of abortions:

> We must link family planning to the debate about abortion. We all know in our hearts that if we had a fraction of the campaign and the lobbying force that has rightly supported the issue of abortion behind the issue of family planning, things would be very different.
>
> (ORC 21 June 1990: 1166)

Other speakers drew attention to the irony that at the same time as access to abortion was being debated, financial constraints on 'family planning' services were being announced. Of course, it is important that the link between contraceptive services and abortion should be emphasised. But, as Holland *et al.* (1990) have noted in relation to HIV and AIDS, health education campaigns have done little to disrupt the dominant construction of heterosexual encounters as inevitably involving penetrative sex; and, in emphasising individual responsibility for 'safer sex', the campaigns have failed to acknowledge the social pressures – very different for women and men – 'which constrain people's talk and behaviour in sexual encounters' (ibid.: 1). In the same way, debates on 'family planning' or increased funding of contraception services, are unlikely to have much impact on requests for abortion unless they take account of the social context in which decisions to use contraception are made.

101

6

THE EXPERIENCE OF ABORTION

Claims about the experience of abortion, about the reasons women have abortions and about its effects on them, have featured prominently in the abortion debates. On the one hand, it is claimed that women have abortions for trivial reasons and that they are seriously damaged by the procedure. On the other hand, women are presented as 'deserving of' abortion, as thinking seriously about their decision and as being relatively unaffected by the experience. This chapter is concerned with psychological and psychiatric research relevant to these claims. The first part will highlight features of this research – outlined in Chapter 1 – which limit its usefulness and which shape the representation of abortion, and women's responses to it, in relatively narrow ways. The second part will examine women's and men's experience of abortion, but from a broader perspective than is usually adopted by traditional research.

PSYCHOLOGICAL RESEARCH ON ABORTION

The first notable feature of the research is its highly individualistic stance: it provides little analysis of the social context in which unwanted pregnancy and abortion are experienced. Women's responses to abortion, for example, have often been represented via attempts to measure hypothesised individual intrapsychic characteristics, such as shame, relief, anxiety or depression. Some researchers, for example, Speckhard and Rue (1992: 108), imply that negative states following abortion have no cultural component, arguing instead that 'grief following pregnancy loss is a human, not necessarily a . . . religiously . . . induced . . . phenomenon'. Other researchers do acknowledge the social and cultural context, but in a highly attenuated way which avoids detailed discussion of the relationship between culture and the experience of abortion, and which tends to present the social context as an idiosyncratic aspect of an individual's experience. Adler *et al.* (1992), for example, suggest that in interpreting research on post-abortion experience, the 'entire context' of the abortion must be considered. The closest they come to acknowledging culture, however, is a reference to 'experience with protesters' and 'whether the pregnancy was the result of rape', but with no suggestion that these events are systematically related to gender, to power, and to the cultural construction of abortion. Similarly, Adler (1992: 22) talks of women who 'may... not engage in planning [to avoid pregnancy]' and suggests that 'such an attitude could arise from a general fatalistic orientation towards life, or from specific experiences related to [women's] reproductive history'. This account offers little acknowledgement of the ways in which women's socially subordinate position is likely to have systematic and repeated effects on their reproductive experience, including their access to and use of contraception.

Other researchers have transferred 'culture' into the heads of individual women, so that it becomes another intrapsychic variable. Clare and Tyrrell (1994), for example, talk of women who seek abortion having 'cultural attitudes'. Similarly, Marecek (1987: 91) described women who showed 'fatalism and moralistic reasoning', such as believing that pregnancy is the price women have to pay for having sex or that ending pregnancy by abortion is evading a just punishment. As we have seen, however, discourses which link sex and motherhood and which construct abortion as a deviant and unnatural act – indeed as an evasion of a just punishment – are culturally pervasive and are central to the abortion debates. Yet when women draw on these discourses in talking about their experiences, they are merely described by Marecek as being under 'misapprehensions' which are to be 'refuted', as if the individual woman's understanding of her situation were somehow deficient or irrational.

The second feature of the psychological literature on the experience of abortion is closely related to the focus on individual women: it is the striking emphasis on negative or pathological aspects of women's responses to abortion. Wilmoth *et al.* (1992), for example, reviewed fifteen studies of the psychological consequences of abortion. Amongst them, these measured a total of fifty-two outcome variables. Of these, forty-two were wholly negative (e.g. depression, shame, guilt, paranoia, anxiety); five referred to relief; three could have been positive or negative. Only one unequivocally positive variable – happiness – was mentioned, in two studies. This preoccupation with negative outcomes is also evident in Miller's (1992) review of theoretical models of 'possible long-term consequences' of abortion, although neither Wilmoth nor Miller draw attention to this feature. Of seven models discussed by Miller, the contents of five are wholly negative and do not seem to allow for other than negative responses to abortion; one, the 'crisis' model, allows both negative reactions and 'relief', and one, the 'learning' model, allows both positive and negative behaviour change following abortion. The only positive change suggested by Miller, however, is women's improved contraceptive practice.

This focus on negative outcomes is quite explicit, but the normalising of negative psychological outcomes of abortion is often more subtle than this. For example, researchers often use neutral headings such as 'psychological effects of abortion' when their text is entirely about negative effects. And Posavac and Miller (1990: 15) claimed that the 'most central question' in their review of 'what the literature reveals on the topic of the psychological effects of abortions' was 'whether the authors of published literature observed sizeable rate [*sic*] of negative reactions after abortion'; they did not say why this question was more central than any other. Similarly, a complex range of responses to abortion may be described only in relation to the presence or absence of psychological distress.

A third feature of the literature is its neglect of gender. Yet paradoxically the research focuses almost entirely on women. Men may appear peripherally, for example in women's reports of their partner's role in the abortion decision, but they are largely invisible in discussions of the psychological consequences of abortion. In spite of this intense focus on women, the significance of gender to abortion is rarely discussed. It is as if women's relationship to abortion were mediated entirely by the biological givens that only women become pregnant and only women have abortions, but that these had little psychological or social significance.

Finally, the psychological literature on the experience of abortion is characterised by a belief in the power of 'pure' science to overcome the 'taint' of the social and moral prejudice which surrounds abortion. This issue will be discussed in more detail in Chapter 7, but it is notable that there are frequent references in the literature to 'the most rigorous research designs', to 'methodologically sound research' and to 'the best scientific studies', where it is clear that this language is intended to convey the researchers' objectivity and to distance them from any particular social or moral stance on abortion. The research is based on a traditional model of scientific psychology, discussed in Chapter 1, in which being rigorous or scientific is often seen as involving the transformation of complex contexts and experiences to numbers or to lists of discrete variables such as religion, ethnicity, social support, and so on. While all of this may give an appearance of rigour and order, it is often at the expense of obscuring the cultural and psychological diversity which lies beneath one category label or one set of numbers and may involve ignoring much important information.

The remainder of the chapter will present an account of women's and men's experience of abortion in which both gender and the cultural context are more visible than they have been in most psychological research. This does not mean that traditional research has no place in a more contextual account. If women who have abortions have answered researchers' questions in particular ways, it is still important to know what these are, even if we reject the theoretical assumptions of the models underlying the research.

BEFORE AN ABORTION: MAKING THE DECISION AND REQUESTING AN ABORTION

In keeping with the very negative ways in which abortion has been construed, deciding to have an abortion is often presented as inevitably painful and traumatic for women. In the parliamentary debates, for example, it was claimed that '[abortion] is a decision that women agonize about' (ORC 24 April 1990: 235) and that 'it is a traumatic decision for the mother and father of the potential child to conclude that there should be an abortion' (ORC 24 April 1990: 243). Another MP referred to 'the thousands of women who take the difficult and traumatic decision to have an abortion' (ORC 24 June 1990: 246). Similarly, Maitland (1984) described the decision as 'a decision of despair; it is a grievous pain for a woman to face the fact that the world is intolerable for her and her child' (cited in Neustatter 1986: 33), while Neustatter herself claimed that the abortion decision was 'profoundly painful and complex' (ibid.: 41).

How women who have abortions feel about their own decisions will be discussed in more detail in the next section, but it is worth noting that, in contrast to these extremely negative claims, the large majority of women surveyed by Osofsky *et al.* (1973) said that they did not find their decision to have a first trimester abortion difficult: only 12 per cent said that the decision was difficult. However, 51 per cent of women surveyed who had abortions after the first three months of pregnancy said that they found the decision difficult. The fact that so many women who have early abortions claim not to find the decision difficult is perhaps consistent with reports that many of them seem to make the decision very soon after suspecting or confirming their pregnancy. Allen (1981) reported that 73 per cent of the women in her sample had visited their doctor to discuss an abortion before the eighth week of pregnancy and that most of them had already made their decision by then. More strikingly, Smetana and Adler (1979) found that 92 per cent of the variance in the abortion decision (i.e. whether women in their sample did or did not have abortions) was accounted for by the woman's intention to have, or not have, an abortion, stated before they knew the result of a pregnancy test. Holmgren (1994) similarly found that 70 per cent of the women in her sample had made the decision to have an abortion before the pregnancy was confirmed.

Although men have not been very visible in the abortion debates, they are more visible in women's accounts of their decision-making about abortion. Miller (1992) reported that 52 per cent of women listed their 'spouse' as the most important person with whom they had discussed the abortion. The next most frequently listed person was 'male friend' and some of these were probably sexual partners. Eighty-five per cent of women in Major *et al.*'s (1990) sample had told their partners about the abortion, although it is not clear to what extent the decision was shared. By contrast, only 25 per cent of a sample of Northern Irish women travelling to Britain for a legal abortion, had talked to their partners about what they were doing (Axby 1994).

When women are asked why they decided to have an abortion, their answers, as we might expect, are very varied. Torres and Forrest's (1988) survey of almost two thousand women suggests that their stated reasons for having abortions can be grouped into those involving personal characteristics (e.g. not old enough; not ready for the responsibility; health problems) and those involving the woman's circumstances such as relationship with her partner, financial worries and desire to continue education (Russo *et al.* 1992). In a reanalysis of these data, Russo *et al.* showed that different groups of women tended to give different reasons for

105

deciding to have an abortion: for example, women who were already mothers were likely to give education and job related reasons and more likely to cite responsibilities to others and their partner's unemployment; adolescents were more likely than adult women to say they were not ready for child-rearing. Of course, women do not give just one reason when they are asked why they chose abortion; not surprisingly, attempts to correlate specific reasons to the abortion decision in large samples of women show that the relationship between the decision and any one reason is usually weak (Miller 1992). The complexities of women's decision-making about abortion will be explored further in the next section through an idea which crops up frequently in discussions of abortion – 'ambivalence'.

Ambivalence and the abortion decision

It has often been suggested that women are 'ambivalent' about their decision to have an abortion; indeed, Lemkau (1988) has claimed that ambivalence is the norm for women who have abortions. The same idea is implied by book titles such as Francke's (1978) *The Ambivalence of Abortion* and Neustatter's (1986) *Mixed Feelings: The Experience of Abortion*. Yet as we have seen, the majority of women claim not to find the decision to have an early abortion difficult; the decision seems to be made at a very early stage and the majority claim to be 'very certain' about their decision (Miller 1992). How might these apparently conflicting positions be reconciled? There are several possibilities. First, the *idea* that women are ambivalent about having an abortion may be inherent in the extremely negative way in which abortion is constructed: how could anyone not be ambivalent about a decision which, though it seems necessary, has been variously described as a 'tragedy', a 'traumatic decision', the 'lesser of two evils' and a 'deeply painful decision'? Claims that women are ambivalent may also be a necessary part of a legislative system in which decision-making power about abortion lies with doctors and not with women themselves. I argued in Chapter 3 that one means of justifying medical involvement in the abortion decision was to present women as emotional and confused and as needing guidance in making the 'correct' decision, in other words, as not having a clear view about terminating their pregnancy.

An alternative explanation for the conflicting positions of women's reported certainty and commentators' emphasis on ambivalence, is that when women talk to doctors or fill in research questionnaires, they overstate their certainty about their decision, and de-emphasise ambivalence, because they are afraid that otherwise their request for an abortion may be refused. And, after the abortion, they may maintain a stance of certainty as a means of reducing conflict between their emotions and their behaviour. Allen (1981), for example, noted that some of the women in her sample had...'kept their doubts to themselves' lest their request be refused. Indeed, Hadley (1996: 184) has claimed that 'the minute women mention ambivalence...the anti-abortion lobby triumphantly crystal-lises these feelings as symptoms of permanent psychological trauma'. Fletcher

(1994) also suggests that women are fearful of speaking about their confused feelings because this could be used to 'prove' that abortion should be restricted.

This suggests that although the *idea* of ambivalence can be seen as being produced by, indeed as being necessary for, negative social constructions of abortion, it may also reflect some women's experience. But this does not necessarily mean that ambivalence and 'confused feelings' are intrinsic to or a 'natural' part of abortion; nor does experiencing a variety of emotions about the decision necessarily conflict with feeling certain about the decision. In exploring this issue further, it is helpful to return to the earlier discussion of psychology's tendency to provide decontextualised analyses of abortion. In keeping with this, 'mixed feelings' about abortion have been conceptualised in intrapsychic terms as 'personal conflict', which seems to take place in the woman's head, when her decision conflicts with her 'personal values'; women are thus described as 'being conflicted' about their pregnancies (Adler *et al.* 1992; Major and Cozzarelli 1992). Although these analyses do acknowledge that a woman's decision to have an abortion may conflict with the values of her family, her religion, or her culture, the analyses remain mainly at an individual level and offer no clear way of understanding the relationship between the social construction of abortion and women's experience of their decision. An alternative approach to the relationship between culture and psychological experience has been suggested by Henriques *et al.* (1984), Hollway (1989) and Shotter (1993); this may be helpful in understanding why 'mixed feelings' about the abortion decision are not uncommon and in clarifying the relationship between women's feelings about their decision and the social construction of abortion.

Ambivalence and the social construction of abortion

Shotter (1993) has argued that individual responses to particular situations should be thought of as the 'marking off' of aspects of collective debate and communal thinking, but which in our society are redefined psychologically as individual attributes or possessions. Similarly, Henriques *et al.* (1984) and Hollway (1989) have strongly criticised the idea of the 'unitary rational subject', which has dominated psychological theory, and have argued instead that each of us is simultaneously positioned in relation to multiple and often contradictory discourses and the social practices produced by them. In line with this, Wasielewski (1992) has argued that the social context of an experience is a major factor in determining which emotions are reported in a given situation. Thus, women who are pregnant in adverse circumstances may experience to some degree or another all the emotions about pregnancy which are culturally mandated. The ways in which these ideas can help clarify women's feelings about their decision to have an abortion will be considered, first, in relation to discourses surrounding motherhood, second, in relation to women's moral reasoning and, third, in relation to women's encounters with counsellors and doctors when they request abortions.

The abortion decision and discourses of motherhood

I emphasised in Chapter 3 that motherhood has traditionally been constructed not simply as a means, but as *the* means of feminine fulfilment. Maintaining this presentation, of course, requires that the risks and challenges of motherhood should be de-emphasised and that the discourses surrounding women who reject motherhood should be mainly negative. Perhaps it is not surprising, then, that even women who are certain that they will have an abortion should, nevertheless, be the recipients of some of the positive discourses which surround pregnancy and motherhood. These positive definitions are more publicly available to some groups of women than to others, but this does not mean that women in a variety of circumstances cannot privately experience the positive emotions which 'should' be engendered by pregnancy, as the following accounts by women who had abortions show:

> When I found out I was pregnant I felt good, right, excited. It was a crazy feeling really because my life at the time was absolutely not set up to have a child. I couldn't have coped financially or practically without huge difficulty. But still a primitive unthinking bit of me was delighted to find that I actually functioned like a woman, that my body could create a baby.
>
> (Neustatter 1986: 4)

> I didn't want a child. I had never wanted one and our marriage had been happy and contented without. Then I got pregnant because of contraceptive failure and although I knew I did not want a child, that this situation was in every sense a mistake, I did feel a strange pleasure in the idea that if I did nothing a child could develop. But that didn't seem reason to give birth to a child who was not wanted.
>
> (ibid.)

> I have three children and I felt sure I didn't want more, but when I got pregnant something inside me was making me feel good about it. I think it was the memory of the fact that whenever I was pregnant before it had been the right thing, we'd been thrilled. But... [i]t really did seem to me that this pregnancy was a choice between me and the baby.
>
> (Neustatter 1986: 16–17)

Ambivalence and women's moral reasoning

One of the key aspects of the abortion debates was the moral status ascribed to women: they were often presented as having abortions for 'trivial' or 'specious' reasons and as putting their own 'convenience' ahead of the rights of the unborn child. I suggested that psychological theory had implicitly supported the idea of women's moral inferiority by presenting as superior particular forms of moral reasoning which appeared more typical of males than females. What Kohlberg

(1976) called conventional reasoning – based on concern for individual outcomes and on shared norms and values – was deemed inferior to reasoning based on universal rules and principles. Yet, as Gilligan (1982) has pointed out, it is precisely by their care and concern for specific others, rather than by their adherence to abstract universal rules, that women both judge themselves and are judged. Gilligan argues that the abortion decision affects both the woman herself and others to whom she is close, and 'engages directly the critical moral issue of hurting... it raises precisely those questions of judgement that have been most problematic for women' (1982: 71). We can see this process operating in several ways to produce 'mixed feelings' when women consider abortion. First, the decision may conflict with the woman's desire not to harm the foetus, reinforced by the cultural message that abortion is 'murder'. It is interesting to note here that women's decisions about abortion seem not to be related to their moral concerns about it (Smetana and Adler 1979), so that for some women, 'mixed feelings' seem inevitable:

> I have always disagreed with [abortion]. My friend had it done a lot of years ago and I thought, it's killing a baby, a wee innocent baby. But when it comes to yourself you come to terms with it, you realise.
>
> (McEvoy and Boyle, in preparation)

> I didn't like the idea of abortion, it does seem like murder to me, but even so, it was preferable to destroying two grown people's lives.
>
> (Neustatter 1986: 20)

This last statement – that abortion was preferable to destroying the lives of two adults – highlights another way in which the moral reasoning surrounding the abortion decision involves conflicting desires and obligations. As Gilligan (1982) has emphasised, women have traditionally been enjoined to maintain connection with others, yet it is clear that pregnancy can threaten this. Torres and Forrest (1988), for example, found that 23 per cent of women in their sample mentioned that their partner's desire for the abortion had contributed to their decision. The potential threat pregnancy brings to a relationship is shown more directly in these accounts:

> He made no secret of his wish to be free, not to have commitments or ties... When I told him... he immediately suggested an abortion.
>
> (Neustatter 1986: 10)

> I got pregnant because of a broken sheath. My husband was livid and told me to get rid of it or he would divorce me and not pay maintenance for the child. I imagined my husband going off with another woman and being happy with her while I would be alone at night.
>
> (ibid.: 24)

> I had always condemned everyone who had an abortion. To me it was callous... But the tables turned when I found myself pregnant by my

boyfriend who really didn't want the baby. I knew what a terrible smear it would be on his family to have an illegitimate child and what a start to adult life it would be for him if he had to give up studying to look after me and a baby. So I too became callous.

(ibid.: 29)

My husband was furious and would not even talk about the idea of another baby...he said he would leave me if I didn't get rid of the baby.

(ibid.: 30)

I just wanted the child, and I really don't believe in abortions...he made me feel if I didn't have [the abortion] that it would drive us apart.

(Gilligan 1982: 81)

A third way in which the abortion decision might involve conflicting obligations and worries about harm, which might result in ambivalence, is where the decision brings the woman into conflict with what she sees as obligations to herself. Two of the women quoted earlier illustrate this point: 'Alongside this positive feeling was despair about what would happen to *me*' and 'it really did seem to me that this pregnancy was a choice between me and the baby'. As Gilligan has shown, however, women may interpret this concern with themselves as selfish, because it conflicts with the social injunction to care for others:

I had never actually resolved that I was doing it for me. Actually, I had to sit down and admit...'I honestly don't feel that I want to be a mother'...[i]t was just a horrible way to feel.

(Gilligan 1982: 86)

I think it is a matter of choosing which one I know I can survive through...I think it is selfish...I guess it does have to do with whether I would survive or not.
Q Why is this selfish?
Well, you know, it is. Because I am concerned with my survival first, as opposed to the survival of the relationship or the survival of the child, another human being.

(Gilligan 1982: 89)

[Having the abortion] would be an acknowledgement to me that I am an ambitious person...It means that my family would necessarily come second. There would be an incredible conflict about which is tops and I don't want that for myself.

(Gilligan 1982: 97)

A women may have negotiated these conflicts more or less successfully before she tries to arrange an abortion. But it is when she makes public her desire for abortion that she most directly faces what Neustatter (1986: 68) has called the

110

'minefield of morality, emotion and control which exist around the matter'. The next section will look at the ways in which encounters with counsellors and doctors can contribute to the conflicting emotions which may surround a woman's decision to have an abortion.

Ambivalence and encounters with professionals

As we saw earlier, by the time they approach their doctors, most women have already made the decision to have an abortion; as would be expected, few women report that discussions with their doctors are an important part of the decision-making process. In spite of this, there is an implicit assumption that the woman has not made her decision at this point, or that her decision might be wrong. This shows itself in two ways. The first is through legislation which requires doctors to make the final decision about an abortion, at least in British law, regardless of what the woman has decided for herself. The second is by the requirement or expectation that the woman undergoes counselling before finally deciding whether to request an abortion. As I emphasised in Chapter 3, it is not a matter of suggesting that women should be deprived of the opportunity to talk over their decision, but in choosing to require or just routinely offer counselling for some decisions and not others, governments and professionals provide powerful messages about which choices are seen as normal and desirable and which are seen as personally and socially problematic. Counselling may also function subtly and perhaps unintentionally, to place women in positions of blame or vulnerability about their pregnancy and abortion, and thus encourage women to feel more negatively or more ambivalently about their decision than they did before the encounter with a professional. Lazarus (1985), for example, talks of pre-abortion counselling being used routinely to inform women of birth control methods, although as we have seen, lack of knowledge may have little to do with whether contraception is used effectively. One counsellor, cited by Neustatter (1986: 47), suggested that although few women who had abortions had made the wrong decision 'that doesn't mean they won't suffer...I tend to stress that sadness and grief is a normal response to abortion'. Another claimed that 'I always say to a client, however old or young, or whatever the circumstances, that she will grieve for what has had to happen...In a sense we are all involved in bereavement counselling' (ibid.: 105). These counsellors are in a difficult position, and it is understandable that they should want to normalise what some women may feel. They run the risk, however, of presenting the abortion decision as naturally and inevitably associated with suffering and grief and of encouraging women who do not react in this way to see themselves as deviant.

Nevertheless, many women speak positively about abortion counselling. In Allen's (1985) study, 86 per cent of women who had spoken to counsellors at a charitable abortion service had found the experience helpful. What is striking about some women's accounts, however, is the relief and gratitude they express at being able to talk without being judged, and at having their decision supported:

> The counsellor was really nice...I thought she would disapprove of abortion because she had a child, but she didn't.
>
> (Neustatter 1986: 40)

> The counsellor was marvellous. She was the first person I'd been able to talk to. She was patient and kind without being patronizing.
>
> (ibid.)

These accounts contrast sharply with some women's experience of consulting their doctors to request an abortion and the accounts of these women show clearly how the medical encounter can function to induce conflicting emotions about the abortion decision. Neustatter (1986) found that women who had NHS consultations were much more likely to report negative experiences than were those who saw practitioners in the private or charitable sector:

> He went on about how silly I had been and how people who took care didn't get pregnant.
>
> (Neustatter 1986: 51)

> I wanted to ask the gynaecologist what was going to happen but I couldn't do anything but weep after he'd called me a stupid, immoral child who would have to suffer for my mistake.
>
> (ibid.)

> My husband is a violent man who has hit me often and it wasn't easy to avoid having sex when he wanted it. I didn't want to get pregnant as I already had two small children...and I was desperate to leave him...My doctor didn't want to know about all that: he was just disgusted, really disgusted with me and he told me so.
>
> (ibid.: 61)

> He called me promiscuous and lectured me for ten minutes. Then he said if he helped me, he didn't want to see me in this state again.
>
> (ibid.: 73)

These, and the following accounts of women's negative encounters with their doctors (Neustatter 1986) emphasise the extent to which the doctor's definitions of the situation may conflict with the woman's, and the ways in which the encounter helps to produce 'mixed feelings':

> He told me I was trying to fix the law to suit myself and that all these women killing babies was a sign of the times...I began to feel very upset and uneasy.
>
> (ibid.: 34)

He gave me the most painful internal I've ever had and scarcely spoke except to say how much he disapproved of abortion. I felt so disgusting and dirty after that.

(ibid.: 51)

[He treated me] like a moron, he told me that if I was going to have intercourse of course I would get pregnant. And although I pointed out that the man had been taking what is called precautions, he ignored it. He gave me a really painful examination – like he was punishing me – then he said he would help me this once. I went out feeling ghastly and indebted to him, which I didn't like.

(ibid.: 65)

The consultant suggested I was killing a baby because I wanted to go on having a comfortable life. In fact we have no money and little space for another child... I had felt quite confident that... I was making the right decision... Suddenly I saw him expressing the way the world would judge me. I just wanted to hide myself away feeling everyone would see me as selfish and evil.

(ibid.)

The abortion decision – an overview

Women make decisions about abortion against what Wasielewski (1992: 119) has called a 'backdrop of contradictory definitions of abortion'. And, although many women still achieve 'certainty' about their decision, they may be in a relatively weak position in developing their own definition of the decision. Women access abortion services from a dual position of weakness. They are supplicants who must convince a powerful other (usually male) that their reasons for wanting abortion are adequate. They are also the recipients of discourses which construct women as maternal and nurturing, but also as potentially irrational, immoral and as properly sexual only under certain narrowly defined conditions. Many women are acutely aware of all this when they consider abortion. This is no doubt one of the reasons why they so often express relief and gratitude when they are treated courteously and sympathetically. When they are treated badly, it is often through the use of discourses which were prominent in the legislative debates: discourses of irrationality ('he treated me like a moron') and immorality ('he said he was disgusted with me'; 'he said I was trying to twist the law for my own convenience'). It is also striking that some women, perhaps accurately, see themselves as being punished ('he gave me the most painful examination'). Not surprisingly, there are very few reports of women openly challenging these definitions of their situation during the medical encounter.

There is another factor which obstructs women in developing a consistent definition of and reaction to their abortion decision. When women consider abortion, they engage in reasoning which is predominantly 'contextual and

113

narrative' (Gilligan 1982) rather than absolutist or rights-based. They do not, as Hadley (1996: 79) has put it, 'act out a law court in their heads'. Instead, they consider their own and their partner's circumstances, their future plans, their resources for raising a child and so on. It is not that rights-based reasoning is absent, but that it must constantly be balanced against the reality of the woman's life. Yet the abortion debate is often conducted around the issue of rights: the right to life versus the right to choose. When context does enter the debates, it is often in an extreme form: women who have been raped; women living in poverty; women whose health is threatened by additional children. And, as we have seen, moral reasoning based on rights or universal principles has been presented as superior in psychological theory; its prominence in the abortion debates also suggests its high social status. Women can therefore find it difficult to gain, or may see themselves as undeserving of, cultural support for reasoning rooted in their life circumstances. The right to life discourse positions them as potential murderers. Wasielewski (1992: 119) suggests that advocates of the 'right to choose' have not diminished the emotional consequences of the abortion decision, but have 'simply provide[d] additional definitions of the situation which support and advance the rights of women to feel thankful, relieved and in control of their bodies (at least temporarily)' (parenthesis in original). But of course women do not, in law, have the right to choose, so that this discourse may be of little use to a woman seeking abortion from a doctor who does not share that view.

This analysis suggests that reports of 'mixed feelings' are indeed likely to be a frequent feature of the decision to have an abortion. It also suggests, however, that the complexity of women's decision-making, and their emotional response to it, cannot adequately be conveyed as somehow intrinsic to abortion or as reflecting 'personal conflicts'. Nor should ambivalence be seen as incompatible with feeling certain about the decision. Instead, we see women often treading a precarious path through multiple and competing constructions of abortion, at times in situations where they have little power to impose definitions of their own.

AFTER AN ABORTION: PSYCHOLOGICAL RESPONSES

The extent of conflict about how women react to abortion is well illustrated by the following statements:

> No less than 90 per cent of aborted women [sic] experience moderate to severe emotional and psychiatric stress following an abortion.
>
> (Mann 1987, cited in Reardon 1987)

> The weight of the evidence is that legal abortion as a resolution to an unwanted pregnancy, particularly in the first trimester, does not create psychological hazards for most women undergoing the procedure... [there] is persuasive evidence that abortion is usually psychologically benign.
>
> (Adler et al. 1992: 1198, 1203)

114

It is difficult to find evidence in support of the first claim, but Adler *et al.*'s claim is based on reviews of what they call 'the best scientific studies of abortion outcome' (ibid.: 1195). Much of this research involves women's brief self-reports of their reactions to abortion or their scores on standard scales such as the Beck Depression Inventory. Lazarus (1985), for example, gave questionnaires to almost 3,000 women who had had abortions at one clinic during 1976 and 1977 and reported results from a random sample of 292. The majority (76 per cent) said that they felt only relief following the abortion; only 10 per cent described their overall subjective experience as negative. Miller (1992) asked a smaller sample of women (64) whether they had experienced 'significant' emotional upset after the first few weeks following the abortion. Seventy-eight per cent reported none, 10 per cent reported 'much'. Eighty-two per cent said that in the same circumstances, they would have the abortion again. Major and Cozzarelli (1992) reported that 85 per cent of over 500 women obtained scores indicating only mild or no depression immediately post-abortion, and that for those women who attended for a follow-up visit three weeks later, this figure had risen to 90 per cent. Similarly, only 1.5 per cent of a sample of just over 6,000 women studied by Frank *et al.* (1985) were judged to require psychiatric treatment within three weeks of having an abortion.

These studies, of course, suggest that some women do experience more serious negative reactions after abortion. This has led to attempts to identify 'risk factors' which seem to make negative reactions more likely. The most frequently cited factors are: allegiance to religious or cultural groups which do not support abortion; length of pregnancy; difficulty in making the abortion decision; lack of social support for the decision; regarding the decision as being externally imposed and having previously had psychiatric treatment (Osofsky and Osofsky 1972; Adler 1975; Bracken 1978; Adler and Dolcini 1986; Zolese and Blacker 1992; Congleton and Calhoun 1993; Clare and Tyrrell 1994).

Recent psychological research on women's reactions to abortion has tried to move away from the medical model and the pathologising of abortion implied in earlier work. Instead, abortion has been reconceptualised within a 'normal' framework of 'stress and coping'. Adler *et al.* have described this approach as assuming that:

> unwanted pregnancy and abortion are...potentially stressful life events, events that pose challenges and difficulties to the individual but do not necessarily lead to psychopathological outcomes. Rather, a range of possible responses, including growth and maturation as well as negative affect and psychopathology can occur.
>
> (1992: 1197)

Similarly, Major and Cozzarelli (1992: 124) have suggested that 'psychosocial factors that have been found to predict coping with stressful life events in general ought to be important for predicting how well women cope with abortion in particular'. Amongst these factors are a belief in one's ability to cope, social support, and attributions of blame for a stressful life-event. In line with this,

115

Mueller and Major (1989) found that women's post-abortion scores on the Beck Depression Inventory and on a Mood Scale were related to their beliefs about their ability to cope with the abortion. They found also, as expected, that women's beliefs about coping were related to perceived social support. And women who attributed their pregnancy to their character (rather than to their behaviour or to some aspect of the situation) scored significantly higher on the BDI after the abortion than women who did not. Cohen and Roth (1984) also used this stress and coping model in categorising women's 'coping style' following abortion, in terms of cognitive and behavioural approach or avoidance. 'Approach' included talking about the abortion and thinking of ways to avoid its happening again; 'avoidance' included staying away from reminders of the abortion and trying not to talk about it. Women using approach strategies reported a decrease in anxiety from just before to just after the abortion.

This research, and that based more explicitly on a pathology model, has been useful in counteracting assertions that the majority of women are psychologically harmed by abortion. But the research retains a view of women's responses to abortion which is extremely narrow and individualistic and which, in spite of the supposed normalising influence of the stress and coping model, remains implicitly pathological and deficit-based. Both models rely on constructions of women's responses to abortion in terms of internal attributes such as depression and anxiety, which at certain 'levels' are categorised as disorders. The stress and coping model also introduces a new set of inferred individual attributes said to influence responses to abortion, such as attribution styles, self-efficacy and coping skills. Neither model draws attention to the ways in which structural conditions shape women's responses to abortion, while attempts to present abortion as a stressful event like any other run the risk of obscuring even further its particular relations to gender and power.

Cultural influences on responses to abortion

Wasielewski (1992) has suggested that the ideologies which surround abortion predominately cultivate feelings of fear, anger, guilt, shame, embarrassment and humiliation, but also of relief and gratefulness. We have seen some of the ways in which both women and professionals draw on discourses which would be expected to relate to these emotional experiences and which position women as killers, as selfish, as irrational and inappropriately sexual, but also as deserving of 'help'. These constructions of abortion – and of women who have abortions – continue to be influential after the abortion in the ways women talk about themselves:

> I didn't like myself for [having the abortion], I didn't feel good about it and the fact that I was exercising my right to choose did not heal the pain I felt at having ended a life.
>
> (Neustatter 1986: 38)

Sometimes I think to myself that I am doing a wrong thing... I don't feel that I should ever sit in church again.

(McEvoy and Boyle, in preparation)

Women who do not have negative feelings after the abortion may castigate themselves for this 'lack':

I'm not going to let myself get down and I feel, I don't like saying this because I feel that maybe it's a bit cruel, but what I've never had I'll never miss.

(ibid.)

It's just that I don't feel any sorrow or anything for the baby, I don't, just relief... I feel as if I should be having some feelings after it. I feel absolutely heartless, I don't feel as if I have killed a baby, I don't feel that at all. I feel as if I've had a tooth out but that's terrible.

(ibid.)

I realized after about six weeks that I just hadn't thought about the abortion. But that made me feel dreadful. I went into an awful depressed guilty state and I made myself think about it.

(Neustatter 1986: 96–7)

I have no regrets *at all*. Sometimes I worry about that, perhaps I should feel some guilt or something.

(Neustatter 1986: 90–1, italics in original)

Other women, while not criticising themselves, still see negative feelings as likely or inevitable:

I am a very positive person and I feel that I will be OK. Now I don't know, you don't know how you'll feel, you don't know how your hormones will react.

(McEvoy and Boyle, in preparation)

You know you hear about these stages after death, stages of mourning... I'll be waiting on the next stage. Maybe it won't come, but I'll be waiting on it. And if it does come, waiting to see if there is another one.

(ibid.)

Some women go further than criticising themselves for having an abortion, or for having particular feelings about it, and see themselves as deserving of punishment for their choice:

You feel guilty and upset about the whole thing. That you might feel sad and feel a loss, the fact that it was your choice means that you have no rights to these feelings, you can't justify them.

(McEvoy and Boyle, in preparation)

117

[After the abortion] I felt I had no right to just be happy; I felt I had failed by getting pregnant and not wanting it and that I had to be punished for that.

(Neustatter 1986: 92)

While they were performing my abortion something happened and they managed to damage me inside. It ended up with an emergency hysterectomy. Of course it was horrifying and I was very shocked at first, but then I felt a kind of relief. I felt that I had paid for having aborted that child.

(ibid.: 98)

Cultural constructions of abortion not only shape women's emotional reactions to it but also encourage secrecy. Neustatter (1986) has remarked on the paradox of abortion's high public profile and its position as a shameful secret in many women's lives. Whether women involve even their partners may be related to the pervasiveness of cultural sanctions against abortion. Major *et al.* (1990) found that 85 per cent of their US sample had told their partners about the abortion; by contrast, Axby (1994) reported that only 25 per cent of a sample of women from Northern Ireland, who had abortions in England, had discussed with their partners what they were doing. Women in the United States experience both very positive and very negative definitions of abortion or at least of women's 'right to choose'; in Northern Ireland there is virtually no public opposition to very negative cultural constructions of abortion. Interestingly, Speckhard and Rue (1992) reported that 89 per cent of a sample of US women who said they were 'highly stressed' by abortion, feared that others would find out about the abortion; this casts some doubt on these authors' presentation of abortion as intrinsically highly stressful for women. The extent to which some women fear being judged harshly – or worse – is clear from their comments about keeping the abortion secret:

My fear of being caught, that is why I thought I'd better not do it, for fear of being caught. That's basically it.

(McEvoy and Boyle, in preparation)

If anyone found out they would say that I was a tramp, a murderer, that I'd deserve a curse... And in my head I keep thinking that something will happen to my kids.

(ibid.)

I know four girls who had it done. They told a few other people and to this day these people don't speak to them and say 'she had an abortion, that bitch had an abortion'.

(ibid.)

[My friends] would be the first to disown me and they would be the first to

118

say you're bad for doing that, and they would tell people that I did it, sort of to punish you.

(ibid.)

I felt very lonely. I think something like that makes you very aware how difficult it is doing something which goes against society's code of practice.

(Neustatter 1986: 42)

I had the abortion but felt extremely guilty for my actions...I often wonder what other people would think of me if they knew what I had done.

(Wasielewski 1992: 116)

Wasielewski (1992: 101) has suggested that one of the most important factors which will influence women's reactions to abortion is 'the power to ideologically define the abortion context'. Certainly, the women in McEvoy and Boyle's Northern Irish sample did not feel that they had the power to define their situation; they talked instead of strongly negative constructions of abortion being 'hammered' and 'pounded' into them, being 'rammed down your throat'. And, as we have seen, women may request an abortion holding a particular view of their situation, only to have it dismissed and replaced by a definition based on derogatory discourses of women's sexuality and morality. Part of the power of these definitions, of course, is that they draw on culturally pervasive assumptions about women's morality and rationality which women seeking abortion have probably already encountered, and which, at some level, they fear will be used against them when they request an abortion. All a woman has to offer against this cultural edifice is her own conviction that abortion is the right decision for her present circumstances. One woman in McEvoy and Boyle's sample expressed the difficulties of resisting these 'public' definitions:

I feel very fortunate that this has happened to me now at twenty-eight rather than at twenty-two or twenty-three. I'm more able to handle it, more able to cope with putting what other people think about it out of my mind. If I had been younger I would have been bullied into having a child. Maybe not bullied by anyone, but bullied by what society thinks.

In spite of these difficulties, the majority of women do seem to 'cope' with abortion, to the point where even a US Surgeon General, who did not support liberal legislation, nevertheless testified to Congress that the problem of the development of significant psychological problems related to abortion was 'minuscule from a public health perspective' (Koop 1989: 211, cited in Adler *et al.* 1992: 1202). This statement, of course, does not capture the complexity of women's responses to abortion, nor convey anything about the context in which abortion is experienced by women. Nevertheless, four factors can be identified which may account for the 'minuscule' public health problem of negative psychological reactions to abortion. The first is the availability of social support

119

from any source for the woman's decision, whether from partners, friends, family or professionals. This factor emerges again and again as an important influence on women's responses to abortion; it is not difficult to see why if social support consists in others, or even just one other, validating the woman's definition of her situation. A second factor may be that the majority of women seem to be convinced that their decision is right for their circumstances. There are important exceptions to this, where women feel that the decision is being imposed by others, whether partners, family or professionals. For example, until 1990, pregnant women in the British army, navy or airforce were made to choose between abortion and abandoning their career, on the grounds that members of the armed forces had to be 'ready for action' at a moment's notice. And Phoenix (1990) has argued that black women, and particularly black teenagers, are referred to abortion services in disproportionate numbers after a first antenatal visit. Not surprisingly, women who feel that the abortion decision was in some way forced on them are likely to be amongst those who show negative reactions afterwards. But when abortion seems to the woman the right decision, then her knowledge of her own circumstances and of how she would be affected by continuing her pregnancy may offer some resistance to competing constructions of her decision. Wasielewski (1992) has suggested a third factor which may help account for many women's apparently successful negotiation of the competing discourses which surround abortion. Drawing on Weigert's (1991) analysis of 'mixed emotions', Wasielewski argues that action accompanied by a 'stoic acceptance' of mixed feelings – said by Weigart to be a relatively rare response to ambivalence – is actually quite usual in women facing unwanted pregnancy, if only because of the unavoidable consequences of inaction. Wasielewski argues further that because women have the status of a marginalised social group, often with little power publicly to define their experiences, they 'already have strategies for acting in spite of mixed messages about the self which result in ambivalence' (Wasielewski 1992: 124). Perhaps, then, one of the 'coping skills' which contribute to women's 'adjustment' to abortion, is their previous experience of negotiating conflicts between their own experience and dominant constructions of themselves and their situation.

Finally, women's success in dealing with abortion may be influenced by its role in bringing about positive psychological changes. The possibility of abortion having positive effects is occasionally mentioned in the literature; but, as we have seen, the effects are more often described in terms of the presence or absence of negative psychological reactions or, at most, as 'relief' or 'more efficient use of contraception'. As Neustatter (1986) has pointed out, however, abortion is often a situation in which a woman, perhaps for the first time, takes control of her life and makes a decision about when and under what circumstances she will have children. Lazarus (1985) noted that some women saw the experience as showing that they had the strength to deal with a crisis or as increasing their understanding of their body; one woman described it as 'a very liberating experience' (ibid.: 146). Women in Neustatter's study also expressed positive responses, often to do with feeling more independent and less passive:

I felt a confidence in myself I hadn't before. I found too that I didn't need to play the 'little girl', the helpless female to my partner so much.

(Neustatter 1986: 112)

Emotionally, I'm a much stronger person now. The experience has made me take more control of my life.

(ibid.: 114)

I felt a kind of pride in myself for actually having sorted out the whole thing. I felt I was able to do things in a way I hadn't felt before.

(ibid.: 113)

For other women, abortion involves re-thinking their attitudes to moral issues and to other people:

My friend had an abortion a few years ago and I suppose I wasn't there for her when she wanted someone to talk to. She's downstairs now. She's here for me.

(McEvoy and Boyle, in preparation)

I have always disagreed with it. My friend had it done . . . and I thought it's killing a baby, a wee innocent baby but when it comes to yourself, you realise.

(ibid.)

I had always felt that abortion wasn't right . . . afterwards I felt sort of humble – I knew I wasn't the same person any more. I couldn't judge others any more and I had to start thinking about lots of other things . . . I had had set ideas about.

(Neustatter 1986: 100)

As Neustatter remarks, no one would choose abortion as a growth experience. But what these accounts, and others quoted in this section, emphasise is the need to consider women's experience of abortion more comprehensively and contextually than the psychological literature has so far achieved.

Abortion for foetal abnormality

The experience of women who have abortion following detection of foetal abnormality is likely to be different in some important ways from the experience of women who have abortions for other reasons. The abortion is more likely to happen later in pregnancy; the pregnancy is more likely to have been planned and wanted, but the woman is less likely to be subjected to criticism of her moral judgement or her sexual behaviour.

There is evidence that women who have abortions after the first three months of pregnancy are more likely to experience psychological distress than are those who have earlier abortions (Blumberg *et al.* 1975; Bracken and Kasl 1975; Adler *et al.* 1992). Certainly, the physical experience of later abortion, where labour may be induced and the woman gives birth to the foetus, seems likely to be more stressful than a vacuum aspiration performed under general anaesthetic earlier in pregnancy. It is difficult, however, to separate out the effects of the procedure itself from other aspects of late abortion. Osofsky *et al.* (1973), for example, found that 51 per cent of 200 women who had abortions in the second three months of pregnancy reported that the decision was difficult, compared with only 12 per cent having earlier abortions. And, although there is no research which looks directly at the impact of 'wantedness' on response to abortion, Major *et al.*'s (1985) study of the 'meaningfulness' of the pregnancy may be relevant here: they found that women who rated their pregnancy as 'highly meaningful' reported more physical complaints immediately after the abortion, and anticipated more psychological distress, than did women who rated their pregnancies as less meaningful.

This research did not look specifically at women who had late abortions or abortions for foetal abnormality, but it seems reasonable to assume that women who have later abortions for foetal abnormality do not just experience a different abortion procedure from women who have earlier abortions for other reasons; they are also in a very different psychological situation in terms of the wantedness and intendedness of the pregnancy. Kolker and Burke (1993) have emphasised this aspect of abortion for foetal abnormality and have suggested that the psychological impact of early abortion for abnormality has been underestimated. Not only is the woman still losing a wanted pregnancy, but ultrasound scans have altered the meanings which surround the foetus early in pregnancy and heightened awareness of its existence as a 'separate' being.

Although many women do experience psychological distress following abortion for foetal abnormality, we cannot assume – any more than with abortion for other reasons – that the woman has made the 'wrong' decision. On the contrary, women interviewed by Kolker and Burke (1993) stressed that, although the experience had been worse than expected, they would make the same choice again in similar circumstances. These women were also concerned that public discussion of their distress would be used by anti-abortion groups as an argument to limit access to abortion; given the extent to which this argument *has* been used to try to restrict abortion, the women's concern is probably justified.

The social context of abortion for foetal abnormality

Women who have abortions following the detection of foetal abnormality are placed in a very different social position from those who have so-called elective abortions. The extent to which this is the case is emphasised by the recent (1996) much publicised case of a British woman who requested termination of one foetus in a twin pregnancy: media reports repeatedly referred to the abortion of a 'healthy' foetus, as if this itself provided grounds for judging the woman's request.

This language, however, reflects strong social support for abortion on the grounds of foetal abnormality. Green *et al.* (1993) found that 84 per cent of a sample of pregnant women believed abortion should be available if there was a 'strong chance the baby will be handicapped', compared to 55 per cent approval for abortion where the woman 'is unmarried and does not want this pregnancy'. Jowell *et al.* (1991) obtained similar results with a British general population sample: 90 per cent supported abortion in the case of foetal 'defect' compared to 54 per cent when the woman decided she did not want the baby. Even in communities such as Northern Ireland, where there are strong social and legal sanctions against abortion, similar relative results have been obtained although the absolute level of support for abortion for any reason is lower (ibid.).

Abortion for foetal abnormality is inextricably linked to screening programmes for the detection of foetal abnormality. Richards and Green (1993) suggest that screening techniques are now usually perceived as an integral part of antenatal care and accepted as such by women. When abnormalities are detected, however, they are almost always untreatable (Green and Richards 1993). Hadley (1996) has argued that the success of the programmes is therefore measured by the number of terminations carried out. This link between screening and termination is sometimes referred to by doctors in medical consultations:

I mean, obviously if you have the test done, the understanding is on your side as well that you will act on the results if they are found to be abnormal.

(Marteau *et al.* 1993: 6)

Do you understand that if you don't want a termination there is no reason going through with [the screening tests]?

(ibid.)

Similarly, Eggert and Rolston (1994b) noted that medical staff in Northern and Southern Ireland tend not to inform women of the availability of screening tests, because abortion is unlikely to be offered if abnormalities are detected. All of this suggests that information about foetal abnormality can be of no possible use to a woman except to 'instruct' her to terminate the pregnancy.

In spite of these close links between screening and abortion, Marteau *et al.* (1993) found that abortion was mentioned in only nine of twenty-five recorded consultations between pregnant women and their obstetricians in which amniocentesis was discussed. Moreover, screening was presented in these consultations as the 'rational' choice, although the women's views on the abortion, which it was assumed would follow the detection of abnormality, were never elicited. For example, the probability that the woman was carrying a foetus with Down's syndrome was presented as a 'risk', i.e. as a value judgement, as something unquestionably to be avoided, rather than as a probability. And similar probabilities of Down's syndrome, and of miscarriage as a consequence of amniocentesis, were sometimes presented in very different ways, so that a probability of 1:100 for miscarriage was described as 'small'; 'very small' and 'very rare', while a probability of 1:160 for Down's syndrome was described as 'high'.

Both Marteau *et al.* and Richards and Green (1993) have emphasised how difficult it may be for women to refuse screening if it is offered, particularly in a context where screening is presented as the rational or obvious choice. Indeed, Green *et al.* (1992) found in one hospital that women who rejected a biochemical screening test (maternal serum alpha-feto-protein) were given an additional anomaly scan – presented as routine – as an alternative way of detecting neural tube defects. It seems very likely, then, that some women who would not favour abortion for themselves, will nevertheless undergo screening procedures to detect foetal abnormality. Certainly, the proportion of people who claim that they themselves would have abortion for foetal abnormality is consistently lower that the proportion who believe abortion should be available in these circumstances (Evers-Kiebooms *et al.* 1993; Green *et al.* 1993). These figures, however, are at odds with the observation that, in practice, almost all women choose abortion if it is offered for foetal abnormality (Green and Richards 1993). This may partly be because hypothetical questions about behaviour are very different from real choices: just as some women who have 'elective' abortions say that finding themselves pregnant made them think differently about abortion, so too do women carrying abnormal foetuses (Neustatter 1986; Kolker and Burke 1993). Yet, it is also possible that part of the discrepancy is due to the way the screening process is structured, and to the implicit assumption that the woman will have an abortion if foetal abnormality is detected.

Research on abortion for foetal abnormality has tended to concentrate on women's experience, in much the same way as more general research on abortion. The final part of this chapter will consider the experience of male partners of women who have abortions, including abortions for foetal abnormality.

MEN'S EXPERIENCE OF ABORTION

Men, of course, contribute to the creation of pregnancies which are terminated; but they are also psychologically central to abortion in at least two other important ways.[1] The first is in their role in decision-making. The extent to which women say that they discussed the decision with their partner varies from study to study; as we have seen, male involvement may be less in communities with strong social and legal sanctions against abortion. Miller (1992) found that women listed 'spouse' more often than any other group (doctors, friends, parents, etc.) as the most important person with whom the decision was discussed; no doubt the figure would have been higher if the term 'partner' had been used. It is also clear from women's accounts that men play an important role in constructing the pregnancy as unwanted. Twenty-three per cent of women in

---

1 A small number of men have become involved in their partner's abortion by mounting legal challenges to the decision (for discussion of some of these cases, see Fegan 1996 and Hadley 1996).

Torres and Forest's (1988) sample, for example, reported that one of their reasons for having an abortion was that their husband or partner wanted them to. In some cases, of course, this will be one of many factors taken into account in the woman's decision; in others, the man's rejection of the pregnancy may be the major reason for the abortion.

A second way in which men are central to the experience of abortion is in the support they provide for their partners. Indeed, one of the most consistent research findings is that women who believe they have been supported by their partners experience more positive responses to abortion than those who do not (Bracken *et al.* 1974; Shusterman 1979; Moseley *et al.* 1981; Major *et al.* 1990). Major *et al.* (1992) also showed an interactive effect of men's and women's expectancies about coping with abortion: men's expectancies about coping were strongly related to ratings of their partner's depression immediately after the abortion, but only if the woman also had low expectations about coping.

In spite of the importance of men's role in abortion, there have been very few studies of men's experience of abortion. Neustatter (1986) commented on the difficulty of finding out about men's experience: only thirty men were recruited for her study through advertisements inviting them to talk about their experiences, compared with 200 women. Neustatter also commented on the homogeneity of the male sample. Whereas the women varied in age, class and ethnicity, the men were mainly white and middle class, and the large majority saw themselves as supportive of their partners. Shostack *et al.*'s (1984) sample was similarly restricted, consisting of men who had accompanied their partners to the clinic. As Neustatter points out, we have very little direct information therefore about the experience of men who were less supportive, or those who insisted that the abortion be kept secret, or who left or threatened to leave the relationship when their partner became pregnant.

A major theme which emerges from the accounts we do have is that of men's uncertainty about their role in abortion, and their dismay at what they see as the absence of a constructive role for them. As one man said:

> I simply don't have a clue what to say to her. After all, it's her body. Who am I to tell her what I want her to do? But I know if I don't say anything she'll think I'm trying to impose on her...I ended up saying I'd support her whatever she wanted but that feels a real cop-out.
>
> (Haslam 1996: 212–13)

Other men have reported similar dilemmas:

> I wanted to say, 'Look, it's my baby too', but that wouldn't have been fair on [my partner]. Even though I felt very mixed up, I didn't let on in case she felt I was undermining her.
>
> (*New Woman*, February 1996)

> I acquiesced when she said she wanted to have an abortion. Looking back I wonder if I was right, if she really did want to go ahead, whether she

would have liked me to express some positive feelings. It haunts me that I might have misread her.

(Neustatter 1986: 122)

The lack of a clear role for men in the abortion decision is also evident in their reports of feeling excluded or marginalised from the abortion process, at the same time as feeling responsible for the pregnancy. Part of this concern seems to involve wanting acknowledgement that pregnancy and abortion are also meaningful for men. It also involves guilt over the fact that it is their partner, and not themselves, who is having to abort the pregnancy they helped create.

A second theme from these accounts is that of the intense feelings many men experience about the abortion. One man in Neustatter's sample described as 'rubbish' the idea that men do not feel much about abortion; all the men interviewed would have welcomed the opportunity to talk to someone about their situation, but few had felt able to at the time. A third theme, noted by Neustatter, is the relative absence in men's accounts of concern about the morality of abortion, or about 'the destruction of life'. This is a particularly interesting area for future research, not because it suggests that women are more 'moral' than men about abortion, but because it may reflect the very different ways men and women are culturally positioned in relation to life, its preservation and destruction. As I emphasised in Chapter 3, it is men who have traditionally occupied the role of socially sanctioned killers while women have been positioned as the nurturers and preservers of life. The decision to abort a foetus may therefore have very different social meanings for men and women in terms of the destruction of life.

Men and abortion for foetal abnormality

Black (1991) has pointed out that men's reactions to abortion for foetal abnormality have received little attention from researchers; Sjögren (1992) suggests that the same is true of pre-natal screening. Sjögren interviewed twenty men whose wives had had amniocentesis or chorionic villus sampling (all tests were negative). More than half the men (65 per cent) considered that their involvement in the procedure, in terms of obtaining information and decision-making, was weak or moderate, and many were critical of the lack of information they received on the procedures. Sixty per cent of the men claimed to have experienced 'hardly any' fear that the test would indicate foetal abnormality, yet 65 per cent claimed to have had considerable fear before the pregnancy that they would have a disabled child. Minimising fear while waiting for the results might have helped some men maintain the rationalist position which was evident from the interviews. One man, for example, claimed that he 'had to take a rationalist attitude because his wife was very anxious'; another claimed that his main role was 'to give some advice' (ibid.: 201). This public split between reason and emotion was also noted by Cooke (1995) in interviews with couples where the woman had had an abortion because of foetal abnormality. Cooke argued that the theories of grief often applied in such situations are implicitly gendered and are based mainly on women's reactions to loss. Cooke identified two major discourses of grief in couples' accounts of their responses to the abortions: 'grief must be expressed' and 'grief is dangerous'; women drew mainly on the former and men on the latter. These discourses correspond to the 'expressive' and 'avoidant' styles of response to the loss of a child identified by other researchers (Black 1991). The gender differences suggested by Cooke were also apparent in Black's (1991) interviews with women who had had abortions for foetal abnormality. Thirty-two per cent of the women reported that, one month after the abortion, their male partners talked 'little' or 'not at all' about their feelings, and many women described their dissatisfaction over the discrepancy between their and their partner's willingness to talk about what had happened. One woman reported that her partner 'just has so many opinions about it, instead of sympathy' (ibid.: 28), while another claimed that '[men] experience this great loss...and then a week later they're concentrating on something totally different and the loss is gone' (ibid.: 27). As Black points out, however, some women saw men's reluctance to talk as a preference for a different coping style, and not as an indication of lack of distress. This is supported by Cooke's (1995) study, in which men drew on the 'grief is dangerous' discourse to provide a positive and future-oriented construction of the so-called 'avoidant' coping style.

Two main conclusions can be drawn from this brief discussion of men's experience of abortion. The first is that men, as well as women, experience unwanted pregnancies, although there has been virtually no research into why men – albeit indirectly – seek abortions. The second is that men and women are not only positioned differently in relation to abortion in the obvious biological way, they also occupy very different cultural positions. As well as highlighting this specific issue, this chapter has criticised traditional psychological and psychiatric research on abortion for its general neglect of social context and gender issues, and for begging important questions by focusing on the negative aspects of abortion. Alternative accounts presented here of the abortion experience highlight the limited nature of much previous research. The final chapter looks at the implications of this wider view of abortion for future research and ultimately for psychology's relationship to social policy.

7

PSYCHOLOGY, ABORTION AND SOCIAL POLICY

Because abortion is closely regulated by law, the psychological study of abortion inevitably becomes linked with social policy. There are, however, considerable differences in the extent to which psychological societies in different countries have made this link explicit. For example, the British Psychological Society has never issued a statement on abortion or had any official involvement with the issue. In 1992, the Psychological Society of Ireland issued a statement entitled 'Abortion: Social Context and Psychological Consequences'. The statement highlighted the lack of psychological research on abortion in Ireland (the PSI was unable to find any at all) and reviewed research conducted in other countries on women's decision-making about, and responses to, abortion. The statement also drew attention to the possible consequences of refused abortion and to trends in public opinion on abortion in Ireland. Although the statement could be interpreted as supporting a liberal approach to abortion legislation, the PSI stopped short of an explicit policy statement.

In contrast with this limited public involvement in abortion policy, the American Psychological Association (APA) has been extensively involved in the issue of abortion in the United States. As early as 1969, the APA Council of Representatives adopted a resolution identifying termination of pregnancy as a mental health and child welfare issue. The Council also resolved that abortion be considered a 'civil right of the pregnant woman, to be handled as other medical and surgical procedures in consultation with her physician' (Adler *et al.* 1992). The APA's view of abortion as a mental health and welfare issue was strongly supported by the 1973 Supreme Court ruling *Roe* v. *Wade*:

> The detriment that the state would impose upon the pregnant woman by denying this choice altogether is apparent...Maternity or additional offspring, may force upon the woman a distressful life and future. Psychological harm may be imminent. Mental and physical health may be taxed by childcare.

The following brief description of US psychologists' involvement in the development of abortion law will focus on the two major areas of psychological activity: adolescent abortion and women's psychological responses to abortion.

128

PSYCHOLOGISTS' INVOLVEMENT IN ABORTION LEGISLATION

The US Supreme Court has made a number of rulings on the issue of abortion requests by girls and young women under the age of 18 (minors). The first such decision, in 1976 (*Parenthood of Central Missouri* v. *Danforth*) established that minors, like adult women, had a constitutional right to privacy in abortion decisions. Several aspects of the judgement, however, suggested that these rights might be more easily challenged than those of adult women. First, the Court argued that state infringement of minors' rights to privacy in the abortion decision could be justified if the state could show *significant* interest in regulation; for adult women, the state's interest must be *compelling*. Second, three members of the Court indicated their approval of infringements on privacy in order 'to protect children from their own immature and improvident decisions' (Melton and Russo 1987: 69). Subsequent judgements have focused on the issue of psychological maturity and its relationship to parental and judicial involvement in abortion decisions. These judgements clearly involve assumptions about adolescent psychology (and, it should be emphasised, about female adolescent psychology) notably assumptions about decision-making and about the effects of abortion. Yet, as Lewis (1987: 84) has pointed out, 'The Supreme Court has generally avoided a systematic review of relevant research and has relied instead on its collective intuition regarding the abilities and needs of minors'.

In response to this situation, the APA's Division 37 (Child, Youth and Family Services) established a committee to review and disseminate psychological research relevant to the assumptions made by the Supreme Court. Three other APA Divisions (Population and Environmental Psychology, the Psychology of Women and the American Psychology Law Society) were also involved in the committee's work, which has been widely disseminated through official channels, media reports and academic publications (e.g. Melton 1986, 1987; Lewis 1987; Melton and Russo 1987; APA 1987). The research discussed by the committee concerned studies of adolescent decision-making; adolescents' responses to abortion and to its alternatives, and the likely impact on girls and young women of parental notification clauses and judicial procedures for by-passing these.

The second major area of psychological involvement in US abortion policy concerns the psychological responses to abortion of women in general. When mental health aspects of abortion were emphasised in the 1973 ruling *Roe* v. *Wade*, it had been assumed that *restricting* access to abortion was detrimental to women's welfare. Subsequently, anti-abortion groups had claimed the opposite – that *having* abortions was damaging to women's mental health. In 1987, President Reagan directed his Surgeon General, Everett Koop, to prepare a report on the psychological and medical impact of abortion on women. Wilmoth (1992) has suggested that the request was made in a context in which pro-choice and anti-abortion groups had reached a stalemate on the abortion issue, and where neither group could see a clear route to furthering their legislative goals.

Certainly, it is not difficult to discern a possible agenda behind the presidential directive: the Surgeon General himself had co-authored an anti-abortion book a few years earlier (Koop and Schaeffer 1983), while the original proposal for the research report had come from the President's Advisor on Domestic Affairs, known to be a strong critic of abortion (Wilmoth 1992). As part of the process of preparing the report, APA representatives presented both oral and written testimony to the Surgeon General's Office on methodological issues in research on psychological responses to abortion; in 1989, an APA panel was convened to review 'the best scientific studies of abortion outcome' (Adler *et al.* 1992: 1195) and its members testified on this issue in congressional hearings (Adler 1989; David 1989). Published accounts of the research reviews (Adler *et al.* 1990; Adler *et al.* 1992) concluded that abortion 'is not likely to be followed by severe psychological responses' and that 'there is persuasive evidence that abortion is usually psychologically benign' (1992: 1194, 1203).

In spite of these conclusions, Wilmoth (1992: 4) has suggested that the scientific debate on the public health consequences of abortion has 'reached an impasse'; in other words, the psychological evidence, although presented as 'persuasive', did not resolve the impasse which had originally led to commissioning the report. Moreover, Wilmoth noted that state legislation continued to be introduced and passed requiring that women seeking abortion be informed of the medical and psychological risks. The new impasse was brought about partly by the Surgeon General's refusal to issue an official report on the psychological sequelae of abortion. Instead, he concluded in a letter to President Reagan that 'despite diligent review... the scientific studies do not provide conclusive data on the health effects of abortion on women' (cited in Adler *et al.* 1992: 1195). In later testimony to Congress, the Surgeon General stated that, from a public health perspective, the psychological risks of abortion were 'minuscule'; an unofficial draft report, however, emphasised the methodological limitations of the research and concluded that 'it is neither reasonable nor advisable to rely on prevailing opinion, based on flawed studies, to conclude whether or not psychological risks are associated with abortion' (cited in Wilmoth 1992: 3).

The Surgeon General's refusal to reach a clear conclusion on the issue of psychological responses to abortion certainly contributed to the impasse on the scientific debate, but it was not the only factor involved. As Wilmoth points out, both pro-choice and anti-abortion groups were able to present the research on women's psychological responses to abortion as consistent with their positions, at times citing the same study (David *et al.* 1981) in support of opposite conclusions. Both groups claimed that the other's ideology had influenced their interpretation of the literature. Mueller and Major (1989: 1067), for example, claimed that the psychological effects of abortion put forward by 'abortion foes' were based on research which was 'ideologically guided and methodologically flawed'. But, almost identically, Speckhard and Rue (1992: 97) argued that the APA's position on abortion was 'an unwarranted overgeneralization' based on methodologically flawed research, and that having 'gone on record' as supporting abortion, the APA might find it difficult to re-examine its position.

Wilmoth *et al.* were not optimistic about resolving the impasse over psychological responses to abortion and their policy implications. They suggested two main reasons why 'decisions about public health policy related to the psychological sequelae of abortion will remain in the political arena' (1992: 61). The first concerns methodological and conceptual problems of conducting research 'to resolve the debate about the psychological sequelae of abortion' (ibid.). Wilmoth *et al.* have described what they believe to be the essential elements of a 'sound prevalence study' of post-abortion consequences. These include a large and representative sample recruited to control for the many variables thought to relate to psychological responses to abortion. The instruments used to assess each (intrapsychic) response to abortion would be 'administered uniformly across the country at the same time interval post-abortion' (Wilmoth *et al.* 1992: 50). This study, however, would still leave unanswered the issue of the 'essential cause of post-abortion consequences' (Wilmoth 1992: 6). Wilmoth *et al.* suggest that clarification of this would involve longitudinal studies which assessed women's state prior to the abortion, as well as comparisons with groups undergoing other kinds of surgery, and assessment of prior and concurrent life-events which might affect psychological state.

Not surprisingly, Wilmoth *et al.* are sceptical that studies like these will ever be carried out, not least because of their cost. But even if they were, Wilmoth *et al.* suggest that we should still be at a policy impasse over abortion because of the 'emotional volatility of the issue' (1992: 61). By this they mean that policy decisions on abortion are dependent on values which may render irrelevant research evidence on psychological responses to abortion. In the face of this pessimism, and of the impasse in the scientific debate, it is important to examine models of the relationship between research and policy-making which seem to underlie these discussions about adolescent abortion and women's psychological responses to abortion.

RESEARCH AND POLICY: MODELS OF THE RELATIONSHIP

The models which have traditionally informed discussions of abortion research and abortion policy have two major features. The first is an assumption that research has the potential to 'resolve' issues such as the psychological effects of abortion, but the reason it has not yet done so is that current research is methodologically and conceptually inadequate. Wilmoth *et al.*, for example, argue that 'the research is flawed in ways that prevent it from *conclusively* establishing either the prevalence of the mental health consequences following abortion or the cause of mental health consequences' (1992: 38, my italics). Miller (1992: 79) has expressed a similar view: 'Unfortunately, a great deal of the work [on the psychological consequences of abortion] is unsystematic, lacking in rigour and therefore inconclusive'. This idea that conclusive data are potentially obtainable is also implied by Gardner *et al.*'s comment that in advising policy makers, psychologists should 'withhold the rhetoric of certainty unless [they] are certain and either restrict [their] assertions to those matters on which [they] have certainty or freely acknowledge [their] doubts' (1989: 901).

The second feature of these traditional models of research and policy is that they make a clear distinction between the disinterested nature of scientific research and the partisan, value-laden nature of policy-making. In this model, the role of the researcher is to provide objective data which may nevertheless be ignored or misrepresented in pursuit of political goals. Chelimsky (1991), for example, suggests that researchers 'define [a] decision as a conclusion resulting from a set of objectively derived premises'. By contrast 'a decision maker often wants to look only at selected premises and may rule out even the consideration of other information to keep it from getting in the way of important political purpose' (ibid.: 227). The APA sees a similarly objective role for the researcher when it suggests that the decision to provide an official statement on an issue should take account of whether 'accurate, valid and factual information' is available about the issue (Gardner *et al.* 1989: 899). Adler *et al.* reflect this statement in their discussion of the formation of an APA panel to examine 'relevant psychological considerations in abortion':

> It was recognised that differing moral, ethical and religious perspectives impinge on how abortion is perceived. Our mission, however, was not to assess values but to consider the best available scientific evidence on psychological responses to abortion.
>
> (1992: 1194)

The supposed objectivity of the researcher and the impression that their task is the disinterested pursuit of facts, is further maintained by the use of terms such as 'research findings' or by claims that research can 'accurately reveal' (e.g. Adler *et al.* 1992; Kendler 1993), as if researchers simply uncovered what was already 'out there' awaiting discovery. Abandoning this idea of a disinterested researcher 'uncontaminated' by values (Kendler 1993) poses a considerable threat because of the loss of authority psychology could suffer as a result. For example, Gardner *et al.* ask why, if our 'scientific evaluations are filtered through our political values...anyone who disputes our politics [should] accept our science?' (1989: 899). Kendler expresses similar fears:

> If society's confidence is lacking because the knowledge claims offered either are contradictory or are perceived as political statements instead of scientific evidence, then psychology will sacrifice its ability to contribute to the amelioration and resolution of social conflicts that reflect moral differences.
>
> (1993: 1052)

There are two major problems with this traditional view of science and its

132

relationship to social policy. The first is that *all* knowledge claims are uncertain and provisional, including those made by natural scientists (see, for example, Lakatos and Musgrave 1970; Chalmers 1990; Harding 1991). Lakatos (1970) has argued that there is no such thing as a critical or conclusive experiment or research study, and showed that scientists routinely ignore or explain away contradictory data in developing and retaining their theories. His point was not to criticise these scientists, but to emphasise that they could not behave otherwise, given the illusory nature of certainty in science. Thus, the idea that psychology can assist the development of policy by 'seeking empirical and theoretical truth' (Kendler 1993) is based on a misrepresentation of the nature of science and an underestimation of the theoretical uncertainty of the natural sciences on which psychology seeks to model itself. The extent of this uncertainty is obscured for two reasons. One is that few of us have the necessary specialist knowledge to understand the theoretical issues involved. The second reason – more important for this discussion – is that the uncertainty or the choice of one theory over another has few social consequences and is therefore not a matter of great public concern. If, however, we awoke to a world where the validity or otherwise of Einstein's theory of relativity could influence abortion policy, then the public would become very interested indeed and we would see heated public discussion of the theory's anomalies, of the accuracy of measuring instruments, and so on. Indeed, it is not far-fetched to suggest that if the perceived shape of the earth could determine abortion policy, there would be fierce controversy over definitions of 'round' and accusations of ideological influence on experimental procedures. This is not to suggest that some data might not be more reliable than others or that some theories might not have stronger empirical support than their rivals. The point is that the inherent uncertainty of science *together with* the social importance of a research area such as abortion make controversy over the interpretation of data, however carefully gathered, inevitable. And within the traditional model of the role of psychology in policy making there is little that can be done to resolve the resulting stalemate. Instead, psychologists are faced with a very narrow conception of their role in relation to social policy, which leaves them feeling permanently either slighted (when they believe their conclusive data have been rejected for political reasons) or inadequate (when they have no certainty to offer policy makers).

The second major problem with the traditional model of the research–policy relationship is its neglect of the role of values in psychological research. The idea that psychology should offer objective, factual or accurate data to policy makers implies that such data should be free from the influence of social values. As we saw earlier, the necessity of this separation has been repeatedly stressed in discussions of psychology's role in policy development. In these discussions, the problem of values in psychological research is seen as a problem of individuals who allow their personal beliefs to influence their research. Gardner *et al.* (1989), for example, distinguish between our roles as citizens, who may hold particular social beliefs, and as psychologists, who should not allow these beliefs to influence the presentation of scientific evidence to policy makers. Similarly, Kendler (1993) suggests that a 'towering obstacle' to offering persuasive information on the effects of different social policies is whether psychology is capable of providing information which is free of the *'individual researcher's'* political or value commitments (emphasis added). Kendler suggests that we might ask researchers to state their values so that their knowledge claims can be judged within those standards. But, given that he calls such statements 'confessions', few researchers would be encouraged to make them.

The major problem with this individualised approach to values is that it entirely overlooks the issue of *institutionalised* values – values inherent to psychology itself. It has been strongly argued that far from being a value-free activity, the production of psychological knowledge is embedded in a complex and usually unarticulated structure of beliefs and assumptions which influence what is questioned and what taken for granted: how a subject matter is conceptualised; how research questions are framed; what is seen as evidence, and so on (Braginsky 1985; Albee 1986; Prilleltensky 1989; Ussher 1991, 1992). Prilleltensky (1994) has emphasised that for psychology to ignore this value system is not to step outside it, to be neutral, but to reinforce it because the system is inextricably linked to the interests of those who produce and use knowledge. Tizard (1990) has argued that institutional values should be of greater concern than the values of individual researchers because their pervasiveness makes them much more difficult to identify. In line with this, Sarason (1981) has described a process of 'socialization' by which psychologists learn not to deviate from the existing intellectual and ideological order and thus often unconsciously endorse and maintain it.

The crucial importance of this issue for psychology's relationship to abortion policy can be seen by considering Smart's (1989, 1991) arguments about legal epistemology. Talking about women's relationship to law, Smart has argued that the law hears what is said about women only to the extent that what is said about them derives from the same world view or, as Smart has put it, occupies the same 'epistemological space' as the law itself. Thus, when psychologists are invited to participate in the legislative process for abortion, or when psychological research is used in developing abortion law, it will be on terms set by the law itself. In the same way, if psychologists want to be listened to, then Smart's argument suggests that they must frame their submissions in terms which do not conflict with the law's own. But at least until now, this requirement has not created any problems for psychology (or psychiatry) precisely because these disciplines were already operating within the same 'epistemological space' as the law. It is unlikely that this reflected psychology's influence on legislators; rather, it reflects the fact that in many important ways, both psychology and the legislature subscribe to broadly similar ideologies. Thus, when Ronald Reagan's Surgeon General asked the APA to provide evidence on the extent of abortion's harmful effects on women, there was no need to carry out the research: it had already been done. Indeed, as I showed in Chapter 6, the issue of abortion's potential to inflict psychological harm on women had often preoccupied researchers more than any other. The fact that this research involved assumptions about women, about motherhood and abortion, and about the conceptualisation of emotional responses to life-events, was never articulated. Instead psychologists presented and legislators accepted the research as a taken for granted (if imperfect) means of answering a taken for granted question.

The nature of the implicit assumptions which have guided psychological and psychiatric research on abortion – and on many other topics – has already been described. The assumptions are manifest in an intense focus on decontextualised individuals; in the case of abortion, these individuals are almost always women. Indeed, so strong is psychology's focus on individuals that even the issue of values in psychology is reduced by some writers to a discussion of individual attributes. The implicit assumptions are also manifest in psychology's tacit focus on negative aspects of abortion; in a tendency to pathologise negative reactions to abortions and to rely on a relatively narrow set of research questions and methods. The extent to which these assumptions are widely shared can be seen by the fact that both pro-choice and anti-abortion researchers and advocates have derived many of their arguments from them. Both sides have been preoccupied with abortion's potential to produce negative effects; both sides have been concerned with the minutiae of methodology to the point where Speckhard and Rue (1992) were able to argue that the mean number of methodological flaws in a sample of studies of women's reactions to abortion was 6.9. And when these researchers suggested a new diagnostic category of 'Post-abortion Syndrome' (PAS) (Speckhard and Rue 1992), they were able to draw on widely accepted psychological theories which conceptualised emotional responses as diagnostic categories, as well as on the specific category of post-traumatic stress disorder. Thus, although pro-choice researchers were well aware that the idea of PAS was being introduced as a potential means of restricting women's access to abortion, they had little theoretical defence against it. The fact that, in important ways, pro-choice and anti-abortion researchers occupy the same 'epistemological space' has contributed to the impasse in the scientific debate highlighted by Wilmoth (1992) just as much as has the nature of scientific research: neither side questions the other's premises, while the inherent uncertainty of scientific knowledge ensures that each side will always be able to question the other's conclusions.

What alternatives are there to this way of approaching the relationship between research and policy? Weiss (1977) has argued that the relationship is much more complex and diffuse than is suggested by traditional accounts. These accounts imply what Weiss calls a 'linear model' of the relationship between research and policy in which one study or set of studies has a direct influence on law and policy. Such models, of course, derive from the rationalist view of research discussed earlier, in which 'research is truth and researchers are the passers of the flame' (ibid.: 7). As we have seen, linear models are both simplistic and unrealistic; they match neither the conduct of research nor the conduct of policy making (see also Chelimsky 1991). Weiss argues that we should instead view the relationship between research and policy as one of reconceptualisation – in which research changes the way we look at an issue, challenges received wisdom, converts practices seen as benign into social problems (e.g. drinking and driving; sexual harassment, etc.). The term 'enlightenment' has also been used in this context, but Weiss is rightly sceptical of the value judgement inherent in it. To see the relationship between research and policy as one of reconceptualisation, of course, suggests that research should be seen as a process of conceptualisation rather than one of discovery; as such, Weiss's model fits well with critiques of the idea of value-free research. The reconceptualisation model does not mean that there is never a direct relationship between social/psychological research and policy, only that it is the exception rather than the rule. The model does suggest, however, that the relationship in terms of a particular topic may be very long-term and that the influence of research on policy may not be discernible for some time.

Viewing research–policy links in this way has two important implications. The first is that researchers need not be deterred by the fact that policy makers appear to ignore their work or to be working to an agenda at odds with the researchers'; research may still have long-term influence provided it is in some way brought to public attention. The second implication is that whether researchers approve it, intend it, or are even aware of it, their theories and methods may have influence – for good or ill. As Prilleltensky (1989: 795) has emphasised, psychology 'is intermingled in social life in countless forms'. Some of these are obvious, as when psychologists appear in the media advising people on child-rearing, relationships, employment, etc. Others are more subtle and require complex concepts such as Foucault's 'disciplinary power' to illuminate them. In the next section, I shall examine these processes of influence in relation to abortion and suggest some ways in which psychological research might lead to reconceptualising abortion. Before I discuss these, however, one point needs to be made clear. Psychological theory and research cannot be used to deduce in some logical way what abortion policy ought to be. But we cannot prevent psychological research and theory from influencing abortion law; nor can we prevent abortion law from influencing women and men both socially and psychologically. It is because of this that we have a responsibility to articulate the assumptions which underlie research and theory and to try to ensure that they do not provide a narrow and unrepresentative account of abortion.

PSYCHOLOGY, SOCIAL POLICY AND THE RECONSTRUCTION OF ABORTION

I mentioned in Chapter 2 Sheldon's (1993) suggestion that the law operates by constructing its own image of the legal subject which it then seeks to regulate. The appropriateness of any law may then be judged by the extent to which it 'matches' its constructed subjects. For example, if women are constructed as 'asking for it' or as liable to 'cry rape', and if men are constructed as having conjugal rights over women or as being unable to control their sexual impulses beyond a certain point, then rape legislation will be preoccupied with protecting men from false or unreasonable accusations. In the case of abortion, we can identify two aspects of the constructed female subject who is regulated by law. First, she is potentially irrational, vulnerable and deserving of help, or she is potentially selfish and immoral. In either case, she cannot be entrusted with the abortion decision. Second, the subject is embedded in an individual health system, rather than in a socio-political process which has psychological effects.

As we have seen, psychology's relationship to this constructed female subject is complex. She was certainly not 'invented' by psychological theory; but psychological theory and research have arguably played an important role in maintaining and reproducing the subject and in apparently providing scientific credibility for what might otherwise be seen as a set of social beliefs and opinions. Psychology has contributed to the female subject of abortion legislation in three major ways. The first is by focusing almost entirely on women in abortion research; I shall argue later that this focus on women has allowed legislation to take certain forms which might otherwise be questioned. A second way in which psychology has contributed to the construction of the female subject of abortion legislation is by providing in co-operation with psychiatry extensive means to conceptualise and measure women's weaknesses, together with the theoretical models which predict negative consequences of abortion. And by focusing so strongly on the negative consequences of abortion even if only to show that few women experience them, psychological research conveys the impression of 'women at risk', even when they are implementing decisions they believe are in their own best interests. In other words, psychological research has reinforced the view that women cannot be trusted to make constructive decisions about their lives. Third, psychological research has reinforced the view of the legal subject as embedded in an individual health system. It has done so by providing a largely individualistic account of abortion with very limited discussion of the cultural context in which abortion is experienced.

The construction of the female legal subject of abortion is, of course, inseparable from the construction of abortion itself. I have emphasised the extremely negative construction of abortion which is apparent in the debates, where abortion is presented as a tragic and deviant option. One of the more obvious ways in which psychology has contributed to this negative construction is by its focus on the potentially negative effects of abortion; but it has contributed more subtly in at least two other closely related ways. One is by its neglect of the topic of abortion. Neglecting a topic does not necessarily imply a negative view of it, but the combination of neglect of abortion and attention to motherhood and infertility, does create an impression of maternity as the norm and abortion as the deviant exception. This construction of motherhood as the norm is the second indirect way in which psychology has contributed to a view of abortion as deviant. As I have shown, the construction of motherhood as standard takes a number of forms – from implicitly assuming that adults are parents to failing to provide a normative account of 'post-natal depression'.

How can this traditional construction of the female legal subject of abortion be challenged? Weiss's (1977) reconceptualisation model of the relationship between research and policy suggests that one constructive strategy is to offer research which encourages the public and policy makers to look at an issue in a different way, to ask different questions or to seek different answers from those which have traditionally served. The four suggestions to be offered here are intended to encourage that process.

1 Make men more visible in abortion research

Supporters of liberal abortion legislation have been cautious of discussing men's role in abortion, given attempts made in the United States to develop legislation on spousal notification or consent, and given some men's legal challenges to their partner's abortions (Fegan 1996; Hadley 1996). Nevertheless, there are at least two reasons why men's involvement in abortion should be highlighted, but without implying that male partners should have the right to prevent or force an abortion. The first is that much of the content of the abortion debates, of legislation and of research is dependent on particular constructions of *women* in spite of the fact than men help create pregnancies which are aborted; they contribute to the definition of the pregnancy as unwanted and if they do not want the pregnancy to continue, they benefit from the abortion. If these roles were highlighted and researched, it would be more difficult to maintain the view that abortion is intrinsically harmful, that it is sought for trivial reasons, or that it is necessary to prevent mental illness. This is not because men's reasons for seeking abortion are 'better' than women's or because they are psychologically 'stronger' in the face of abortion. Rather, it is because there is no cultural tradition of construing 'man' as weak and irrational in relation to reproduction, or as potentially immoral in his disregard of the right to life. Of course, individual men may be labelled as feckless or immoral, but we do not have access to a set of derogatory discourses which link 'man' to reproduction in the same way that such discourses link reproduction and 'woman'. Focusing more on men's role in abortion would also require us to confront the very different discourses which surround socially sanctioned killing, depending on whether it is initiated by men or women. As we saw in Chapter 6, men rarely mentioned the moral issue of the destruction of life when asked about their experience of abortion, yet this issue was a strong theme in many women's accounts. If this difference is reliable, then it would be difficult to understand without reference to the gendered nature of socially sanctioned killing.

A second reason for encouraging research on men's role in abortion is that it would highlight men's contribution to the creation and prevention of unwanted pregnancies and perhaps lead to more research on men's use of contraception. I argued in Chapter 5 that the prevention of pregnancy has traditionally been viewed as primarily women's responsibility; the fact that it is women who directly and publicly seek abortion, and the practice of linking abortion counselling to contraceptive 'education', can reinforce this view. Yet, if more attention were to be paid to men's role in the construction of pregnancies as unwanted, and if they were also to be seen as seeking abortions, albeit indirectly, then the obvious question to ask would be: if they did not want the pregnancy, why did they not prevent it? At the very least, a shift in research focus to include men would force us to recognise that abortion is a *gender* issue, and that the assumptions which surround it arise neither from a morally neutral concern with the sanctity of life, nor wholly from a concern with the health of individuals who just happen to be women.

2 Develop a new theoretical framework for abortion decision-making

Discussion of women's reasons for having abortions has featured prominently in the debates, but often in terms of whether the reasons are good or bad, important or trivial. Women's own accounts of their reasons have not been very visible in these discussions. As Russo *et al.* (1992: 200) have emphasised, psychological research has an important role to play in ensuring that policy makers 'learn to appreciate the meaning of abortion from the point of view of the women concerned'. There is a danger, however, that the task of such research will be seen as providing evidence that women's reasons for choosing abortion are actually 'good' and that the women are deserving of abortion. This places women on the defensive, having to prove that they are not having abortions for 'mere convenience', and ultimately having to emphasise their weaknesses rather than their strengths and aspirations. Russo *et al.* do not entirely avoid this problem: having discussed the educational, occupational and economic disadvantages of single parenthood, they suggest that 'when nearly one in five unmarried mothers say they are seeking abortions to avoid single parenthood, the data suggest they are doing so *for good reasons*' (ibid.: 199, my italics). An alternative or complementary approach would involve challenging the distinction between 'trivial' and 'important' reasons for abortion and between 'deserving' and 'undeserving' women. Such an approach allows us to ask a very different set of questions. For example: What assumptions about women lie behind the distinction? Who decides what criteria to use in making it? Who is entitled to apply it? What are its social and psychological consequences? Why do we not make a similar distinction between important and trivial reasons for forcing a woman to bear an unwanted child? I have already suggested that making men's role in abortion more visible would force us to confront the gendered basis of discussions about reasons for seeking abortion. Gilligan's (1982) research on moral reasoning is also very relevant here and would provide one useful theoretical framework for future research on abortion decision-making. Gilligan has argued that the social supremacy of rights-based moral reasoning rests not on the fact that it is an intrinsically higher form of reasoning, but on its socially constructed superiority to more contextual and personalised modes of reasoning. Moreover, some aspects of their context which women will consider in choosing abortion, such as preferring to pursue a career rather than motherhood or preferring only one child when they could afford several, are already surrounded by derogatory discourses of selfishness and convenience which may function as a form of social control. As I emphasised in Chapter 3, many supporters of liberal legislation circumvented this problem only by presenting women as weak and vulnerable and presenting abortion as a form of therapeutic intervention. These structural aspects of abortion decision-making need to be acknowledged by future research, otherwise researchers will continue to operate within a conceptual system which is literally man-made, in trying to prove that women are not 'really' selfish when they choose abortion.

3 Provide a more balanced account of the experience of abortion

The experience of abortion can have a wide range of psychological consequences, yet researchers have often prejudged this issue and focused only on potentially negative outcomes. This tendency to narrow the field of investigation has been reinforced by the use of quantitative methods. As Hollway (1989) has pointed out, such methods limit what can be known about a person. They do so either by providing pre-set questions and/or a limited answer format, and by converting complex data into a simplified numerical form. Taken together, these practices have resulted in a limited and very narrow account of the experience of abortion. Future research needs to adopt a more open approach which makes fewer assumptions about the experience and which allows women themselves, and their partners, more control of the content of their responses.

4 Adopt a more contextual approach to abortion research

This final suggestion is implied in the previous three, but it is so important that it merits separate consideration. Psychology's individualistic and ahistorical account of abortion is not simply a matter of theoretical preference. I have argued that it has important social and psychological consequences, not least in facilitating the presentation of women as weak and vulnerable in relation to abortion, and in obscuring the potential links between the social construction of abortion and women's experience of it. I have also suggested that attempts to adopt a less pathological 'stress and coping' model of abortion have done little to change this situation.

A contextual approach to abortion research creates the potential for a major shift in policy debates. In an individualised framework, the argument that abortion should be restricted because women are psychologically damaged by it is usually answered by the claim that most of them are not. This quickly leads to disagreements over methodological niceties of the research and, in the case of pro-choice researchers, to an approach which cannot afford to look too closely at the very negative effects of abortion on some women, but which paradoxically focuses on negative effects by emphasising their absence. An individualised framework also makes it difficult to comment on the policy implications of research which links socio-cultural factors such as religious affiliation to responses to abortion. Wilmoth (1992: 7), for example, claims that 'the pro-choice side believes the consequences of abortion are the result of socio-cultural factors, the type and circumstances of the abortion, hormonal changes associated with the end of pregnancy, and conditions of the woman preexisting the abortion'. Yet the 'logical' policies which he suggests follow from this include only 'better pre- and post-abortion counselling, and research to develop less time-consuming, painful, and invasive abortion procedures' (ibid.). A contextual approach which emphasises the relationship between the social construction of abortion and women's responses to it, directs policy discussions to the effects of the debates themselves and legislation on women's and men's experience of abortion. Similarly, the ideas that women need abortion to prevent mental disorder or that some abortions are abortions of convenience, are made problematic by analyses which stress the social origins and social functions of these claims.

The role of traditional research in abortion policy

Although I have been critical of traditional psychological research on abortion, this does not imply that such research cannot play a constructive role in the debates. On the contrary, it can be argued that the APA's use of research on women's responses to abortion played an extremely important role in maintaining access to abortion in the United States because the evidence presented made it difficult to sustain the argument that abortion is harmful to most women. This use of research is a good example of Posavac and Miller's claim about the appropriate use of research on women's responses to abortion: while such research 'cannot determine the desirability of policies that are contingent on moral and political beliefs [it] may be able to clear the air of unfounded assertions' (1990: 14). This may be rather optimistic, but such research can at least provide strong challenges to assertions based, for example, only on samples of women who claim to have been damaged by abortion. Kendler (1993) has suggested another approach in which psychologists' contribution is to 'throw light' on the empirical consequences of adopting particular policies. David et al. (1988), David (1992), Russo et al. (1992) and Sobol and Daly (1992) have provided important examples of this approach through discussions of the potential consequences of alternatives to abortion such as adoption or bearing an unwanted child.

In considering the value and limitations of using research in these ways, apart from the fact that the results will never be conclusive, it is useful to recall Smart's (1991) and Weiss's (1977) suggestions about the relationship between policy and research. Smart's argument that policy makers will listen to 'outsiders' only to the extent that they share the same 'epistemological space' suggests that, if we stray too far from legislators' conceptual frameworks, we will not be heard. And Weiss suggests that the process of reconceptualisation through research may be very long-term. Thus, research whose conceptual framework overlaps with the present framework of the law may be an essential part of the process of influence, at least in the short term. Ultimately, however, such research has serious limitations: in policy debates it tends to be reactive rather than proactive, responding to legislators' agendas rather than setting its own; by adopting a value-neutral stance it fails to confront the values it shares with the legal system and thus perpetuates them. Finally, such research does little to challenge the law's construction of the female 'legal subject' of abortion or to recognise psychology's participation in this process.

A major aim of this book has been to examine psychology's relationship with abortion from a number of different perspectives. The visible aspect of this relationship is limited, especially in Britain. There is, however, an extensive but less visible relationship between psychology and abortion which shows itself in the use of psychological theory and research in legislative debates and in the contribution of psychological research to the construction of the weak and vulnerable female subject of abortion legislation. The fact that this aspect of psychology's relationship to abortion has been largely unacknowledged does not make it any less powerful; on the contrary, it increases its power. Psychology, as much as the law itself, has helped prevent women from approaching abortion other than from a position of weakness, and has helped deny them access to ways of talking and thinking about their experiences which do not emphasise pathology. Psychology has also obscured the gendered basis of abortion by treating as a kind of error variance the fact that only women have abortions, while it is largely men who decide whether they may have them.

If psychology has been reluctant to acknowledge or examine the extent of its relationship to abortion, it has also been reluctant to use its analytical tools to examine the extraordinary strength of feeling which surrounds the topic. I hope I have shown here that psychology not only has a responsibility to acknowledge the ways in which its research and theories construct 'abortion' and women's experience of it, but also that psychology has a great deal to contribute to our understanding of the controversies and sensitivities which characterise abortion.

BIBLIOGRAPHY

Adler, N. E. (1975) 'Emotional responses of women following therapeutic abortion', *American Journal of Orthopsychiatry* 45: 446–54.
—— (1982) 'The abortion experience: social and psychological influences and artifacts', in H. S. Friedman and M. S. Di Matteo (eds) *Interpersonal Issues in Health Care*, New York: Academic Press.
—— (1989) 'The medical and psychological impact of abortion on women', Testimony on behalf of the American Psychological Association before the Subcommittee on Human Resources and Intergovernmental Operations, Committee on Government Operations, US House of Representatives, 101st Congress, 1st session, 16 March 1989.
—— (1992) 'Unwanted pregnancy and abortion: definitional and research issues', *Journal of Social Issues* 48: 19–35.
Adler, N. E. and Dolcini, P. (1986) 'Psychological issues in abortion for adolescents', in G. B. Melton (ed.) *Adolescent Abortion: Psychological and Legal Issues*, Lincoln: University of Nebraska Press.
Adler, N. E., David, H. P., Major, B. N., Roth, S. H., Russo, N. F. and Wyatt, G. E. (1990) 'Psychological responses after abortion', *Science* 248: 41–4.
—— (1992) 'Psychological factors in abortion: a review', *American Psychologist* 47: 1194–1204.
Ainsworth, M. D. S. (1974) 'Infant–mother attachment and social development: socialization as a product of reciprocal responsiveness to signals', in M. P. Richards (ed.) *The Integration of the Child into a Social World*, Cambridge: Cambridge University Press.
Albee, G. W. (1986) 'Towards a just society: lessons from observations on the primary prevention of psychopathology', *American Psychologist* 41: 891–8.
Allen, I. (1981) *Family Planning, Sterilisation and Abortion Services*, London: Policy Studies Institute.
—— (1985) *Counselling Services for Sterilization, Vasectomy and Termination of Pregnancy*, London: Policy Studies Institute.
American Psychological Association (APA) Interdivisional Committee on Adolescent Abortion (1987) 'Adolescent abortion: psychological and legal issues', *American Psychologist* 42: 73–8.
Axby, H. (1994) *Client Survey: Women Attending From Northern Ireland*, London: Marie Stopes International UK Clinics.
Azjen, I. and Fishbein, M. (1980) *Understanding Attitudes and Predicting Social Behaviour*, New York: Prentice-Hall.
Badinter, E. (1981) *The Myth of Motherhood*, London: Souvenir Press.
Bean, P. (1980) *Compulsory Admissions to Mental Hospitals*, Chichester: Wiley.
Beck, J. G. and Davies, D. K. (1987) 'Teen contraception: a review of perspectives on compliance', *Archives of Sexual Behaviour* 16: 337–69.

143

Bennett, E. (1983) 'The biasing effect of possession of information on clinicians' subsequent recognition of client information', unpublished M.Sc. thesis, North East London Polytechnic.

Black, R. B. (1991) 'Women's voices after pregnancy loss: couples' patterns of communication and support', *Social Work in Health Care* 16: 19–36.

Blumberg, B. D., Globus, M. S. and Hanson, K. H. (1975) 'The psychological sequelae of abortion performed for a genetic indication', *American Journal of Obstetrics and Gynecology* 122: 799–808.

Bowlby, J. (1973) *Attachment and Loss*, New York: Basic Books.

Boyle, M. (1993a) 'The abortion debate: a neglected issue in psychology', *Psychologist* 6: 106–9.

—— (1993b) 'Sexual dysfunction or heterosexual dysfunction?', *Feminism & Psychology* 3: 73–88.

—— (1994) 'Gender, science and sexual dysfunction', in T. R. Sarbin and J. Kitsuse (eds) *Constructing the Social*, London: Sage.

Bracken, M. B. (1978) 'A causal model of psychosomatic reactions to vacuum aspiration abortion', *Social Psychiatry* 13: 135–45.

Bracken, M. B. and Kasl, S. V. (1975) 'Delay in seeking induced abortion: a review and theoretical analysis', *American Journal of Obstetrics and Gynecology* 121: 1008–19.

Bracken, M. B., Hachamovitch, M. and Grossman, G. (1974) 'The decision to abort and psychological sequelae', *Journal of Nervous and Mental Disease* 158: 154–62.

Braginsky, D. D. (1985) 'Psychology: handmaiden to society', in S. Kock and D. E. Leary (eds) *A Century of Psychology as Science*, New York: McGraw Hill.

Brewer, C. (1977) 'Incidence of post-abortion psychosis: a prospective study', *British Medical Journal* 19 February 1977: 476–77.

Bromham, D. R. and Cartmill, R. S. V. (1993) 'Are current sources of contraceptive advice adequate to meet changes in contraceptive practice? A study of patients requesting termination of pregnancy', *British Journal of Family Planning* 19: 179–83.

Brooks, B. (1988) *Abortion in England: 1900–1967*, Beckenham: Croom-Helm.

Brownmiller, S. (1976) *Against our Will: Men, Women and Rape*, Harmondsworth: Penguin.

Bruch, M. A. and Hayes, M. J. (1987) 'Heterosexual anxiety and contraceptive behaviour', *Journal of Research in Personality* 21: 343–60.

Callahan, D. (1970) *Abortion: Law, Choice and Morality*, London: Macmillan.

Caplan, P. J. (1989) *Women's Masochism: The Myth Destroyed*, London: Mandarin.

Cates, W., Smith, T. C., Rochat, R. W. and Grimes, D. A. (1982) 'Mortality from abortion and childbirth. Are the statistics biased?', *Journal of the American Medical Association* 9 July 1982: 192–5.

Chalmers, A. (1990) *Science and its Fabrication*, Milton Keynes: Open University Press.

Chapman, L. J. and Chapman, J. (1982) 'Test results are what you think they are', in D. Kahneman, P. Slovic and A. Tversky (eds) *Judgement Under Uncertainty: Heuristics and Biases*, Cambridge: Cambridge University Press.

Chelimsky, E. (1991) 'On the social science contribution to governmental decision-making', *Science* 254: 226–31.

Chilman, C. S. (1985) 'Feminist issues in teenage parenting', *Child Welfare* 64: 225–34.

Chodorow, N. (1978) *The Reproduction of Mothering: Psychoanalysis and the Sociology of Gender*, Berkeley CA: University of California Press.

Chodorow, N. and Contratto, S. (1982) 'The fantasy of the perfect mother', in B. Thorne (ed.) *Rethinking the Family*, New York: Longmans.

Clare, A. W. and Tyrrell, J. (1994) 'Psychiatric aspects of abortion', *Irish Journal of Psychological Medicine* 11: 92–8.

Clark, M., Forstner, I., Pond, P. A. and Tredgold, R. F. (1968) 'Sequels of unwanted pregnancy', *Lancet* 2: 501–3.

Cohen, L. and Roth, R. (1984) 'Coping with abortion', *Journal of Human Stress*, 10: 140–5.

Comfort, A. (ed.) (1987) *The Joy of Sex*, London: Quartet Books.

Congleton, G. K. and Calhoun, L. G. (1993) 'Post-abortion perceptions: a comparison of self-identified distressed and non-distressed populations', *International Journal of Social Psychiatry* 39: 255–65.

Connell, R. W. (1994) 'The state, gender and sexual politics: theory and appraisal', in H. L. Radtke and H. J. Stam (eds) *Power/Gender: Social Relations in Theory and Practice*, London: Sage.

Contratto, S. (1984) 'Mother: social sculptor and trustee of the faith', in M. Lewin (ed.) *In the Shadow of the Past*, New York: Columbia University Press.

Cooke, P. (1995) 'An investigation into the differences in the experience of men and women who lose a baby through termination for fetal abnormality', unpublished M.Phil. thesis, Manchester Metropolitan University.

Cott, N. (1978) 'Passionlessness: an interpretation of Victorian sexual ideology, 1790–1850', *Signs: Journal of Women in Culture and Society* 4: 219–36.

Coward, R. (1984) *Female Desire: Women's Sexuality Today*, London: Paladin.

Cvetkovich, G. and Grote, B. (1983) 'Adolescent development and teenage fertility', in D. Byrne and W. A. Fisher (eds) *Adolescents, Sex and Contraception*, Hillsdale NJ: Lawrence Erlbaum.

Darmon, P. (1985) *Trial by Impotence*, London: Chatto and Windus.

David, H. P. (1989) 'The medical and psychological impact of abortion on women', Testimony on behalf of the American Public Health Association before the Subcommittee on Human Resources and Intergovernmental Operations, Committee on Government Operations, US House of Representatives, 101st Congress, 1st session, 15 March 1989.

—— (1992) 'Born unwanted: long-term developmental effects of denied abortion', *Journal of Social Issues* 48: 163–81.

David, H. P. and Matejcek, Z. (1981) 'Children born to women denied abortion: an update', *Family Planning Perspectives* 13: 32–4.

David, H. P., Rasmussion, N. and Holst, E. (1981) 'Postpartum and postabortion psychotic reactions', *Family Planning Perspectives* 13: 88–93.

David, H. P., Dytrych, Z., Matejcek, Z., and Schuller V. (1988) *Born Unwanted: Developmental Effects of Denied Abortion*, New York: Springer.

Derrida, J. (1978) *Writing and Difference*, Chicago: University of Chicago Press.

Diggory, P. (1970) 'Experience with the new British law', in R. E. Hall (ed.) *Abortion in a Changing World*, vol. 1, New York: Columbia University Press.

Doerr, E. and Prescott, J. W. (eds) (1989) *Abortion Rights and Fetal Personhood*, Long Beach CA: Centerline Press.

Duncan, G., Harper, C., Ashwell, E., Mant, D., Buchan, H. and Jones, L. (1990) 'Termination of pregnancy: lessons for prevention', *British Journal of Family Planning* 15: 112–17.

Dworkin, R. (1993) *Life's Dominion. An Argument about Abortion and Euthanasia*, London: HarperCollins.

Eddy, D. M. (1982) 'Probabilistic reasoning in clinical medicine: problems and opportunities', in D. Kahneman, P. Slovic and A. Tversky (eds) *Judgement Under Uncertainty: Heuristics and Biases*, Cambridge: Cambridge University Press.

Eggert, A. and Rolston, B. (1994a) (eds) *Abortion in the New Europe*, London: Greenwood.

—— (1994b) 'Ireland', in B. Rolston and A. Eggert (eds) *Abortion in the New Europe*, London: Greenwood.

Ehrenreich, B. and English, B. (1979) *For Her Own Good: 150 years of Experts' Advice to Women*, New York: Doubleday.

Ellworthy, S. (1996) *Power and Sex: A Book about Women*, Shaftesbury: Element.

Enloe, C. (1983) *Does Khaki Become You? The Militarization of Women's Lives*, Boston MA: South End Press.

Evers-Kiebooms, G., Denayer, L., Decruyenaere, M. and Berghe, H. van den (1993) 'Community attitudes towards prenatal testing for congenital handicap', *Journal of Reproductive and Infant Psychology* 11: 21–30.

Faludi, S. (1992) *Backlash: The Undeclared War Against Women*, London: Chatto and Windus.

Fegan, E. V. (1996) ' "Fathers" fetuses and abortion decision-making: the reproduction of maternal ideology in Canadian judicial discourse', *Social and Legal Studies* 5: 75–94.

Feyerabend, P. (1978) *Against Method*, London: New Left Books.

Fleissig, A. (1991) 'Unintended pregnancies and the use of contraception: changes from 1984 to 1989', *British Medical Journal* 302 (19 January): 147.

Fletcher, R. (1994) 'Women speak out against the great unmentionable', *Irish News*, 8 April 1994.

Flower, M. (1989) 'Neuromaturation and the moral status of human fetal life', in E. Doerr and J. W. Prescott (eds) *Abortion Rights and Fetal Personhood*, Long Beach CA: Centerline Press.

Forssman, H. and Thuwe, I. (1966) 'One hundred and twenty children born after application for therapeutic abortion refused', *Acta Psychiatrica Scandinavica* 42: 71–8.

Foucault, M. (1977) *Discipline and Punish: The Birth of the Prison*, New York: Pantheon.

—— (1979) *The History of Sexuality. Vol. 1: An Introduction.* London: Allen Lane.

—— (1980) *Power/Knowledge: Selected Interviews and Other Writings 1972–1977*, C. Gordon (ed.), Hemel Hempstead: Harvester Wheatsheaf.

Francome, C. (1994) 'Gynaecologists and abortion in Northern Ireland', *Journal of Biosocial Science* 26: 389–94.

Francke, L. B. (1978) *The Ambivalence of Abortion*, New York: Random House.

Frank, P. I., Kay, C. R., Wingrave, S. J., Lewis, T. L. T., Osborne, J. and Newell, C. (1985) 'Induced abortion operations and their early sequelae', *Journal of the Royal College of General Practitioners* 35: 175–80.

Freidson, E. (1970) *The Profession of Medicine: A Study of the Sociology of Applied Knowledge*, New York: Harper and Row.

French, M. (1986) *Beyond Power: On Women, Men and Morals*, London: Sphere Books.

—— (1992) *The War Against Women*, London: Hamish Hamilton.

Freud, S. (1977) [1925] 'Some psychical consequences of the anatomical distinction between the sexes', in J. Strachey (ed. and transl.) *On Sexuality: Three Essays on the Theory of Sexuality*, vol. 7, Harmondsworth: Pelican Freud Library.

Furedi, A. (1995) (ed.) *The Abortion Law in Northern Ireland*, Belfast: Family Planning Association Northern Ireland.

Gallup (1990) *Political Index Report No. 353*, London: Gallup Social Surveys.

Gardner, W., Scherer, D. and Tester, M. (1989) 'Asserting scientific authority: cognitive development and adolescent legal rights', *American Psychologist* 44: 895–902.

Gerrard, M., Gibbons, F. and McCoy, S. B. (1993) 'Emotional inhibition of effective contraception', *Anxiety Stress and Coping* 6: 73–88.

Gilligan, C. (1982) *In a Different Voice: Psychological Theory and Women's Development*, 1st edn, Cambridge MA: Harvard University Press.

—— (1993) *In a Different Voice: Psychological Theory and Women's Development*, 2nd edn, Cambridge MA: Harvard University Press.

Ginsburg, F. (1984) 'The body politic: the defense of sexual restriction by anti-abortion activists', in C. S. Vance (ed.) *Pleasure and Danger: Exploring Female Sexuality*, London: Routledge and Keegan Paul.

Goggin, M. L. (ed.) (1993a) *Understanding the New Politics of Abortion*, Newbury Park CA: Sage.

—— (1993b) 'Introduction: a framework for understanding the new politics of abortion', in M. L. Goggin (ed.) *Understanding the New Politics of Abortion*, Newbury Park CA: Sage.

Granberg, D. (1978) 'Pro-life or a reflection of conservative ideology? An analysis of opposition to legalised abortion', *Sociology and Social Research* 62: 421–3.

Green, J. M. and Richards, M. P. M. (1993) 'Psychological aspects of fetal screening and the new genetics', *Journal of Reproductive and Infant Psychology* 11: 1–2.

Green, J. M., Snowden, C. and Statham, H. (1993) 'Pregnant women's attitudes to abortion and prenatal screening', *Journal of Reproductive and Infant Psychology* 11: 31–9.

Green, J. M., Statham, H. and Snowden, C. (1992) 'Screening for fetal abnormalities: attitudes and experiences', in T. Chard and M. P. M. Richards (eds) *Obstetrics in the 1990s: Current Controversies*, London: MacKeith Press.

Griffiths, M. (1990) 'Contraceptive practices and contraceptive failures among women requesting termination of pregnancy', *British Journal of Family Planning* 16: 16–18.

Guth, J. L., Smidt, C. E., Kellstedt, L. A. and Green, J. C. (1993) 'The sources of anti-abortion attitudes: the case of religious political activists', in M. L. Goggin (ed.) *Understanding the New Politics of Abortion*, Newbury Park CA: Sage.

Hadley, J. (1996) *Abortion: Between Freedom and Necessity*, London: Virago.

Hafner, J. (1994) *The End of Marriage: Why Monogamy Isn't Working*, London: Arrow Books.

Halva-Neubauer, G. A. (1993) 'The States after *Roe*: no "paper tigers" ', in M. L. Goggin (ed.) *Understanding the New Politics of Abortion*, Newbury Park CA: Sage.

Hamill, E. and Ingram, I. M. (1974) 'Psychiatric and social factors in the abortion decision', *British Medical Journal* 9 February 1974: 229–32.

Hansen, S. B. (1993) 'Differences in public policies toward abortion: electoral and policy context', in M. L. Goggin (ed.) *Understanding the New Politics of Abortion*, Newbury Park CA: Sage.

Harding, S. (1986) *The Science Question in Feminism*, Ithaca: Cornell University Press.

—— (1991) *Whose Science? Whose Knowledge? Thinking From Women's Lives*, Milton Keynes: Open University Press.

Hare-Mustin, R. T. and Marecek, J. (1988) 'The meaning of difference: gender theory, post-modernism and psychology', *American Psychologist* 43: 455–64.

Haslam, D. (1996) *Coping with a Termination*, London: Mandarin.

Henriques, J., Hollway, W., Urwin, C., Venn, C. and Walkerdine, V. (1984) *Changing the Subject*, London: Methuen.

Hite, S. (1981a) *The Hite Report on Male Sexuality*, New York: Ballantine Books.

—— (1981b) *The Hite Report: A Nationwide Study of Female Sexuality*, New York: Dell.

HL v. *Matheson* 450 US 398 (1981).

Holland, J., Ramazanoğlu, C., Scott, S., Sharpe, S. and Thompson, T. (1990) *Don't Die of Ignorance . . . I Nearly Died of Embarrassment*, WRAP Paper 2, London: Tufnell Press.

—— (1991) *Pressure, Resistance and Empowerment: Young Women and the Negotiation of Safer Sex*, WRAP Paper 6, London: Tufnell Press.

Hollway, W. (1989) *Subjectivity and Method in Psychology: Gender, Meaning and Science*, London: Sage.

Holmgren, K. (1994) 'Repeat abortion and contraceptive use: report from an interview study in Stockholm', *Gynecological and Obstetric Investigations* 37: 254–9.

Hopkins, J., Marcus, M. and Campbell, S. B. (1984) 'Post-partum depression: a critical review', *Psychological Bulletin* 95: 498–515.

Howard, G. S. (1985) 'The role of values in the science of psychology', *American Psychologist* 40: 255–65.

Ingelhammer, E., Moller, A., Svanberg, B., Tornbom, M., Lija, H. and Hamberger, L. (1994) 'The use of contraceptive methods among women seeking a legal abortion', *Contraception* 50: 143–52.

Jamous, H. and Peloille, B. (1970) 'Changes in the French university hospital system', in

J. A. Jackson (ed.) *Professions and Professionalization*, Cambridge: Cambridge University Press.

Jeffreys, S. (1985) *The Spinster and Her Enemies: Feminism and Sexuality 1880–1930*, London: Pandora Press.

—— (1990) *A Feminist Perspective on the Sexual Revolution*, London: Women's Press.

Jelen, T. (1984) 'Respect for life, sexual morality and opposition to abortion', *Review of Religious Research* 25: 220–31.

Johnson, T. (1972) *Professions and Power*, London: Macmillan.

Jowell, R., Witherspoon, S. and Brook, L. (1991) *British Social Attitudes: 7th Report*, Aldershot: Gower.

Kantner, J. and Zelnick, M. (1972) 'Sexual experiences of young unmarried women in the US', *Family Planning Perspectives* 4: 9–18.

Kaplan, H. S. (1974) *The New Sex Therapy : Active Treatment of Sexual Dysfunctions*, London: Ballière Tindall.

Kendler, H. H. (1993) 'Psychology and the ethics of social policy', *American Psychologist* 48: 1046–53.

Kennedy, H. (1992) *Eve was Framed: Women and British Justice*, London: Chatto and Windus.

Kennedy, I. (1983) *The Unmasking of Medicine*, London: Granada.

Kent, S. K. (1990) *Sex and Suffrage in Britain: 1860–1914*, London: Routledge.

Kenyon, F. E. (1969) 'Termination of pregnancy on psychiatric grounds: a comparative study of 61 cases', *British Journal of Medical Psychology* 42: 243–54.

Kohlberg, L. (1976) 'Moral stages and moralization: the cognitive developmental approach', in T. Lickona (ed.) *Moral Development and Behaviour Theory: Research and Social Issues*, New York: Holt, Rinehart and Winston.

—— (1981) *The Philosophy of Moral Development*, San Francisco: Harper and Row.

Kolker, A. and Burke, B. M. (1993) 'Grieving the wanted child: ramifications of abortion after prenatal diagnosis of abnormality', *Health Care for Women International* 14: 513–26.

Koop, C. E. and Schaeffer, F. A. (1983) *Whatever Happened to the Human Race?* Westchester IL: Good News.

Krishnamoorthy, S., Trlin, A. D. and Khoo, S. (1983) 'Contraceptive risk-taking among never-married youth', *Australian Journal of Sex, Marriage and the Family* 4: 151–7.

Lakatos, I. (1970) 'Falsification and the methodology of scientific research programmes', in I. Lakatos and A. Musgrave (eds) *Criticism and the Growth of Knowledge*, Cambridge: Cambridge University Press.

Lakatos, I. and Musgrave, A. (1970) *Criticism and the Growth of Knowledge*, Cambridge: Cambridge University Press.

Larson, M. (1977) *The Rise of Professionalism*, California: University of California Press.

Lazarus, A. (1985) 'Psychiatric sequelae of legalized elective first trimester abortion', *Journal of Psychosomatic Obstetrics and Gynaecology* 4: 141–50.

Lee, S. (1995) 'Abortion law in Northern Ireland: the twilight zone', in A. Furedi (ed.) *The Abortion Law in Northern Ireland*, Belfast: Family Planning Association Northern Ireland.

Lees, S. (1986) *Losing Out: Sexuality and Adolescent Girls*, London: Hutchinson.

—— (1995) *Rape on Trial*, Harmondsworth: Penguin.

Lemkau, J. P. (1988) 'Emotional sequelae of abortion', *Psychology of Women Quarterly* 12: 461–72.

Lerner, G. (1986) *The Creation of Patriarchy*, New York: Oxford University Press.

Lewin, M. (1984) 'The Victorians, the psychologists and psychic birth control', in M. Lewin (ed.) *In the Shadow of the Past*, New York: Columbia University Press.

Lewis, C. C. (1987) 'Minors' competence to consent to abortion', *American Psychologist* 42: 84–8.

Lipman-Blumen, J. (1994) 'The existential bases of power relationships: the gender role case', in H. L. Radtke and H. J. Stam (eds) *Power/Gender: Social Relations in Theory and Practice*, London: Sage.

Livingston, J. A. and Rankin, J. M. (1986) 'Propping up the patriarchy: the silenced soldiering of military nurses', *Women and Therapy* 5: 107–19.

Luker, K. (1975) *Taking Chances: Abortion and the Decision not to Contracept*, Berkeley CA: University of California Press.

—— (1984) *Abortion and the Politics of Motherhood*, Berkeley CA: University of California Press.

Lupton, D. (1994) *Medicine as Culture: Illness, Disease and the Body in Western Societies*, London: Sage.

McCance, C. and McCance, P. F. (1970) 'Abortion or no? Who decides? An enquiry by questionnaire into the attitudes of gynaecologists and psychiatrists in Aberdeen', *Seminars in Psychiatry* 2: 352–60.

McCance, C., Olley, P. C. and Edward, V. (1977) 'Long-term psychiatric follow-up', in G. Horobin (ed.) *Experience with Abortion: A Case Study of North East Scotland*, Cambridge: Cambridge University Press.

MacCannell, D. and MacCannell, J. F. (1993) 'Violence, power and pleasure: a revisionist reading of Foucault from the victim perspective', in C. Ramazanoğlu (ed.) *Up Against Foucault. Explorations of Some Tensions Between Foucault and Feminism*, London: Routledge.

McCarthy, B. (1994) 'Warrior values: a socio-historical survey', in J. Archer (ed.) *Male Violence*, London: Routledge.

Maccoby, H. (1982) *The Sacred Executioner: Human Sacrifice and the Legacy of Guilt*, London: Thames and Hudson.

McDougall, W. (1913) *An Introduction to Social Psychology*, 7th edn, London: Methuen.

—— (1923) *Outline of Psychology*, New York: Scribner's.

McEvoy, J. and Boyle, M. (1997) 'Exporting abortion: a psychological study of Northern Irish women's experience of abortion in England'. Paper presented at the Annual Conference of the British Psychological Society Psychology of Women Section, Loughborough University.

McIlroy, L. (1936) 'The sociological and medical aspects of induction of abortion', *Journal of State Medicine* 44: 334.

McKenna, G. (1995) 'On abortion: a Lincolnian position', *Atlantic Monthly* September 1995: 51–68.

Maitland, S. (1984) *In Vitro Veritas*, St Mary's, Bourne Street, London (cited in Neustatter (1986).

Major, B. and Cozzarelli, C. (1992) 'Psychosocial predictors of adjustment to abortion', *Journal of Social Issues* 48: 121–42.

Major, B., Mueller, P. and Hildebrandt, K. (1985) 'Attributions, expectations and coping with abortion', *Journal of Personality and Social Psychology* 48: 585–99.

Major, B., Cozzarelli, C., Testa, M., Sciacchitano, A. M. and Mueller, P. (1992) 'Male partners' appraisals of undesired pregnancy and abortion: implications for women's adjustment to abortion', *Journal of Applied Social Psychology* 22: 599–614.

Major, B., Cozzarelli, C., Sciacchitano, A. M., Cooper, M. L., Testa, M. and Mueller, P. M. (1990) 'Perceived social support, self-efficacy and adjustment to abortion', *Journal of Personality and Social Psychology* 59: 452–63.

Manpower Planning Advisory Group (MPAG) (1990) *Clinical Psychology Project: Full Report*, MPAG London: Department of Health.

Marecek, J. (1987) 'Counselling adolescents with problem pregnancies', *American Psychologist* 42: 89–93.

Marshall, H. (1991) 'The social construction of motherhood: an analysis of childcare and parenting manuals', in A. Phoenix, A. Woollett and E. Lloyd (eds) *Motherhood: Meanings, Practices and Ideologies*, London: Sage.

Marteau, T. M., Plenicar, M. and Kidd, J. (1993) 'Obstetricians presenting amniocentesis to pregnant women: practice observed', *Journal of Reproductive and Infant Psychology* 11: 3–10.

Martin, E. (1991) 'The egg and the sperm: how science has constructed a romance based on stereotypical male-female roles', *Signs: Journal of Women in Culture and Society* 16: 485–501.

Masters, W. H. and Johnson, V. E. (1970) *Human Sexual Inadequacy*, London: Churchill.

Maxwell, C. and Boyle, M. (1995) 'Risky heterosexual practices amongst women over 30: gender, power and long-term relationships', *AIDS Care* 7: 277–93.

Medawar, P. (1984) *Pluto's Republic*, Oxford: Oxford University Press.

Meier, K. J. and McFarlane, D. R. (1993) 'Abortion politics and abortion funding policy', in M. L. Goggin (ed.) *Understanding the New Politics of Abortion*, Newbury Park CA: Sage.

Melton, G. B. (ed.) (1986) *Adolescent Abortion: Psychological and Legal Issues*, Lincoln: University of Nebraska Press.

—— (1987) 'Legal regulation of adolescent abortion: unintended effects', *American Psychologist* 42: 79–83.

Melton, G. B. and Russo, N. F. (1987) 'Adolescent abortion: psychological perspectives on public policy', *American Psychologist* 42: 69–72.

Metson, D. (1988) 'Lessons from an audit of unplanned pregnancies', *British Medical Journal* 297 (8 October 1988): 904–6.

Miles, R. (1992) *The Rites of Man: Love, Sex and Death in the Making of the Male*, London: Paladin.

Miller, W. B. (1992) 'An empirical study of the psychological antecedents and consequences of induced abortion', *Journal of Social Issues* 48: 67–93.

Mills, J. (1991) *Womanwords: A Vocabulary of Culture and Patriarchal Society*, London: Virago.

Minturn, L. (1989) 'The birth ceremony as a rite of passage into infant personhood', in E. Doerr and J. W. Prescott (eds) *Abortion Rights and Fetal Personhood*, Long Beach CA: Centerline Press.

Mohr, J. (1978) *Abortion in America*, New York: Oxford University Press.

Morell, C. M. (1994) *Unwomanly Conduct: The Challenges of Intentional Childlessness*, New York: Routledge.

Morgan, L. (1989) 'When does life begin? A cross cultural perspective on the personhood of fetuses and young children', in E. Doerr and J. W. Prescott (eds) *Abortion Rights and Fetal Personhood*, Long Beach CA: Centerline Press.

Morrison, D.M. (1985) 'Adolescent contraceptive behaviour: a review', *Psychological Bulletin* 98: 538–68.

Moscucci, O. (1990) *The Science of Woman: Gynaecology and Gender in England, 1800–1929*, Cambridge: Cambridge University Press.

Moseley, D. T., Follingstad, D. R., Harley, H. and Heckel, R. V. (1981) 'Psychological factors that predict reaction to abortion', *Journal of Clinical Psychology* 37: 276–9.

Mueller, P. and Major, B. (1989) 'Self-blame, self-efficacy and adjustment to abortion', *Journal of Personality and Social Psychology* 57: 1059–68.

Muir, K. (1991) *Bridging the Gender Gulf*, The Times, 1 February 1991.

Neustatter, A. (with Newson, G.) (1986) *Mixed Feelings: The Experience of Abortion*, London: Pluto Press.

Niven, C. (1988) 'Labour pain: long-term recall and consequences', *Journal of Reproductive and Infant Psychology* 6: 83–7.

Northern Ireland Abortion Law Reform Association (1989) *Abortion in Northern Ireland: The Report of an International Tribunal*, Belfast: Beyond the Pale Publications.

Office for National Statistics (1996a) *Series AB No. 21*, London: HMSO.

—— (1996b) *Monitor: Population and Health AB 96/7* (21 November), London: HMSO.

150

Ortner, S. (1974) 'Is female to male as nature is to culture?', in M. Rosaldo and L. Lamphere (eds) *Woman, Culture and Society*, Stanford CA: Stanford University Press.

Osofsky, J. D. and Osofsky, H. J. (1972) 'The psychological reaction of patients to legalized abortion', *American Journal of Orthopsychiatry*, 42: 48–60.

Osofsky, J. D., Osofsky, H. J. and Rajan, R. (1973) 'Psychological effects of abortion: with emphasis upon immediate reactions and follow-up', in H. J. Osofsky and J. D. Osofsky (eds) *The Abortion Experience*, Hagerstown MD: Harper and Row.

Petchesky, R. P. (1984) *Abortion and Woman's Choice: The State, Sexuality and Reproductive Freedom*, New York: Longman.

Phoenix, A. (1990) 'Black women in the maternity services', in J. Garcia and R. Kilpatrick (eds) *The Politics of Maternity Care: Services for Childbearing Women in Twentieth Century Britain*, Oxford: Oxford University Press.

—— (1991) 'Mothers under twenty: insider and outsider views', in: A. Phoenix, A. Woollett, and E. Lloyd (eds) *Motherhood: Meanings, Practices and Ideologies*, London: Sage

Phoenix, A., Woollett, A. and Lloyd, E. (eds) (1991) *Motherhood: Meanings, Practices and Ideologies*, London: Sage

Piaget, J. (1965) [1932] *The Moral Judgement of the Child*, New York: The Free Press.

Pilger, J. (1995) *All Right on the Night*, Guardian, 31 March 1995.

Planned Parenthood of Central Missouri v. *Danforth* 428 US 52 (1976).

Pleck, J. H., Sonenstein, F. L. and Ku, L. C. (1990) 'Contraceptive attitudes and intention to use condoms in sexually experienced and inexperienced adolescent males', *Journal of Family Issues* (Special Issue: *Adolescent Sexuality, Contraception and Childbearing*) 11: 294–312.

Pollack, S. (1985) 'Sex and the contraceptive act', in H. Homans (ed.) *The Sexual Politics of Reproduction*, Aldershot: Gower Publishing.

Posavac, E. J. and Miller, T. Q. (1990) 'Some problems caused by not having a conceptual foundation for health research: an illustration from studies of the psychological effects of abortion', *Psychology and Health* 5: 13–23.

Prescott, J. W. (1978) 'Abortion and the "right to life": facts, fallacies and frauds', *Humanist* July/August 1978: 18–24.

Prescott, J. W. and Wallace, D. (1978) 'Abortion and the "right to life": facts, fallacies and frauds. II: Psychometric studies', *Humanist* November/December 1978: 36–42.

Prilleltensky, I. (1989) 'Psychology and the status quo', *American Psychologist* 44: 795–802.

—— (1994) 'Psychology and social ethics', *American Psychologist* 49: 966–7.

Quilliam, S. (1994) *Women on Sex*, London: Smith Gryphon.

Radcliffe-Richards, J. (1982) *The Sceptical Feminist*, Harmondsworth: Penguin.

Ramazanoğlu, C. and Holland, J. (1993) 'Women's sexuality and men's appropriation of desire', in C. Ramazanoğlu (ed.) *Up Against Foucault: Explorations of Some Tensions Between Foucault and Feminism*, London: Routledge.

Ransom, J. (1993) 'Feminism, difference and discourse: the limits of discursive analysis for feminism', in C. Ramazanoğlu (ed.) *Up Against Foucault: Explorations of Some Tensions Between Foucault and Feminism*, London: Routledge.

Raymond, J. (1982) 'Medicine as patriarchal religion', *Journal of Medicine and Philosophy* 7: 197–216.

Reading, A. E., Cox, D. N. and Sledmere, C. M. (1982) 'Issues arising from the development of new male contraceptives', *Bulletin of British Psychological Society* 35: 369–71.

Reardon, D. C. (1987) *Aborted Women: Silent No More*, Westchester IL: Crossway.

Rich, A. (1976) *Of Woman Born: Motherhood as Experience and Institution*, New York: W. W. Norton.

Richards, M. P. M. and Green, J. M. (1993) 'Attitudes toward prenatal screening for fetal abnormality and detection of carriers of genetic disease: a discussion paper', *Journal of Reproductive and Infant Psychology* 11: 49–56.

Roe v. *Wade* (1973) 410 US 113, reproduced in E. Doerr and J. W. Prescott (eds) (1989) *Abortion Rights and Fetal Personhood*, Long Beach CA: Centerline Press.

Rose, N. (1989) *Governing the Soul: The Shaping of the Private Self*, London: Routledge.

Ruddick, S. (1989) *Maternal Thinking: Toward a Politics of Peace*, Boston MA: Beacon Press.

Russo, N. F., Horn, J. D. and Schwartz, R. (1992) 'US abortion in context: selected characteristics and motivations of women seeking abortions', *Journal of Social Issues* 48: 183–202.

Sarason, S. B. (1981) *Psychology Misdirected*, New York: Free Press.

Sawicki, J. (1991) *Disciplining Foucault: Feminism, Power and the Body*, New York: Routledge.

Schinke, S. P. (1984) 'Preventing teenage pregnancy', in: M. Hersen, R. M. Eisler and R. M. Miller (eds) *Progress in Behavior Modification*, vol. 16, New York: Academic Press.

Schnell, F. (1993) 'The foundations of abortion attitudes: the role of values and value conflicts', in M. L. Goggin (ed.) *Understanding the New Politics of Abortion*, Newbury Park CA: Sage.

Scull, A. T. (1979) *Museums of Madness: The Social Organisation of Insanity in Nineteenth Century England*, London: Allen Lane.

Sheldon, S. (1993) ' "Who is the mother to make the judgement?" The constructions of woman in English abortion law', *Feminist Legal Studies* 1: 3–22.

—— (1996) 'Subject only to the attitude of the surgeon concerned: the judicial protection of medical discretion', *Social and Legal Studies* 5: 95–112.

Shields, S. (1984) 'To pet, coddle and "do for": caretaking and the concept of maternal instinct', in M. Lewin (ed.) *In the Shadow of the Past*, New York: Columbia University Press.

Shorter, E. (1985) *Bedside Manners: The Troubled History of Doctors and Patients*, New York: Simon and Schuster.

Shostack, A., McLouth, G. and Seng, L. (1984) *Men and Abortion: Lessons in Love*, New York: Praeger.

Shotter, J. (1993) *Cultural Politics of Everyday Life*, Milton Keynes: Open University Press.

Showalter, E. (1987) *The Female Malady: Women, Madness and English Culture*, London: Virago Press.

Shusterman, L. (1979) 'Predicting the psychological consequences of abortion', *Social Science and Medicine* 13A: 683–9.

Sjögren, B. (1992) 'The expectant father and prenatal diagnosis', *Journal of Psychosomatic Obstetrics and Gynaecology* 13: 197–208.

Smart, C. (1989) *Feminism and the Power of Law*, London: Routledge.

—— (1991) 'Analysing law: the challenge of feminism and postmodernism', paper presented at conference entitled *Women's Studies in the European Community*, European University Institute, Florence, January 1991.

Smeal, E. (1995) *Anti-abortion extremists: organised and dangerous*, Glamour, October 1995.

Smetana, J. G. and Adler, N. E. (1979) 'Decision-making regarding abortion: a value x expectancy analysis', *Journal of Population* 2: 338–57.

Smith, J. (1993) *Misogynies*, London: Faber and Faber.

Smith, R. (1981) *Trial by Medicine*, Edinburgh: Edinburgh University Press.

Sobol, M. P. and Daly, K. J. (1992) 'The adoption alternative for pregnant adolescents: decision making, consequences and policy implications', *Journal of Social Issues* 48: 143–61.

Sorensen, R. C. (1973) *Adolescent Sexuality in Contemporary America*, New York: World.

Speckhard, A. C. and Rue, V. M. (1992) 'Post-abortion syndrome: an emerging public health concern', *Journal of Social Issues* 48: 95–119.

Spender, D. (1985) *Man Made Language*, 2nd edn, London: Routledge.

Spensky, M. (1992) 'Producers of legitimacy: homes for unmarried mothers in the 1950s', in C. Smart (ed.) *Regulating Womanhood: Historical Essays on Marriage, Motherhood and Sexuality*, London: Routledge.

Stock, W. (1988) 'Propping up the phallocracy: a feminist critique of sex therapy and research', in E. C. Cole and E. D. Rothblum (eds) *Women and Sex Therapy: Closing the Circle of Sexual Knowledge*, New York: Harrington Park Press.

Tew, M. (1990) *Safer Childbirth?*, London: Chapman and Hall.

Tizard, B. (1990) 'Research and policy: Is there a link?', *Psychologist* 3: 435–40.

Torres, A. and Forrest, J. D. (1988) 'Why do women have abortions?', *Family Planning Perspectives* 20: 169–76.

Torres, A., Forrest, J. D. and Eisman, S. (1980) 'Telling parents: clinic policies and adolescents' use of family planning and abortion services', *Family Planning Perspectives* 12: 284–92.

Turner, B. S. (1995) *Medical Power and Social Knowledge*, 2nd edn, London: Sage.

Urwin, C. (1985) 'Constructing motherhood: the persuasion of normal development', in C. Steedman, C. Urwin and V. Walkerdine (eds) *Language, Gender and Childhood*, London: Routledge and Keegan Paul.

Ussher, J. M. (1989) *The Psychology of the Female Body*, London: Routledge.

—— (1991) 'Positivistic science and social policy: A contradiction in terms?', *Educational and Child Psychology* 8: 23–5.

—— (1992) 'Science sexing psychology: positivistic science and gender bias in clinical psychology', in J. M. Ussher and P. Nicolson (eds) *Gender Issues in Clinical Psychology*, London: Routledge.

—— (1993) 'The construction of female sexual problems: regulating sex, regulating woman', in J. M. Ussher and C. D. Baker (eds) *Psychological Perspectives on Sexual Problems: New Directions in Theory and Practice*, London: Routledge.

Venn, C. (1984) 'The subject of psychology', in J. Henriques, W. Hollway, C. Urwin, C. Venn, and V. Walkerdine (eds) *Changing the Subject*, London: Methuen.

Vickers, J. (1994) 'Notes towards a political theory of sex and power', in H. L. Radtke and H. J. Stam (eds) *Power/Gender: Social Relations in Theory and Practice*, London: Sage.

Washington, A. C., Rosser, P. L. and Cox, E. P. (1983) 'Contraceptive practices of teenage mothers', *Journal of the National Medical Association* 75: 1059–63.

Wasielewski, P. L. (1992) 'Postabortion syndrome: Emotional battles over interaction and ideology', *Humboldt Journal of Social Relations* 18: 101–29.

Watters, W. W. (1980) 'Mental health consequences of refused abortion', *Canadian Journal of Psychiatry* 25: 68–73.

Weigert, A. J. (1991) *Mixed Emotions: Certain Steps Toward Understanding Ambivalence*, Albany NY: State University of New York Press.

Weiss, C. H. (1977) 'Introduction', in C. H. Weiss (ed.) *Using Social Research in Public Policy Making*, Lexington MA: Lexington.

Wight, D. (1992) 'Impediments to safer heterosexual sex: a review of research with young people', *AIDS Care* 4: 11–23.

Wilmoth, G. H. (1992) 'Abortion, public health policy and inforced consent legislation', *Journal of Social Issues* 48: 1–17.

Wilmoth, G. H., Alteriis, M. de and Bussell, D. (1992) 'Prevalence of psychological risks following legal abortion in the US: limits of the evidence', *Journal of Social Issues* 48: 37–66.

Wilton, T. and Aggleton, P. (1991) 'Condoms, coercion and control: heterosexuality and the limits to HIV/AIDS education', in P. Aggleton, G. Hart and P. Davies (eds) *AIDS: Responses, Interventions and Care*, London: Falmer Press.

Witz, A. (1992) *Professions and Patriarchy*, London: Routledge.

Woollett, A. and Phoenix, A. (1991) 'Psychological views of mothering', in A. Phoenix, A. Woollett and E. Lloyd (eds) *Motherhood: Meanings, Practices and Ideologies*, London: Sage.

World Health Organisation (1978) *Technical Report Series. #623: Induced Abortion*, Geneva: WHO.

Zabin, L. S. and Clark, S. D., Jr (1983) 'Institutional factors affecting teenagers' choice and reasons for delay in attending a family planning clinic', *Family Planning Perspectives* 15: 25–9.

Zahave, S., Noy, S. and Bar-On, R. (1986) 'Risk factors in combat stress reaction: a study of Israeli soldiers in the 1982 Lebanon War', *Israel Journal of Psychiatry and Related Sciences* 23: 3–8.

Zellman, G. L. and Goodchilds, J. D. (1983) 'Becoming sexual in adolescence', in E. R. Allgeier and N. B. McCormick (eds) *Changing Boundaries: Gender Roles and Sexual Behaviour*, Palo Alto CA: Mayfield.

Zolese, G. and Blacker, R. (1992) 'The psychological consequences of therapeutic abortion', *British Journal of Psychiatry* 160: 742–9.

NAME INDEX

SUBJECT INDEX